To: Megan

Grandma Jeannett
& Grandpa Del

Dec 2003

# FRONTIER SPIRIT

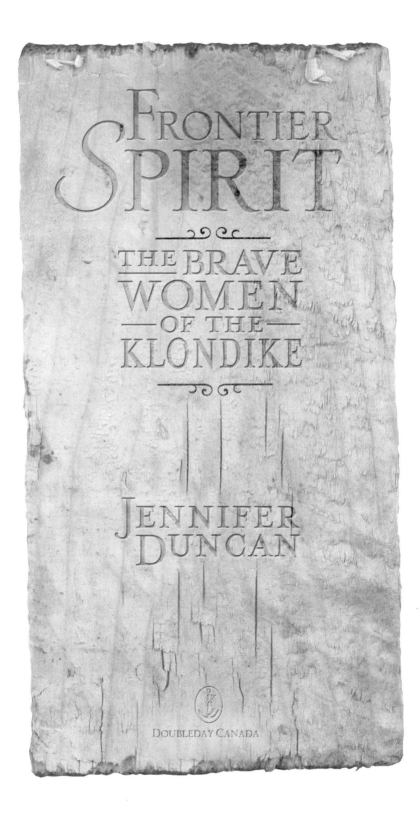

# FRONTIER SPIRIT

## THE BRAVE WOMEN OF THE KLONDIKE

### JENNIFER DUNCAN

DOUBLEDAY CANADA

**National Library of Canada Cataloguing in Publication**

Duncan, Jennifer, 1967–
Frontier spirit : the brave women of the Klondike / Jennifer Duncan.

ISBN 0–385–65904–0

1. Women pioneers—Yukon—Klondike River Valley—History. 2. Women—
Yukon Territory—Klondike River Valley—History. 3. Klondike River Valley
(Yukon)—Gold discoveries. I. Title.

FC4022.3.D85 2003      971.9'102'082      C2003–902154–8
FI095.K5D85 2003

JACKET IMAGE: Dawson City Museum #984R-212-9
JACKET AND TEXT DESIGN: Daniel Cullen
MAP DESIGN: CS Richardson
Printed and bound in the USA

Published in Canada by
Doubleday Canada, a division of
Random House of Canada Limited

Visit Random House of Canada Limited's website: www.randomhouse.ca

BVG 10 9 8 7 6 5 4 3 2 1

To Fifi (Edna Baker Bricker)
kindred spirit and chère grand-mère

# CONTENTS

PREFACE      *1*

1    THE SPELL OF THE YUKON      *5*

2    THE KLONDIKE GOLD RUSH
AND THE "DELICATELY NURTURED"      *41*

3    *Shaaw Tláa:* KATE CARMACK      *63*

4    *Émilie Fortin Tremblay:* THE MOTHER OF THE PRIESTS      *83*

5    *Anna DeGraf:* THE SAMARITAN      *103*

6    *Belinda Mulrooney:* THE MOGUL      *119*

7    *Martha Louise Black:* FIRST LADY OF THE YUKON      *145*

8    *Klondike Kate Rockwell:* QUEEN OF THE KLONDIKE      *167*

9    *Nellie Cashman:* THE MINER'S ANGEL      *195*

10    *Faith Fenton:* THE FAITHFUL CORRESPONDENT      *219*

11    GRANDES DAMES OF DAWSON      *247*

NOTES      *261*

SOURCES      *269*

PHOTO CREDITS      *281*

ACKNOWLEDGEMENTS      *285*

INDEX      *287*

"I long to speak out the intense inspiration that comes to me from the lives of strong women."

—RUTH BENEDICT

"Any woman venturesome enough to join the Klondike Gold Rush was likely to be a handful, not at all content with being regarded as a fragile thing, all sighs and sweetness. Influenced by the feminist spirit of the times, she was ready to assert her rights as a human being equal if not superior to any male."

—RICHARD O'CONNOR

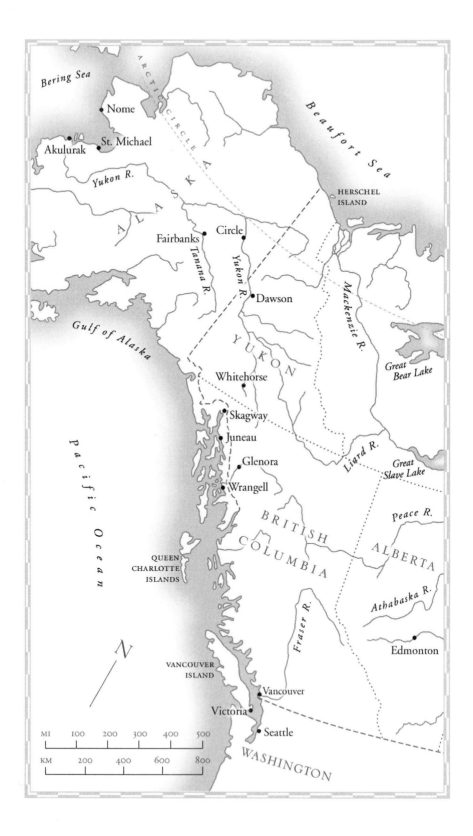

Bering Sea

ARCTIC CIRCLE

Beaufort Sea

Nome

Akulurak

St. Michael

Yukon R.

A L A S K A

HERSCHEL
ISLAND

Fairbanks

Circle

Tanana R.

Yukon R.

Dawson

Mackenzie R.

Gulf of Alaska

YUKON

Great
Bear Lake

Whitehorse

Skagway

Juneau

Glenora

Wrangell

Liard R.

Great
Slave Lake

Pacific Ocean

B R I T I S H

C O L U M B I A

Peace R.

A L B E R T A

QUEEN
CHARLOTTE
ISLANDS

Fraser R.

Athabaska R.

Edmonton

N

VANCOUVER
ISLAND

Vancouver

Victoria

Seattle

WASHINGTON

MI    100    200    300    400    500

KM      200     400     600    800

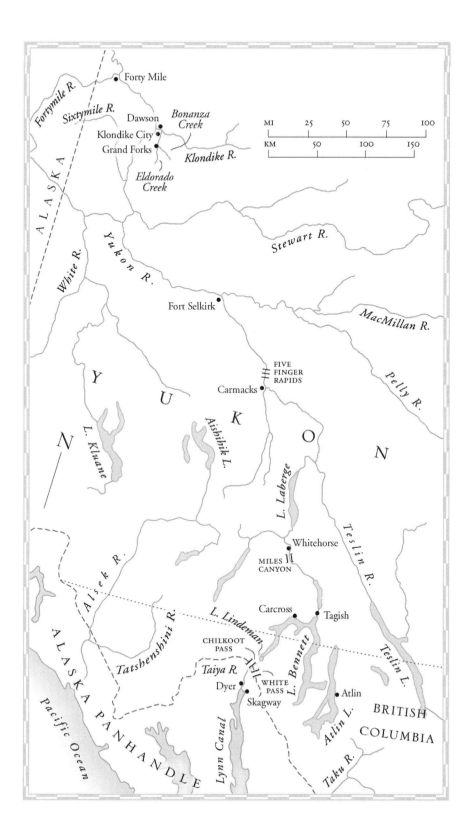

Forty Mile

Fortymile R.

Sixtymile R.

Dawson

Bonanza Creek

Klondike City

Grand Forks

Klondike R.

Eldorado Creek

ALASKA

White R.

Yukon R.

Stewart R.

Fort Selkirk

MacMillan R.

Pelly R.

FIVE FINGER RAPIDS

Carmacks

Y        U        K        O        N

L. Kluane

Aishihik L.

N

Alsek R.

L. Laberge

Whitehorse

MILES CANYON

Teslin R.

L. Lindeman

Carcross

Tagish

Tatshenshini R.

CHILKOOT PASS

Taiya R.

Dyer

L. Bennett

WHITE PASS

Skagway

Atlin

ALASKA   PANHANDLE

Pacific Ocean

Lynn Canal

Atlin L.

Taku R.

Teslin L.

BRITISH COLUMBIA

MI    25    50    75    100

KM        50        100        150

*They say it is no place for a woman. They say many a man has turned back, defeated by the trail to the Klondike goldfields, its creeks to be forded, its waist-deep swamps to be waded through, its steep, treacherous mountains to be scaled. But there she is, a woman, African-American, 19 years old, and nine months pregnant, on the Stikine River Trail in the autumn of 1897. And she is not turning back.*

*After 150 miles, she goes into labour in a First Nations village. The Tagish people have seen many newcomers come pouring over the mountains, but never someone like her. "Another kind of white," they call her.*

*She asks them what they call this lake. They say, "Teslin." She tells them: "This is what I'll call my daughter. For the lake where she was born. For you who have always lived here."*

Lucille Hunter was one of many brave women who stampeded to the Gold Rush. Pausing briefly in Teslin to give birth, Lucille did not wait out the winter as most stampeders did but mushed on for weeks through frigid temperatures with her husband, Charles, their newborn daughter, and their dog team, finally reaching Dawson City on the brink of the new year. Her courage and stamina enabled the family to stake a Bonanza Creek claim before the spring hordes arrived by boat.

Lucille's strength only grew in this wild land. As a widow during the Depression, she would walk 140 miles between her silver mine in Mayo and her three gold mines in Dawson, running these operations single-handedly. After the Second World War, she ran a laundry in Whitehorse, where she died at 94, in 1972.

Like Lucille Hunter, many of the women of the Gold Rush are fascinating characters, with unusual claims to fame.

There were the wives of the first Klondike Kings, like "Bride of the Klondike" Ethel Berry, who spent her honeymoon crossing the Chilkoot Pass during the Gold Trickle, and whose arrival in Seattle in 1897 with $100,000 worth of gold in her bedroll fed the media frenzy that sparked the rush to the goldfields. With her sister Tot Bush, Ethel helped with cooking and panning on the claims that would innovate hydraulic mining methods in the Yukon, and she collected for herself $70,000 of gold nuggets, ending up a wealthy Beverly Hills widow.

There were eccentrics, like Royalist-socialist-feminist activist and poet Marie Joussaye Fotheringham from Belleville, Ontario. Marie had helped organize the Working Girls' Union and had published a volume of her verse before arriving in Dawson, marrying an ex-RCMP officer, snapping up over 30 claims, and being sentenced to two months' hard labour for stealing diamonds from another woman.

There were wealthy tourists Mary Hitchcock and Edith van Buren, who brought up an ice cream machine, a magic lantern, a zither, a mandolin, a bowling alley, a score of live pigeons, two canaries, a parrot, and two Great Dane dogs on their 1897 trip to Dawson.

There were notorious prostitutes like Mae Fields. Mae famously put a gun to her head after being abandoned by her husband. Thwarted by an onlooker, she still made the headlines for the attempt.

Mae supplemented her income as an Orpheum dance hall girl with keeping a house of ill repute, for which she was finally put on trial in 1908.

The lives of women like Lucille Hunter, Ethel Berry, and Mae Fields have largely been sluiced from the popular mythology of the Gold Rush, and mining the nuggets that remain in the riffles is a painstaking task. Because what scanty material exists about these women has already been explored in previous works, I have chosen to focus on the women who have left the most full and interesting accounts of their lives. I wondered:

*Mary E. Hitchcock, on the right, and Edith van Buren*
*with their Great Danes on the steamer to the Klondike in June 1898.*

What kind of woman was drawn to the Gold Rush? What were these women's lives like before and after the Gold Rush? How significant a part did the Gold Rush play in the broader continuum of these women's lives?

I discovered that the women who struggled so hard to get to the Klondike did so because they were already extraordinary in their courage, independence, and craving for adventure. These were women who strove to escape the confines of Victorian propriety and the prison of the domestic sphere. The frontier gave them the greatest opportunity for this emancipation. Whether out on the creeks or in town, these women were able to prove themselves by taking on challenges that weren't offered "Outside." They were also privileged to take part in a sensational historic event. Their time in and around Dawson City remained a pivotal point in their lives.

Shaaw Tláa, known as Kate Carmack, was damaged by the Gold Rush, and her life is a mark of the destruction such rapid colonization wrought on the First Nations communities of the Yukon. For Belinda Mulrooney and Klondike Kate Rockwell, the Gold Rush brought fame and fortune but broke their hearts. Anna DeGraf failed in the quest that sent her to the goldfields, but she succeeded in living a far more exciting life than had she stayed away. For Émilie Tremblay, Nellie Cashman, Martha Black, and Faith Fenton, the Gold Rush led to lives of marked happiness and distinction.

Wherever the Gold Rush took them, all of these women remained under the famous Spell of the Yukon, that mysterious allure stronger than gold or any other kind of fever. I was first drawn to their stories because I had fallen under the same spell, and this enchantment is the key to understanding fully who these women were and what the Klondike gave them.

# 1

## THE SPELL OF THE YUKON

*The author and her brother in Peabody's Photo Parlour, 1998.*

THE WOMEN OF THE KLONDIKE GOLD RUSH FELL UNDER THE SPELL OF the Yukon because they loved its wilderness, its promise, its guts and glory. These were women of courage who had driving ambitions and who sought every opportunity to prove what a woman could do. Like the women of Dawson City today, they demonstrated outstanding resource-fulness, undaunted determination, and a keen hunger for adventure.

I am not one of these women.

It took my brother Jake five years to convince me to come visit him in Dawson City. To all his entreaties—his appeals to sisterly loyalty and his glowing descriptions of a vibrant community, a lifestyle of enviable simplicity and freedom, and a seemingly endless wilderness—I had one reply: "The library is not big enough."

Of course, that was not the whole reason. Like many Outsiders, my impression of the Yukon had been formed largely by the legends of an unrelentingly cold and harsh land of many dangers, almost completely populated by rough, ignorant men. I fully anticipated that someone like me would be eaten alive there.

As a vegetarian, I didn't relish the idea of being surrounded by the *carci* (the plural of "carcass" in Jake-slang, pronounced *cark-eye*) of Jake's moose-hunting trips, trapline, and fish camp. As a feminist, I could conceive of nothing more tiresome than spending my time in the saloon fighting battles that had been won in my milieu decades ago. And, as a graduate school student of postmodern literary theory, I was always far too poor to afford the expensive plane fare. But, in the end, I missed Jake so much that I broke down and booked a ticket. Little did I know I'd become some sort of sourdough over the next five years, exploring ever deeper layers of Klondike culture and discovering a frontier that is much the same as it was in Gold Rush days.

Greenhorns in the Yukon are called "cheechakos," seasoned old hands are "sourdoughs." To become a sourdough, you have to have spent every season of the year in the territory; specifically you must witness the fall freeze-up of the river and the spring breakup of the ice. I remain an ambiguous sourdough, as my seasons have been staggered over separate visits. But I have gone from freeze-up to breakup, and these experiences gave me a rich context from which to understand the lives of Gold Rush women.

When Jake first arrived in the Yukon as a cheechako, it was on a beat-up old motorcycle, with all his belongings packed on with bungee cords. He rode into Whitehorse and suddenly realized all his gear was on fire. He speeded up but the flames still shot out behind him like a bushy tail. Finally he just drove straight into the lake, the speed of his wheels churning up ferocious sprays of dousing water. A classic introduction to the Klondike.

My entrance was much less spectacular. Jake picked me up at the airport in Whitehorse in September 1998, a hundred years after the stampeders made a continuous line over the Chilkoot Pass. In honour of my first visit, he'd taken two weeks off from his salmon restoration projects. He'd become so devoted to protecting the land, rivers, and wildlife in the Yukon that he'd given up winters on the trapline to initiate research studies and had worked 20 hours a day all summer on these.

We spent a night at a hotel before the long drive to Dawson. Jake told me he had worked a trapline not only to live closer to nature but also to demonstrate a vested interest on the part of Canadians to keep wilderness and wildlife wild. He explained that Yukon trappers and fishers, many of whom are First Nations, lobby to keep mining regulations tightly controlled against pollution, to prevent destructive logging and pipeline projects, and to protect traditional lifestyles that keep nature in balance. And after we talked Jake flipped through all the manic satellite channels and settled on the local First Nations station with a sigh of relief. It was a fishing show, filmed in real time, although "fishing" isn't quite accurate, as no fish were caught. In silence, a man motored down the Yukon River in his boat. Jake was riveted. Once in a while he'd get excited and say, "Oh yeah, I've camped at that spot before," or "Caught some big salmon there." It all looked like the same trees and river bank to me. I was ready to stick a fork in my eye out of boredom. This was my first introduction to "Yukon Time," the much slower pace of life up North. During one of my stays in Dawson, there was a town meeting to decide on a proposal to build a town clock. From the opposition came the comment: "But if we get this thing then everyone will know what time it is!" Since this would destroy the entire culture, the plan was dropped.

On Yukon Time, the next morning, we got into Jake's old, red pickup and began the drive to Dawson. For almost six hours we drove, rarely seeing another vehicle on the road. We stopped once, at Braeburn's Lodge, a log cabin heated by a wood stove, and ate sandwiches bigger than a bear's behind. For the entire trip, there were no billboards, no sirens, no streetlights, nothing but breathtaking vistas of white-capped mountains bristling with skirts of orange-leaved and green-needled trees, swishing ribbons of river, flashing hints of moose in the brush. We swooped around a high curve to encounter the startling beauty of the Five Finger Rapids, islands like raised knuckles. We dipped into purple-shadowed valleys and rose to stunningly bright peaks, my stomach leaping like a salmon, my breath catching in my throat, my eyes drying from a reluctance to blink and miss anything.

This was far from the barren, grey, flat tundra that had been my persistent image of the North. This subarctic region is abundant with mountains, boreal forest, and muskeg swamps. Every place I put my foot in the Yukon was a step into the unfamiliar. Boardwalks and dirt roads in Dawson, instead of concrete and asphalt. The rough rocks up mountainsides that shift and tumble under hiking boots. The spongy hillocks of muskeg in the valleys, like slippery mushrooms of frost-raised peat, sprouting from water-bogged mud. The rounded big pebbles of tailing piles in surrounding settlements, enormous hills of rocks left behind by the large dredges that operated along all the creekbeds in this area. The piles are now growing over with soil, grass, even trees, and houses and businesses are being built on them. In the dips between these hills are often tailing ponds, some sporting weeds, grayling, and beaver.

Grouse, raven, hawk, and eagle peer down from the sky. Rabbit, squirrel, fox, porcupine, marten, lynx, wolverine, wolf, bear, caribou, and moose might be glimpsed from trail or road. In season, wild blueberries, cranberries, fireweed, and thousands of different wildflowers, including orchids, may be spotted and picked. Trees are shorter, spindlier, and of less variety but are still plentiful—spruce, aspen poplar, balsam poplar, paper birch, alders, and willows. Far from bare, this primordial landscape is a feast of sharp, tangy scents; bright, rustling flora; and bold wild fauna.

Finally, we pulled up in front of Jake's shack in Bear Creek, just east of Dawson City. Like most of my friends' homes in the Yukon, it is a patched-together homemade affair crowned with moose antlers. There was the dog yard, an outdoor shop set up under a blue tarp, and a doorless outhouse facing the front door (which took getting used to). Everyone has piles of junk around their place because you never know when you might need that old iron bedstand to rig up a sled or roof rack.

Jake's partner, Janice, and his team of sled dogs gave me an enthusiastic welcome, and Jake set me up in my own wall tent—a large white canvas tent with a wood frame and floor, heated with a wood stove. I was used to a kitchen wood stove at my family's farm but never got the hang of this boiler version. I'd fall asleep in heat that could fry grayling and wake in cold that could freeze a grizzly. Usually Jake would be there building up the fire to make himself coffee, saying, "Get up, jug-butt," with the door flap wide open behind him, revealing the frost tipping the brush, the ravens bouncing on birch tree branches, the mist wreathing the mountaintops a stone's throw away. Then he'd make me return the newborn puppy I'd stolen to its mother for feeding. I fell in love with this one puppy who, eyes still sealed, would creep up my chest and suckle my nose.

Jake took me to the firing range at the dump. Hoisting the .22 rifle to my shoulder, I shot off round after round at the target, under Jake's guidance. Brought up in a hippie pacifist household, I got quite the rush shooting the gun—and I swaggered a bit the whole two weeks of my visit. The truth was that the gun was a necessity. If Jake and I got out on the river into the bush, I would have to be prepared to kill a bear if the occasion arose.

We did get out on the river on Janice's day off. The three of us brought four of the seven sled dogs and a box full of puppies on the long yellow boat Jake had built himself. Within minutes of travelling downriver, we could no longer see any signs of civilization. We stopped at an island and the dogs ran wild, their thick husky-Akita fur waving wheat-gold under the long sun. It was wordlessly beautiful. The clean, crisp air invigorating; the unimaginable expanse of the wild unknown all around freeing; the clear silence, with its echoes of breeze and rustle and raven-song, stirring. This was the moment I heard the call of the wild. I have been back and forth across Canada many times, through the Rockies, the Prairies, the Shield, the Great Lakes, the Maritimes. In the Yukon I felt more alive than anywhere else. Gold Rush journalist Faith Fenton described the feeling perfectly: "It may be the greater nearness to the primeval, but light and shadow, gradations of color, curve, form, sound . . . are intensified to a strange and special vividness in the Yukon."[1]

Janice also took me to the old-timey play at the Palace Grand Theatre, where we had our own box in the balcony. Friends of mine claim to have seen the ghost of Klondike Kate here. I think Kate would be pleased that these floorboards are still being trod by troupers.

Janice also brought me to see the high-kicking dancing girls at Diamond Tooth Gertie's Casino, where she did shifts as a blackjack dealer on top of running her own photo parlour all day. The days of the dance halls and headliners like Klondike Kate are long gone. Today Diamond Tooth Gertie's has three shows a night of about five dancers, gaudily anachronistic in costumes and choreography that mix Gay Nineties can-can with modern jazz dancing. A large, gregarious woman plays Diamond Tooth Gertie, singing and hosting. At one point, the women always drag some bashful men up on stage and make them embarrass themselves by following the dance routine, for which a winner is rewarded with the privilege of removing a garter from a dancer's leg. The only real taste of what it might have been like in the glory days comes when the show closes for the season in the fall.

On this night, the tradition is absolute lawlessness. The musicians surprise with new, often satirical, songs; the routines are spiced up with racy bits and scanty costumes; and the dancers go wild—breaking into giggles mid-song, suddenly cutting out from the chorus line to rush the bar and pound back shots of tequila, getting too drunk even to dance. The busting-loose spirit is infectious and it's quite a kick to be in the crowd on this night.

Because I was on vacation, Jake took me to The Pit every night. The Pit was still the centre of everything for Dawson locals. A ratty, eccentric

*The infamous Pit. Check your shotgun at the bar.*

tavern in the pink-fronted Westminster Hotel, with eerie portraits of distinguished town leaders and a giant mural of a Neanderthal version of The Pit surrounded by woolly mammoths on the walls, The Pit is the quintessential frontier saloon where all the wheeling and dealing in town goes down. Everyone mingles here—miners, trappers, fishers, First Nations people, government employees, politicians, business owners. This is where you go if you want to find a job, sell your truck, or slug the guy your wife slept with. Legends abound of people driving their horses or dogsleds through the bar, depending on the season. The house band, The Pointer Brothers, play country and western as only ex-bikers can and have been "held over" for many years.

The Pit was just as I feared. Mostly rowdy, unshaven men who smelled more than manly (few people in the Yukon have running water). But I liked it. Despite the occasional goading "women can't chop wood"-type comment, these men were great storytellers and demonstrated a real respect for women. In fact, of the few women that came to the bar that fall, the ones that turned heads were strongly built and moved with the confidence of muscles that have hiked hard terrain, bucked wood, and hauled water.

This was mating season in the Yukon, when single men look for women to become their bush partners on the trapline for the winter. I was rather shocked by aspects of this custom. Few women have traplines and very few work them alone, as men are known to do. It seems to be common for young women, enticed by the romance of bush life, to be mentored by older men. What's more, some will frankly admit that this is more a pragmatic than romantic arrangement. Two people chopping wood, hauling water, cooking on a wood stove, and feeding dogs can keep each other company and cut the chores in half. Later I would meet women who, with their partners, were raising their families out in the bush, at their traplines or mining camps, but you rarely see these bush couples in the bar.

I had fun with these men, banging my drink down on the table, laughing raucously, punching arms. Jake says of The Pit, "All you need is the price of admission," meaning that as long as you have the cash for your first beer, people will buy you pints all night long. And in some of the other bars, there are still rare occasions when a high roller will ding the bell, signalling that he is buying a round for the whole house, just like in the heyday of the Gold Rush.

During the day, I wandered the little toy town. Dawson City restored itself as a Gold Rush town in 1976, so it's all Victorian façades for the tourists. But this is no Disney version of the frontier. No advertisements or chain stores or fast food restaurants mar the setting, and decrepit log cabins are allowed to rot picturesquely beside the balconied hotels. The streets look much the same today as they do in sepia-toned photographs of the 1890s.

There are no traffic lights, no paved roads, no concrete sidewalks. Pickups are duct-taped together. Everyone wears jeans with plaid flannel shirts and sweatshirts that say "Dawson City" on them. At first I thought, "These people must really love their town." But then I realized that, although this is true, it is also true that these tourist clothes are pretty much the only ones you can buy here.

Having met few women on this trip, my first impression of Dawson City was of a frontier town choked with men whose attitude towards any cheechako was "Are you skookum enough?" *Skookum* is a Chinook word meaning powerful, and it is used in the Northwest in a general way. "It was totally skookum" could mean it was tough, or big, or outrageous. I could see why the territory suited my skookum brother so well, but I was yet to discover how false this picture was, just as false as many versions of the Gold Rush.

I returned the following summer, 1999, for a month. My cousin joined me for the first two weeks. Jake and Janice had moved across the road to a large spread with a pretty and unusual hand-built house. I stayed in the kind landlord's trailer by the pond. Every morning ravens performed a cancan on the roof as if they were dance hall girls at Diamond Tooth Gertie's. Then the seven husky-Akita sled dogs howled and barked as any appreciative audience would. Which got the beaver in the pond at my front door slapping his tail. This Yukon alarm clock unfailingly woke me in time to catch a ride to town.

Once again, I spent most nights in The Pit. But this time it was crowded with young women as well as men. All the students and hippies were up to work at the hotels and bars for the summer, and the town was swinging. With almost 20 hours of daylight and weather as sunny and warm as summer down South, both visitors and locals were going all day and all night, many working three jobs and still carousing for hours after their shifts. Recreational vehicles were lined up for blocks waiting for the ferry that crosses the river to join Dawson City with West Dawson and the highway to Alaska. The boardwalks, stores, and restaurants thronged with smiling people, and the bars resounded with hoots and hollers, just like in Gold Rush days.

Jake scolded us for hanging around town. That's not the Yukon, he said. So while he was sampling upriver, my cousin and I grabbed a canoe and launched it into the Klondike River. Too lazy to paddle, we drifted on the shallow current for four hours, winding around beaver dams and log-jams, spotting squatters in old rusty school buses on the banks, catching sight of a troop of firefighters in orange suits spreading over a mining piling, all the while chased by a golden eagle.

Dawson City conveniently sits where the Klondike River meets the Yukon River, so our canoe trip brought us back to The Pit. On this night, an old trapper with a grizzled white beard was the guest singer, and he sounded like the rusty parts in the Volvo graveyard beside my trailer.

It was the company not the alcohol that drew us here. Bars are the only places to socialize, making Dawson a hard-drinking town, but it is the conversation that entices, with its uniquely northern flavour. Talk is of guns, chainsaws, and pickup trucks. The old-timers tell their stories of excess and deprivation, trying to shock cheechakos with an ancient tale of puppy skins hanging from the rafters during a lean winter.

Many tough-guy stories are still being played out in the Yukon, but sometimes the tough guys are women. A bushwoman I know named Kirsten once tried rafting from a remote trapline back to Dawson during breakup, with disastrous results. She and her partner, known as Hurricane, had had a rough season and were low on food, so they needed to get to town in a hurry. Mushing through wet spring snow in the mountains would take more days than their rations allowed for. Hurricane insisted they raft down, even though it was breakup, exultant at the adventure it would be.

The raft broke up in the raging current, buffeted by slabs of ice. Down into the surging water went everything they owned, including the dog team tied to the raft. Kirsten's hands were so cold that when she tried to cut the dogs free the knife slipped and stabbed her hand.

She was able to rescue only two of the dogs from drowning, but she also saved Hurricane's life. She got to shore and lay on the slippery ice to pull him out as he fought the torrent whirling around him. It took several heart-stopping tries before she could yank him onto the bank beside her. The two were stranded in winter temperatures, dripping wet, with no sled or provisions, in the middle of nowhere. She got a fire going— panicking that her hands were too frozen to even hold a match—and the couple took hours to get dry but managed to avoid frostbite or exposure.

They had days of hiking in front of them before they could reach a cabin where friends lived. There was no trail and they bushwhacked through the mountains. They began the journey lean and hungry from a severely rationed winter. Now they were skeletal with starvation. After a few days, they were so weak that it looked as if they wouldn't make it. Hurricane said they needed to eat their remaining dogs to survive. Kirsten argued for just one more day. The next day, they and their dogs reached the friends' cabin—and the famous bush hospitality that fed and clothed them and got them to town.

After nights of such stories in The Pit, we finally got a break from The Pointer Brothers when it was time for the Dawson City Music Festival. This festival really captures the frontier spirit that began in the Gold Rush and continues today. It seems as if the entire population volunteers to put it together, and musicians from all over the world are welcomed as part of the community. For three days, Dawson is so invaded that the hotels are overflowing and many visitors sleep on the streets in their cars. The whole town lets its hair down. When I went to get money, I found that someone had left a roll of duct tape, an emblem of life in Dawson, on the bank machine, and I saw that inside the closed bank a shirtless guy with a handlebar mustache was stretching with a beer in one hand and a rolled smoke in the other.

Men here like to dance. Soon I was being hurled around inside the festival tent to music by Latin Americans Diego Marulanda & Pacande and by a ska band called the Planet Smashers while whole families two-stepped across the floor, kicking up clouds of dust. Meanwhile, out in the beer garden, the rumours sparked like fireflies, giving an idea of how all those Klondike legends got started. Everyone said that someone named Typhoid Charlie had been murdered.

After one o'clock in the morning, the sun began to set. It would be twilight for a few hours and then sunrise again after only a flash of darkness. I looked up just as a shooting star sledded across the sky to the jagged peak of the Dome, the highest point in the mountains that ring the town. I thought of all the women who'd been here a hundred years earlier, how they too must have been struck into wonder by such a night.

The summer of 1999 was plagued by massive forest fires, which brought scads of firefighters to town. One of the local recruits, a bush-man who'd lived in the Yukon about fifteen years, began to woo me.

I mention this only because the courtship was so quintessentially Klondike. One night we were sitting in the crowded Pit with his and my brother's compadres when Jake yelled down the table at him: "Hey, if you're sweet on my sister, tradition says you'll have to drink a jug of beer out of her gumboot!"

The men grabbed my leg and pulled off my rubber boot, which the waitress filled with beer. My suitor gulped it down to a chorus of cheers, then he traded a wolverine pelt he'd trapped to a South American trader for a knife for himself and unset jewels for me. He invited me back to his shack to see the bearskin rug once worn by the beast he'd shot straight through the nose as it charged him one night.

He took me out to the bridge on the Dempster Highway. Looking down at the big red salmon swimming in pairs below, I finally understood my brother's love for these fish. They looked like animate ripe fruit. When I looked up, a dark grey fox with a squirrel in its mouth was pacing back and forth at the entrance to the bridge, venturing forth then retreating. Finally the vixen got up enough gumption and sidled by us, her black feral eyes never leaving mine.

Seasons change fast in the Yukon. By now, mid-August, the temperature dropped below zero some nights, the leaves were turning colour, and autumn briskness zinged the air.

It was time to go back to Toronto. My suitor drove me to Whitehorse on his Ducati motorcycle. We tore through the mountains, the river appearing and disappearing beside us. So fast that we outran the sharp scent of spruce, so fast that my hair dragged the road when we tilted around corners, so fast that I missed seeing the cow moose in the road that we swerved around. At one point, my boot caught on fire from the tailpipe, and without disturbing the driver I gave my leg a quick shake and extinguished the flames in the chill air whipping past. Almost two in the morning, we were still hours away from our destination, out of gas in front of the closed gas station in Carmacks. We ambled over to the nearest bar and heard a First Nations woman at the karaoke machine give one of the most achingly beautiful renditions of Pasty Cline's *Walking After Midnight* I have ever heard. One of the bartenders gave us a jerry can and we made it to Braeburn's Lodge. Despite five layers of clothes, I was frozen stiff and couldn't move my gloved hands. The kind owner opened up for us. After warming up with hot chocolate, we went back outside. For the first time in my life, I saw the northern lights, twin green streams of light flowing across the immense black sky, merging, separating, undulating against each other. I stood open-mouthed with my head thrown back for what seemed like hours, completely mesmerized.

We made it to the hotel in Whitehorse at four in the morning. The next day, we had just enough time to see Miles Canyon before my flight left. From the bridge across the canyon, I stared into the deep teal-green water as it eddied into whirlpool and rapids, imagining the tens of thousands of men and women who'd braved this canyon in rigged-up rafts and boats, risking their lives and everything they owned to get to the goldfields. We hopped down and across to a little island in the river and peeked around the bend to see stronger rapids farther down. This was the Klondike I was ready to explore.

The following summer, I drove up alone in my aunt's old station wagon, starting my journey on June 1, 2000. Driving across the Canadian Shield, the Prairies, and the Rocky Mountains, it took almost seven days to get to Prince Rupert, where I boarded the ferry to Skagway. As a gift, my father had reserved a stateroom for me with two bunks, a shower, and a window looking directly out over the ocean. Most people sleep out on deck in lounge chairs, dependent on the overhang's heat lamps for comfort in the damp chill that persists all summer. I was grateful for the prospect of a room that would be warm, clean, and most of all, private. I'd spent the night shivering in a flimsy tent in front of a swamp with bikers carousing beside me—but I had woken to see bald eagles nesting atop bare silver trees.

The ferry was hours late and crowded. Another ferry had ignited with an electrical fire in the control room, necessitating a mid-ocean rescue. My ferry had pulled up alongside and plywood boards were gangplanked across the churning waves. Hundreds of cars, recreational vehicles, and trucks drove over these flimsy boards into the safety of my ferry's hold as the Pacific seethed beneath them.

There was a respectable camaraderie aboard. I was too wide-eyed to sleep much and noticed that there seemed to be two sets of passengers, those you only saw in the day and those you only saw at night. By day, a group of male tourists adopted me as their kid sister and taught me to play hearts, our games interrupted as we passed blue-tinged glaciers or leapt up with binoculars to catch the last flip of a whale's tail. After midnight, the ship floated in pure blackness and I went to the bar to argue with Alaskan fishers about the new salmon treaty my brother had supported. When I later read Martha Black's account of her steamship ride, I felt lucky to have travelled in such luxury. She had had to bunk with a gambler and ladies of ill repute:

> The steamer was certainly a has-been. She was dirty, and loaded to
> the gunwales with passengers, animals and freight. Men slept on the
> floor of the saloon and in every corner. The captain was seldom, if
> ever, sober, and there were many wild parties. Poker, blackjack, and
> drinking went on night and day, and our safe arrival in Skagway was
> due probably to the Guiding Hand that looks after children, fools,
> and drunken men.[2]

After two days and two nights on the ferry, I disembarked in Skagway at four in the morning as the dawn spread into thick mists. Like Dawson, Skagway has the appearance of a movie set with its preservation of eccentric frontier facades. Long gone are the days when outlaw Soapy Smith ran this town, so I had no need to fear falling victim to con games or gunshots.

I carried on to the Alaska Highway. Driving slowly through a thick white fog, I had to sense the steepness of the mountains in the strain of my engine, for I could see nothing, not even the road immediately in front. Only once in the hours I drove did another car emerge from the blankness and pass back into it. When I reached the highest summit, near the White Pass, the air cleared briefly and I was startled by sharp banks of snow, ponds frozen a shocking aquamarine, unending vistas of white-crested peaks, all unearthly with a moonlike, unending barrenness. Snow in June!

It took four hours to reach Whitehorse, a two-hour trip on a clear day, then another six to Dawson, crossing bridges over island-studded rivers, careening around sharp corners between mountain and lake, hardly ever seeing another driver. To travel for so long and see only endless ranges of peaks and valleys, knowing you are alone on the only road going, pure of the clutter of modern civilization, it changes you. Every mile brings a greater sense of being stripped down to what is most unambiguously real—the sun in your eyes, the wind on your skin, the whole earth inhaling and exhaling with you.

That summer I finally met the women of Dawson. My brother and Janice had parted, but Janice gave me a weekend job in her store, Peabody's Photo Parlour, and Jake's new partner, Megan, had opened her own store down the street, The Fashion Nugget. Most of the businesses in town are owned and run by women, which is why you don't tend to meet them in The Pit—they are too busy to go out most nights. Every woman I met, young and old, was full of plans and working round the clock. Many had spent time living in the bush, most still lived without electricity, running water, and phone, amenities which I take for granted even in rural Ontario. Some were living in Tent City, the campground across the river, and after a night on the ground in a sleeping bag they would cross on the ferry and somehow arrive at work looking well groomed. Others were raising children in one-room cabins, baking their own bread with a wood stove and hauling water to wash diapers. A few were building their first house.

The town was changing. The old Oddfellows Hall across from Peabody's had been elegantly renovated as the Dawson City Arts Society and now housed an art gallery—The Odd Gallery—a ballroom, offices, and a classroom. Two women, Kim and Wendy, had moved an old bordello from the other side of town to the corner directly across the street from the Oddfellows and converted it into a stylish hotel, Bombay Peggy's, with a swanky pub. An arts scene was forming and beginning to thrive, with a yearly international film festival in February, a summer art festival, a six-month Arts for Employment program, and many cultural events year round organized by the Klondike Institute for Arts and Culture (KIAC). As trapping, fishing, and mining fall from their previous peaks, it is the arts that are drawing new blood to Dawson.

In previous years, many men and women came to Dawson drawn by the bush lifestyle. Some chose this way of life because they wanted to be self-sufficient, part of nature, free of the consumerism and superficiality of the technological world. Others were enamoured of the cachet of bush life and how it seemed to keep the Klondike frontier legends alive. Now it is a cultural renaissance that is attracting young artistically inclined people, especially women. While there is still talk of guns, chainsaws, and trucks, talk about films, books, and paintings is growing louder. These conversations have always occurred among parts of the community, but now they are given a greater place. And I was now enough a part of the community to see these deeper layers, in which women play a much larger role than it looks like on the surface.

There is a strong tradition of volunteerism in the Yukon, and many of the volunteers are women. That summer, I helped make gourmet pizzas for the Music Festival musicians with a dozen other volunteers and I got a behind-the-scenes look at how extremely expert Dawsonites are at putting on any kind of show. If you have ever taken a weekend workshop in anything, you will be invited to provide this service or teach it at the Arts Society. I taught creative writing. There are also classes specifically for women in survival skills like car repair and chainsaw maintenance and operation.

Female friendships build alliances within the community, providing much needed support in this remote area. Most of the women I know have worked at the women's shelter at one time or another. And at the end of the summer, there was a women's festival with concerts by female musicians as well as workshops on belly dancing, dog ownership, making mosaics, and such.

Now that I had wonderful women friends in town, I was invited to the all-female social occasions that left my belly sore from shared laughter and feasts. Many plans were laid at these events, everyone helping each other to achieve their dreams. It was a joy to discover this part of life in the North. I was amazed at how narrow and misguided my initial impressions had been. It rained for 40 days and nights that summer, but I was thrilled to be back in the trailer in Bear Creek, learning this new world.

Just like a century ago, you have to prove yourself before you can really become part of the frontier community and go deeper into the culture. It takes time. And it takes even more time, if you are white like myself, to earn relationships within the First Nations community. The Tr'ondëk Hwëch'in Nation is coming back in force after surviving the colonization that the Gold Rush ushered in and recently settling their land claims. But there remains a sense of social segregation because the two cultures, and their values, are so different, I rarely met First Nations women at the bar or at parties. The two communities do work closely together, though, especially when it comes to the environment.

My brother took a friend and me out to one of his projects, the Chandindu River Salmon Weir. We spent hours going down the river, passing the village at Moosehide, abandoned camps from the mushroom pickers that had swarmed the area in earlier months, and pink-hued cliffs that looked as if they were straining to become flesh. Then we hiked for miles through boggy forest out to the weir-camp. Bush etiquette is such that visitors must never arrive empty-handed or leave unfed. Jake brought fresh supplies. Two welcoming Tr'ondëk Hwëch'in men cooked us bannock and showed our pal how to tag a fish. I watched wide-eyed as the enormous salmon, like a raw, pulsing muscle with eyes and mouth, was calmed in their capable hands.

Jake's friend Mary Ellen Jarvis, a drily witty woman, also took me out on the river, this time upstream to Ancient Voices, the camp that immerses visitors in local Tr'ondëk Hwëch'in culture. It was Mary Ellen's job to travel around to remote fish camps and First Nations communities all over the Yukon, spreading news of in-season fish management and collecting catch information for a territory-wide study that is a result of the Land Claims Agreement. As she talked with the women of the Kormandy family, I played catch with their little girl, respectfully keeping out of the elders' way.

Things happen on the river that you don't get to see in town. And you must exercise some foresight and caution. On the way out, our journey had been interrupted by a couple stranded on an island without gas for their boat. Mary Ellen gave them the fuel to get back to Dawson. Then we saw a huge bear swimming across the river right in front of us, as fast as any Olympic athlete despite her huge bulk.

Another friend also took me out of town for a picnic. We drove on narrow, pot-holed mining roads all over Bonanza and Hunker Creeks, past the Discovery Claim and claims still being worked by lone or family placer miners. Imagining living in these valleys, as Émilie Tremblay did, I could see how isolated these women were, and yet also how free to run into the hills with their skirts hitched up and howl.

It was hard to leave this country of extremes. And not only because I had begun to feel at home. A friend had borrowed my car to drive to Whitehorse and had accidentally smashed the front into another friend's

*The author's car with hood duct-taped shut after a friend smashed it into a highway sweeper. A popular subject for tourist photos.*

highway sweeper. Tourists were taking pictures of my station wagon as the classic Yukon vehicle, its frame slightly twisted, its hood held down by a net of duct tape. It took weeks to get a mechanic an hour and a half outside of town to fix it up.

Luckily, the harsh climate and road conditions have made the RCMP in the North understanding about cars held together with duct tape. The Yukon is now the most policed area in Canada, with double the number of officers per capita of other Canadian provinces and territories, and no one in Dawson locks their homes or vehicles. This was also true in Gold Rush days. Far from lawless, Dawson City was well policed, and while the RCMP may have dismissed some petty infractions, they were hard on actual crime. The community also has its own way of dealing with people who break the rules.

The knowledge that you depend on each other for survival in the most brutal of climates creates a close-knit community that has a generous tolerance for eccentricity and a reluctance to punish bad behaviour. You could grift your neighbour of her savings, seduce her husband, and throw a drink in her face—she'll still stop and help dig your Ski-Doo out of the ditch.

The remoteness of the North does attract rascals—perhaps fleeing the law or more personal demons down South—but the community has its own way of dealing with them. If the haywire tunes up, the past is forgotten. If not, then everyone will still lift a glass with the ne'er-do-well in The Pit, but gradually it will be harder to get a job or a place to rent. Survival here depends on the exchange of favours. People need the help of others to get wood in for the winter, insulate shacks, plow snow from lanes. If you are left out of this exchange, your life will become very difficult. The exclusion is subtle and effective, but it doesn't carry the same sense of judgment that social snubbing does.

And when it doesn't work, there is still the "blue ticket"—running people out of town, a custom begun in the Gold Rush days. I know of two examples, and both cases involved women who were mentally ill and prone to violent outbursts. The community tried to help them for years, and it was only when they had crossed the line into breaking the law many times that the RCMP put them on a bus out of town with instructions not to return. There are no mental health facilities here so the blue ticket is typical of the way the North accepts eccentricities yet draws the line at extremely unacceptable behaviour that threatens the community. The First Nations have also instituted justice circles within the territory's circuit-court system.

This particular summer, one scalawag boarded a string of horses at my brother's then disappeared without paying or providing feed as contracted. Living at the trailer at Jake's was always a circus. Packs of horses wandering by, dogs scrapping underfoot, cats yowling. People were always dropping by to mend fishing nets, borrow tools, use the shop to fix their vehicles, plan for Renewal Resource Council and Salmon Fishing Association meetings, pick up puppies, and share tips on breaking trail, repairing a chainsaw, and building a boat. Even respected First Nations elder Percy Henry dropped by to borrow epoxy for his boat and get horse manure for his garden. As in the Gold Rush days, you must be self-sufficient and learn everything from scratch, and the community is the only real resource you've got.

This was what I missed when driving back across the country in September: the unique women and men that make every day an event; the strong community that accepts everyone and is always there to help someone up; the sense of possibility where anyone can make anything happen without having to tangle with red tape or spend years attaining credentials; and the invigoration of being entirely surrounded by nature, unmediated, wild, free.

In April and May of 2001, I returned to Dawson to do an internship for my teaching certificate. This was my first spring up North. Staying in a camper with broken windows and a door that wouldn't close was not very comfortable when there were both freezing snow on the ground and vicious mosquitoes in the air. I am cold even in humid Toronto summers and did a fair bit of whingeing about the barbarity of winter temperatures in April.

The highlight of my stay was a trip to Top of the World, the border between the Yukon and Alaska, where my friend worked as a customs officer. Some buddies took me up and we picked cranberries from the low bushes on the side of the mountain as the dogs streaked back and forth across the valley. The mountains here had a more melancholy and rugged beauty, all seemed slate and granite grey in shales and pebbles, creasing into deep clefts and peaking into jagged tips. Driving there and back, we passed massive overhangs of solid ice gleaming a spectral greenish white. It really seemed the ends of the earth, not a single pit stop or passing vehicle.

I also got to see my first spring breakup. Almost daily, crossing the Klondike River into town, I watched for the signs. Sure enough, the Klondike fractured into small chunks of ice that pushed up against each other as they struggled to get downstream to the Yukon River. A massive jam of ice was piled at the mouth of the Yukon, shoving at the unbroken sheet that still covered this mightier river, its top layer melting into puddles. Friends who live across the river in West Dawson are stranded there for however long it takes the river to break up or freeze up, depending on the season. With global warming, these processes are longer, more gradual, taking sometimes over a month.

In his early years in Dawson, Jake saw the old kind of breakup. Years ago, the river would break up all at once, cataclysmically. Enormous chunks of ice, some as high as a three-storey building, would crash into each other with the sound of an explosion. For hours, the ear-splitting cracks and crunches, booms and blasts of the breaking ice would echo across the mountains. And then it would be over.

I missed the moment the Yukon first broke. For over a hundred years, this event has always been announced by a siren blaring all through the town as everyone drops whatever they are doing and rushes to the riverbank in cheering crowds. But you can't hear the siren from Bear Creek, where I was working all day at my computer in the camper. I went into town hours later and saw rafts of ice jostling each other as they sluggishly floated past, some elbowed to the bank to stack up in ungainly staircases. It was still a powerful vision. I could taste both the hard ice and the soft water on the wind, feel their different scents mingle in my lungs, sharp cold with hint of cloud and murky cool with tang of mud.

By the beginning of May, spring had settled in. Literally overnight, fuzzy green buds sprouted on the beech and willow trees, a purple crocus appeared in the garden, and the grass was suddenly free of all but a few spots of snow. Just when I would actually enjoy being in my draughty camper, it was time to go.

In September, I drove up North again. I had a proposal approved to design the curriculum for and teach a six-month writing program. And I had a contract to research and write this book. Everything was in order. But order is often an illusion. In northwestern Ontario, I had to bushwhack off-highway for a couple hours to find gas. What I found was a single pump in front of a seemingly deserted marina. I went into the office and found three young men sitting in front of live satellite TV, watching the towers of the World Trade Center collapse. It was September 11. Whitehorse would soon be evacuated because of an apparent plane hijacking and fighter jets would circle the airport. Panic was pervasive.

The rest of the journey had a nightmarish quality. Stranded Americans filled all the hotels and roadside diners. In one town, I had to drive to the outskirts to find the last motel with a room available. But there was a roadblock outside my destination, red lights spinning around atop fire trucks. A police officer approached me. I happened to have a bumper sticker that read "Ladies Sewing Circle and Terrorist Society." This made him laugh. He said there was a problem with a gas main but I could cross the barricade to get to the motel. Sleep was scarce there and everywhere.

I took the direct Yellowhead route this time and reached Liard Hot Springs with relief. A bit nervous about bears, I walked the long ramp across marsh and through forest to sink gratefully into the steaming sulphuric waters, my breath still coming out puffy white in the crisp air. Alone in the natural pool, I became blissfully languid, all my muscles finally relaxing. It was a glorious way to return North.

Almost as soon as I arrived in Dawson, I heard that my grandfather had died. It was strange and uncomfortable to mourn so far from my family, to feel so distant. How much worse it must have been when there weren't telephones, when the mail took months to arrive, when the trip back out would take weeks.

Already the leaves had fallen from the trees. I moved into my own one-room log cabin out in Bear Creek, perfectly spacious, with the electricity and phone lines I needed for my work, and a small oil furnace, called a monitor, so I didn't have to worry about an overloaded or neglected wood stove damaging my computer. But there was no running water, and in this small detail I was to learn what is was to be a sourdough. I hauled water from town in big blue jugs for cooking, dishwashing, and cleaning my face. Once a week, I went to Jake's to bathe in his sulphuric and brackish well water. As for a toilet, I was proud to have my own outhouse.

As soon as I'd set up my place, in early October, I came down with pneumonia. There is no hospital in Dawson, just a nursing station and a doctor's clinic. My illness became so severe that they were afraid I'd die

*The author's rented one-room cabin outside of Dawson City,*
*featuring the classic moose antlers as decoration.*

if they didn't medevac me by helicopter to Whitehorse. Thankfully, a
megadose of steroids saved me this melodrama.

After this inauspicious beginning, I began to work like mad. Over
the winter, on top of researching the book and developing the curriculum, I did some writing for the Klondike Institute for Arts and Culture,
sat on the Dawson City Arts Society selection committee, organized a
small Collage Party to benefit the museum, had two quilts in the Quilt
Show organized by Megan (who had moved in with Jake and was pregnant with their first child), participated in an Artists Trading Card trade
show, and performed in an art video. The activities are a drop in the
bucket compared with the volunteer efforts of most Dawsonites and
demonstrates just how much really goes on in this remote community.

This is the secret of Dawson City. When the ferry is pulled out of
the river and the last tourist has left, there is a lull while everyone pre-
pares for winter. The discotheque, the Palace Grand Theatre, Diamond

Tooth Gertie's Casino, stores and restaurants are closed up until next May. The streets are deserted. A great silent peace descends as the first snow falls. Many locals are busy insulating their ramshackle homes, cleaning up their soon-to-be-buried yards, getting cords of wood in. Then the town bursts into activity from Hallowe'en until New Year's Day. There are movie nights with new independent films, dance performances by troupes from Toronto, art shows with local and international artists, concerts by violinists, talks by the artists-in-residence, readings by the Berton House writer-in-residence, and gatherings, especially costume parties, every weekend.

Because many people don't have phones, they stop into Bombay Peggy's to get the news. Just as in Gold Rush days, everyone is always mad to know who will be staying for the winter; the population so dwindles that each person who remains becomes an important indication of the kind of winter it will be. Gossip is always a welcome distraction in Dawson, but speculation runs rampant when there are fewer people to talk about. Say a pal stops by for tea and his truck stalls. You give him a lift home. The next morning a neighbour will run into someone and say, "Hey, his truck is still in front of her place, think something might be going on there?" By afternoon, every single person in town knows about this and some are convinced there is mischief afoot.

After a grand Hallowe'en party, with all guests in elaborate costumes—I went as a gold nugget—a few people in town were privy to top secret information about when the herds of caribou would be running through the territory. This was to be kept confidential so as to protect the forerunners of the herds. A plan was hatched. The veterinarian invited the two artists-in-residence and myself to drive up the Dempster and see what, as a code word, we were calling "the 'Bou."

It was pitch dark at seven in the morning when we started out. We had all been up until three at a vernissage at the art gallery, so we were sleepy. A cold snap had iced all the trees with glittering adornment. With the wind, it was 20 below, Celsius. As you always must, we brought plenty of gear, because if we broke down there would be nothing and nobody for days of hiking. We packed sleeping bags, lots of chocolate bars, fire-starter, an axe, tools, extra gas, and duct tape.

For hours and hours we drove north in a fierce wind toward the Arctic Circle, the highway edged on each side with swaths of snowy tundra and then ranges of grand mountains. It was a vast white planet. Winter-bleached ptarmigan—notoriously stupid grouse-like birds that usually get crunched under tires—were everywhere, like stacks of paper being blown all over the road. We saw three glorious sundogs, rainbows formed from ice crystals instead of rain. And finally, when parked and

*The Fortymile caribou herd migrating.*

picnicking, we saw seven caribou in the distance through binoculars. If we had come up two days before, we would have been able to walk amongst hundreds of them migrating but now they had scattered. It was well worth it to see even so few, their elegant antlers twitching above graceful bodies as they loped down the mountain and across the tundra. Imagining how far they'd already come and how much farther they would roam, and knowing we were in their land where they were free to live as they had always lived, seemed miraculous.

At this time of year, it is light only for a few hours each day. Faith Fenton gave a very detailed and accurate description in one of her 1899 *Globe* articles:

Through the November days we watched the sunrise, or rather the reflection of it, around the mountain tops at 10 o'clock in the morning. There would be a yellow flush upon a southeastern peak, the clouds trailing about the heights grew rosy and lit the snowy crests into a lovely glow. Then a rim of gold lifted itself above the lofty horizon, just a rim, like the arc of a time-worn wedding ring. It would slip across the southern horizon–a little journey of two hours or less duration–then drop down behind the mountain peaks. Its day's work was done, and only the dying crimson flush remained.

With early December days the golden rim disappeared. Only the yellow and gold light upon the peaks told us that the sun was shining somewhere down below the mountains. Now, in mid-December, we do not see it at all, and the light upon the peaks is very faint and brief, a touch of rosiness at midday and then the afternoon greyness.

But this sunless month is not one of continued night . . . It is grey, as a cloudy day may be. Dark until 9 A.M., twilight until 10, then a grey midday, followed by twilight at 2 P.M., that deepens into night darkness at 3.[3]

In January, the flush reappears, followed by the golden rim, then the full sun again, rising ever higher until the summer solstice's endless days.

Although the winter of 2001–02 was mild, each successive drop in temperature was a shock. Twenty below was a shock that I got used to; 30 below was another shock that I got used to; but 40 below was a shock there was no getting used to. At 40 below, no amount of down-filled and polar fleece layers seems enough. The breath freezes in your throat and lungs. Any exposed skin stings. Muscles stiffen in their swaths of bulky clothes. For my first day at 40 below, I celebrated by making cupcakes and delivering them to pals around town. Then I crawled under my arctic-weight duvet and sleeping bag with my computer and didn't emerge until it warmed up a couple of degrees.

Not to be indelicate, but imagine what it is like to depend on an outhouse in such a climate. If I needed to relieve myself, I would have to put on three layers of clothing—not forgetting hat, scarf, mitts—and clumsily stumble through the pitch dark to my outhouse, which was webbed inside with frost the entire winter. I'd brush the crumbles of snow off the Styrofoam seat. Then came the hard part, taking off my moosehide mitts to unbutton all pants and pull them down. Flesh thus bared would sting even after I got back inside the cabin. I soon relented and got a "honey bucket" for urine in my cabin.

I don't know how my brother and friends have survived 50 below, many times, and sometimes out in the bush. At this temperature, your breath freezes in the air in front of you and falls tinkling like crystals to the ground. Oil freezes in engines. To get your car started, if you don't have electricity, you have to heat up a propane tank by the wood stove, put a tarp over your car, and spend two hours heating up every single part of your engine with a tiger torch without blowing yourself up.

Yukoners say it is a dry cold that is much more bearable than the wet cold of Toronto, which I warmly contest. I never have to wear wool long johns, down ski pants, three sweaters, a down parka, and enormous arctic boots that make you walk like an astronaut when I winter in Toronto. But I certainly did in the Yukon. People who stay on in Dawson are those whose bodies actually *enjoy* the cold. Faith Fenton was clearly one of these: "Fifty degrees below zero—and exhilarating to intoxication. We breathe ozone; we walk on air; of pounds avoirdupois we have none, we are electrical spirits flashing without consciousness of weight or weariness."[4]

There are other dangers in the winter. A coyote ate Megan's cat. A woman was walking her dogs just outside of town and wolves came down and tore them to pieces right in front of her. But the bears are in hibernation so humans are safe.

The season is also one of countless celebrations where friends come together like family. I ate two enormous Thanksgiving feasts, one with 20 close pals at Jake's place, and another at the artists-in-residence house. I had two Christmas dinners as well. One was at the Dawson City Arts Society, and ended in demonstrations of belly-dancing moves on the ballroom floor while listening to Eartha Kitt sing "Santa Baby." The other was cross-river by snow machine with West Dawsonites. All events are charmingly decorated, with gourmet food, and glamorous outfits underneath snow pants and parkas, just like at the peak of the Gold Rush, when Dawson was becoming a cosmopolitan city.

For New Year's Eve, Jake and Megan had a beautiful skating party with snow lanterns ringing their pond, a bonfire circled with benches right on the ice, and sushi arranged decoratively back inside their house. But I went to the Odd Ball at the Arts Society because I'd never been to a ball before. Art students had decorated the elegant room with swaths of gold lamé and fairy lights. It was hard to recognize everyone out of their parkas and shined up in silks and velvets, toasting the new year with champagne. I had brought up a twelve-dollar Goodwill dress especially for this occasion: a white satin 1940s evening gown trimmed with white marabou feathers that made a Dr. Seuss-like swirl on the skirt. As a friend twirled me around like Ginger Rogers, all about us were people swinging each other and laughing under the high chandeliers, filled with the joy of coming together to create a true celebration, as silver stars and green hints of northern lights hung high in the windows, guiding us into the new year.

Such gaiety ends in January, when many locals leave for warmer climes like Thailand, Costa Rica, Mexico. This is the worst month, when the days have been too dark and too cold for too long. I holed up in my cabin with my research and barely emerged until February, which is the best month as the sun returns quickly day by day, infusing you with its energy and warmth.

My favourite day in the winter of 2001–02 was spent dog-mushing on the Klondike River with a chum and his friendly, scruffy team. The beauty of the dogs flowing like mercury around the curves of the trail, their fur rippling dark and golden before me, their paws shooting back sparkles of snow to dew my face. The sled making smooth gliding sounds in the echoing silence and skimming dangerously close to black splits of open water. All around, the unrisen sun tinting the white mountains peach and violet and aqua from the horizon. Sailing on the ice of the river as it is winding into a world so unimaginably unending, white, and wild—I never wanted to do anything else but this again.

This again is the Spell of the Yukon. When all around you are massive heaps of spruced-up mountains, farther than you can imagine never mind see; when the pervasive silence is startled only by the whack of a beaver tail or the rustle of a moose that may never have seen a human; when you know that your axe breaking while you are out in the bush in 70 below temperatures can mean your frozen body might not being found for weeks—a permanent awe infuses you, leaving no room for petty inanities.

Everything is stripped down to what is most important in life. What appeals to me the most about Dawson is its lack of media representations, multinational corporations, and hype. Shopping is not an entertainment.

People make their own fun. No one has seen the newest hot video and nobody cares. Life is unmediated—it is about true grit, not flash.

I began to need some of that true grit as I earned my Klondike name, Jinx Duncan. First, the engine of my car burst into flames on the road back to Bear Creek. Jake was following behind and pulled over to open the hood and yell, "Get everything out of the car! Don't you have any water in there?" I thought, "No, water freezes in the car," then looked around to realize that we were surrounded by water. I began stuffing chunks of snow into the engine, which effectively killed the fire. But my car was also dead. What would I do, living over ten klicks out of town in winter without a car?

I borrowed a friend's old truck, but without four-wheel drive it wouldn't make it into my lane and then it too died. Jake and Megan were in Whitehorse, anticipating the birth of their first child (Dawson doesn't have a hospital so expectant mothers must move to hotels in Whitehorse two weeks prior to the delivery date). Megan's truck was loaned out to a filmmaker in town teaching workshops for the International Film Festival, and it wasn't working either. Luckily, many neighbours kindly gave me rides to and from town with my water jugs and groceries.

The streets of Dawson were filled with motley film crews as everyone participated in producing the shorts that would compete in the Local Yokels part of the festival. My friend K.C. Woodfine had me torturing apples for her art video, *Five Apples.* I volunteered as doorperson for the festival itself and was privileged to see films that came from Mexico, Norway, Israel, Afghanistan, everywhere. As in summer, the town was crowded with strangers, and it was startling to pass people on the boardwalk and not know them. The ballroom at the Arts Society was packed every night. K.C.'s film won Best in Show for local shorts, but the most popular feature-length film was Troy Suzuki's hilarious *Moccasin Square Gardens,* a documentary about the re-creation of the Dawson hockey team's cross-country trip by bicycle, dogsled and train to play against the Ottawa Senators. It captured the Yukon perfectly, its indomitable spirit of goofy, haywire courage, always attempting the impossible and laughing at the stumbles on the climb.

Unfortunately, I had stomach flu the whole festival and found myself at four in the morning at the closing night party miserably ill with no ride home. I put on my gear and headed out in the 30-below cold. It was hard to see the trail in the smoky charcoal darkness, and I was glad as the hours brought lighter and lighter greyness to keep me from slipping down into a frozen tailing pond. It took over two hours to stumble the seven miles back to my cabin but I loved every minute of it. To force myself to meet this challenge, belly queasy with sickness and legs aching with lifting the big, heavy Sorel boots; to be right in the frigid night, not gazing from behind a frosty window; to feel each step make this territory my home—it was sheer glory! Although this small excursion pales in comparison with the feats performed daily by Yukon women both during the Gold Rush and now, it gave me a small taste of what feeds the hunger to pit oneself against these elements.

Not having a car was a real test of endurance. To get water, I'd have to haul my big water jugs over to a neighbour's or the highway to bum a ride into town. I'd fill up the jugs in Peabody's darkroom then have to wait around Bombay Peggy's until I could find a kind soul going back to Bear Creek. It ate up hours and got me into trouble.

One day, Jake drove my jugs and me into town early in the morning. I hung around in the freezing cold by the river until Maximilian's General Store opened. The news there was about who had bought what for Janice's birthday, which was thought to be that day. I stopped by the desktop publishing business to check. Yes, it was her birthday. Damn, I forgot the present at the cabin. I got groceries, running into more pals, then went to Peabody's and said, "Hey, Janice! Happy birthday! Can I fill up my jugs and borrow your car for an hour?" She said sure. I went out back and put the filled jugs and grocery bags in the back seat of her red car. Janice came out and asked if I would watch the store while she ran an errand in her car. I happily manned the till. A friend came in and said everyone would meet at Bombay Peggy's that night for Janice's birthday, then there would be a space-theme costume party out at Bear Creek. Janice returned and said her car was parked out front. I went out and, sure enough, a red car was right there with keys in the ignition. I got in and raced home, dropping off a photo delivery on the way. When I reached my cabin, the phone was ringing. I picked it up.

"Come back right now!" Janice was yelling. "You have stolen a car and the RCMP are looking for you. That wasn't my car!"

I wrapped her present, got back in the stolen vehicle, laughed when I noticed no water jugs in the back seat, and drove to town. I parked the car where I'd found it, slipped five dollars for gas under a seat cushion, and went to give Janice her present. Janice had a good giggle as she described the amusement of the woman who'd come looking for her car, and the RCMP, when she'd explained the situation to them. This time, I got in the right car and drove my supplies home, returning immediately. Within less than an hour, the story was all over town. Rideless, I then had to hang around Bombay Peggy's for hours as every single person who entered pointed at me and said, "Ha! Jinx, the car thief!"

I was jinxed in other ways, too. Twice my heat monitor conked out and it was 30 or 40 below *inside* my cabin, the water in my kettle freezing on the stove and frost forming in the corners of the ceiling. I tried to write in bed under the down covers, fully dressed in parka and snow pants, working on my laptop with fingertips pecking out from fingerless wool gloves.

The funding for the course I was to teach and other expected payments were delayed. For the first time in my life, I couldn't pay my rent or bills on time. My research stalled as I couldn't afford a single photocopy. I was carless and completely penniless and trapped in the Yukon—which is how some people end up living there. Then the summer tenants returned and I had to leave my cabin and move into a wall tent at Jake's, where one of his dogs snuck in and ate my tape recorder so I couldn't even do interviews. To get another tape recorder, I had to wait until my brother went to Whitehorse on business. Then Megan's parents came to visit and needed the wall tent. I began couch-surfing in town.

Murphy must have been a Yukoner for his law definitely prevails in that country. What also prevails, though, is a spirit of goodwill and generosity. The community came through: with loans of cars and gear and money; with rides and meals and comfort; with true friendship that can keep your spirits up even when you are no longer hanging by a thread but just in total free fall. In the end, after a fast and giddy spring, I was able to leave because a sweet neighbour offered to trade me his air miles for my charred carcass of a car. I was even able to pay all my debts because some payments finally came in.

I'm left with a love/hate relationship with the Yukon, which seems natural for a place of such extremes. A climate that veers from the darkest, coldest winter to the brightest, warmest summer. A remoteness that makes things like colour photocopies unobtainable but manages to ship in biscotti to stock the cappuccino bar. A culture wherein people enjoy a sophisticated art installation but leave early to chop wood and load up the stove in their primitive cabins.

The uniqueness of these extremes also creates a certain bigotry, the way some locals see the Yukon as the only place in the world, discounting everywhere else as "Outside." This didn't make sense to me. Although the Yukon enchants me and its spell compels me to return again and again, I can also live happily in Toronto, rural Ontario, Spain, just about anywhere. But in Dawson there is a prevailing attitude that there's something wrong with you if you don't want to live *only* in the Yukon. When you tell people you're leaving, they say: "No, you won't go. You'll be here ten years from now."

I began to understand this attitude when I read historian Charlene Porsild, who writes that the distinctions between Yukon/Outside and cheechako/sourdough originated in the Gold Rush. These divisions made it clear that only those who were committed to spending years in the territory would be fully accepted and so created the strongest community. She also sees that this stance continues today.

As more and more people insisted that I would stay in Dawson, I wondered at the intense loyalty of Yukoners, which expresses how much they love their land, their community, and their northern lifestyle.

I couldn't help but admire the loyal women who organize events in town, run their own businesses, home-school their children out on the trapline, cook huge meals and operate heavy machinery in the mining camps, run sled dogs, make quilts by hand, fix their own snowmobiles, pack a hundred pounds for days of trekking through dense swampy bush. Under the Spell of the Yukon, they face every adversity with cheerful optimism, confidence in their own abilities, and fierce determination to make a difference in this country of rare, raw power.

It was the women of today who inspired me to go back to the Gold Rush days to find women who were just as admirable. Although my research was as thorough as possible, with all resources checked against their original sources, *Frontier Spirit: The Brave Women of the Klondike* is not meant to be a scholarly work. Its purpose is to celebrate these female sourdoughs and their place in the Gold Rush, and to let their stories stand as sources of inspiration to any who might follow them.

Whenever my jinx started to get the best of me, I thought of the motto that Gold Rush women like Martha Black and Klondike Kate would use to keep themselves going: "Mush on and smile." Whatever their faults, whatever the injustices or dangers they faced, these are women who not only mushed on and smiled but who also broke new trail everywhere they ventured, as they rushed headlong into one of the greatest historic events of the nineteenth century.

# 2

## THE KLONDIKE GOLD RUSH
## AND THE "DELICATELY NURTURED"

*A fleet of First Nations women paddling to trade with steamships in 1900.*

Gold! That one word had the power to seize the minds of men and women so that they thought of nothing else. Butcher, baker, corset-maker, few were immune to its glitter of riches, fame, excitement. In the grip of gold fever, tens of thousands from all walks of life, from all over

*Ethel Berry and sister Tot Bush pan gold at the Berry mine.*

the world, left their homes, their families, their professions, to seek their fortune in the Klondike from 1896 to 1900. Swept up in the euphoria, they gambled everything on their dreams of mansions, news headlines, and the thrill of adventure. After an arduous journey through an extreme climate and a demanding wilderness, a few stumbled on exactly what they were looking for. Others lost what little they had. Some lost their lives. But all became the stuff of legend.

The frontier mythology of the Klondike Gold Rush, created by writers like Robert Service and Jack London, celebrates the lone prospector, hungry for gold, struggling courageously against the harshest elements, mightily wresting his fortunes out of the frozen ground; the gregarious gambler, hungry for good times, strewing his nuggets about rowdy saloons as he buys the boys another round, calling for his favourite dance hall girl; and the misfits—tramps and remittance men and outlaws, hungry for everything. If there are women in these tales, they are gold diggers, not gold prospectors. At the time of the Gold Rush, women were called euphemistically the "delicately nurtured" and the feminine mystique was one of fragility and fainting fits. Who could believe such creatures could brave the Yukon frontier?

But women were there in force, if not in equal numbers to the men then in equal spirit. Their story begins not with the intrepid adventurers who joined the stampede to the goldfields. It begins with the strong and knowledgeable women who were already there, who had lived on this land for thousands of years, and who saw no wilderness—only home as far as the eye could see, a home that would be suddenly invaded by hordes of gold seekers. These are the women of the First Nations: the Inuit and the Gwich'in of the north, the Han of the west, the Tutchone of the central region, the Kaska of the east, and the Tagish and Tlingit of the south.

The Gold Rush started with a Gold Trickle in the 1870s, and First Nations women were an integral part of this preliminary period of prospecting. Three of the first major prospectors in the Yukon were Arthur Harper, Leroy McQuesten, and Alfred Mayo, and all married First Nations women who helped them survive in this strange land.

In 1874, Harper, McQuesten, and Mayo established Fort Reliance on the Yukon River six miles downstream from the mouth of the Klondike, the future site of Moosehide, just north of what would be Dawson City. It is this primary trading post that named the surrounding rivers: Fortymile River is 40 miles from the post site, Sixtymile is 60 miles away. Trading in fur and supplies financed the quest for gold.

Harper met his future wife, Seentahna, a Koyukuk woman, the summer of 1874. He was 39 to her 14 years. Called Jennie Bosco Harper, Seentahna helped Arthur set up a trading post in Tanana with Al Mayo and his wife, Margaret, who was Seentahna's cousin. While Arthur went on extensive prospecting trips, sometimes for up to two years, Seentahna maintained her traditional lifestyle and raised their eight children. Then Arthur sent their first seven children down South to be educated, against

Seentahna's objections. In 1895, they separated. Bereft of her children but determined to stay Koyukuk, Seentahna took only her two-year-old son and returned to her community to raise him in her First Nations culture, eventually marrying Robert Alexander of the Nenana First Nations and becoming a potlatch storyteller and honoured elder.

Like Harper, McQuesten, at 42, married a 14-year-old First Nations woman, Satejdenalno, called Katherine or Kate. Satejdenalno was Russian-Koyukuk; her father was a European trader. She attended the nearby Russian Mission school and was fluent in both Russian and Koyukon. While the Harpers and Mayos established the trading post at Tanana, the McQuestens ran Fort Reliance. Then, in 1886, all three couples moved to the Stewart River to found Fort Nelson. When the Gold Trickle gathered force at Fortymile, the McQuestens joined this settlement, where Satejdenalno acted as a liaison between the First Nations and Euro-Americans and hosted social occasions that brought newcomers like Anna DeGraf into the fold. An avid gardener, Satejdenalno was infamous for having attempted to use a moose to pull her plow. When the search for gold ran to Circle City in 1894, the McQuestens followed, opening a store there and having the eighth of what was to become a brood of 11 children, who would be schooled down South. When the news of the Dawson bonanza sent everyone running again, the McQuestens moved to a Victorian mansion in Berkeley, California, where Satejdenalno fit in just as well as she had everywhere in the North. When her husband died in 1910, her business skills enabled her to retain their wealth until her death in 1918.

The arrival of men like Harper, McQuesten, and Mayo ushered in a new era in the Yukon. When mining settlements such as Fortymile were established to accommodate the first small waves of prospectors, European-based law and customs came to town. Some of these new prospectors brought their wives and families. There had already been a minuscule number of white missionary wives in the Yukon, like

Charlotte Selina Bompas, who came in 1865, and the odd white prostitute travelling with groups of miners, like Dutch Kate, who is believed to be the first white woman to cross the Chilkoot Pass. Dutch Kate dressed in men's clothes on the trail but decked herself out in feminine finery once in a First Nations village, becoming a source of fascination for the local people. Anna DeGraf, seamstress, and Émilie Tremblay, miner's wife, also arrived in this Gold Trickle period. The isolation, harsh climate, and lack of basic amenities created real hardship for these women, but they met these challenges with fortitude, meriting respect that made it easier to be the few women among many men.

As white women joined the hunt for gold, alliances with the First Nations began to break down. White men had needed these alliances to build trading partnerships and learn northern survival skills. But in Victorian times, white women were held responsible for keeping their men civilized Christians, and they objected to intermarriage and distanced themselves from women who were not both white and Christian. At first, the white men defended the inclusion of indigenous women: a dance hall owner knocked down his white common-law wife when she kept herself apart from the wives of his customers. But soon white men began to look down upon their comrades who had relationships with First Nations women.

George Carmack, who is known as the man who made the famous discovery that unleashed the Klondike Gold Rush, was married to a First Nations woman, Shaaw Tláa (Kate Carmack). George, Shaaw Tláa, her brother Keish (Skookum Jim), and cousin Kàa Goox (Dawson Charley) had been prospecting for years to no avail. They were camped on a tributary of the Klondike River, just east of where the Klondike meets the Yukon River when, on August 17, 1896, they stumbled upon the greatest find of gold ever seen in the North, huge chunks of glittering metal that would change the world. Naming the creek Bonanza, Carmack rushed to register the find and brag about it in the bar.

Word of the bonanza burned like wildfire through the Yukon and Alaska, and within no time every prospector from this immense, remote area was camped in a tent on the site of what was to become Dawson City, madly staking claims all around. These early birds snapped up Bonanza, Gold Bottom, and Eldorado creeks, working their claims all spring with sluices. By summer, they had a lot to show for their luck and labour: about $30 million from around 50 claims. Panning in the creek for ten minutes could net what a factory worker in the city would work six months for.

The steamer *Excelsior* docked in San Francisco on July 14, 1897, just like any other ship. No one would have guessed that the grubby miners on board, men and women, had a total of half a million dollars' worth of gold in their battered bags. When the news leaked out, masses of onlookers swarmed the docks in the sweltering heat and the media frothed at the mouth. The *Portland* pulled up three days later, to be greeted by cheering crowds and hordes of reporters. This time there was a million dollars of gold, weighing a full ton.

Newspapers ran wild with the story, building tales even taller than the truth, which was towering enough. Newsboys on every corner called out grander and grander headlines. Rumours that you could pick nuggets worth hundreds of dollars off the ground everywhere were recorded as fact. Reports went out as far away as Europe and Australia.

So much misinformation was perpetuated by journalists that those who joined the stampede were often dangerously ill prepared for the arduousness of the journey, the severity of the northern climate, and the possibility of failure. Most people had no idea where the Klondike even was. For years, the Klondike was called Alaska and considered an American territory. A.N.C. Treadgold, of the *Manchester Guardian*, expressed disdain for the quality of reporting, but did acknowledge that "the Klondike country . . . is so difficult for the ordinary traveller that it is small wonder if newspaper correspondents as a whole have sat still at

Dawson or even further away and retailed second-hand information gathered from sources, at best, unreliable."[1] When the Rush was fully under way, female correspondents like Flora Shaw and Faith Fenton did go into the heart of the Klondike and report reliably on conditions there.

The media made the arrival of the two steamers one of the most publicized events of the Victorian age. With the West long conquered, a new frontier offered romance and hope to a world in a deep economic depression. The United States, still on the gold standard, was trying to recover from the Panic of 1873 and the treasury was almost empty. Many Americans had lost their jobs and been evicted from their homes. Even those who were not desperate responded to the dream of easy fortune in an exciting new frontier. The new century loomed and people were restless, easy prey for the sensationalism and sentimentality of the promise of gold.

Gold fever was good for morale and for business. Port towns like Seattle and San Francisco boomed with suppliers and transporters. Almost overnight, Vancouver grew to twice its size and Edmonton to five times its size. Because the Government of Canada ruled that entry to the Yukon would be granted only to those with a year's worth of supplies, warehouses overflowed with stock for the stampeders. Over a hundred steamers were built in early 1898 to carry prospectors north. Publishers put out guidebooks with maps of the best routes and lists of required items.

Some of these guides addressed the needs of women. Female reporters also wrote packing lists for women. In the *Skagway News,* Annie Hall Strong's list included nine kinds of rugged footwear, two pairs of mittens and one pair of gloves, an arctic hood, three denim or heavy duck skirts to wear over bloomers, a Mackinaw, and basic sets of summer and winter clothing. But only one pair of socks!

On March 18, 1898, the Seattle *Post-Intelligencer* offered the simple message: "NO PLACE FOR WOMEN." Under this headline, a man recently returned from the goldfields was quoted: "Women are utterly unfit to fight the battle out there. People in the East have not the least conception of the hardships that have to be endured by those who succeed in reaching the country, not to speak of the horrors of the trail leading into the country . . . It might be set down at once as impossible for women to get into the Yukon by the passes."

Undaunted, women formed their own Gold Rush clubs to plan expeditions. One of these societies was called the Woman's Klondike Expedition Syndicate and another, founded by Chicago patent lawyer Florence King, was named the Woman's Alaska Gold Club. Club members were enthusiastic suffragists who had already broken through barriers to become professionals in their fields.

One of the unique characteristics of the Klondike Stampede is how it attracted men and women from all walks of life: rich and poor, educated and illiterate, urban and rural, skilled and unskilled, single and married. While the images of dance hall girls and prostitutes became synonymous with the Gold Rush, the female stampeders were actually from many different occupations: nurses, doctors, nuns, teachers, scholars, journalists, domestic servants, laundresses, seamstresses, cooks, shopkeepers, restaurant and hotel owners, entrepreneurs, and entertainers. They were from English and French Canada, the southern and northern United States, England, Scotland, Ireland, Wales, Australia, France, Sweden, Denmark, Norway, Germany, Greece, Italy, Poland, Russia, Japan, and China. Some were Asian and African-American, although the majority were of European descent. And they came for the same reasons the men did, out of greed, curiosity, or sheer cussedness.

They would need all the cussedness they had just to get to the goldfields, deep in the interior of the Yukon Territory, far east of Alaska's Pacific shores and far north of the Rocky Mountains. There were different routes, each one long and life-threatening.

The safest and easiest was the all-water route, but this was for the rich, costing more than a thousand dollars. First a steamship took passengers up the Pacific coast to St. Michael, Alaska. There they boarded a riverboat going upriver to Dawson City. On board, passengers indulged in luxurious meals, card games, dances, and concerts. Small wonder that, even at exorbitant prices, it was almost impossible to gain passage on the fully booked boats. But this was the longest and slowest route, about 2,500 miles of ocean and 1,700 miles of river. The boats could only run in the summer, when the river was free of ice, and becoming stranded was a real possibility. In the first year of the stampede, about 2,500 people ended up forced to spend the winter, grievously unprepared, in St. Michael or wherever their steamer had been iced in along the river. Others made it to Dawson too late—the best claims had all been staked. Some one hundred or so foolhardy adventurers, including a few women, got to Yakutat Bay and attempted to cross the Malaspina Glacier. Just over 50 survived.

Another route was to take a steamship up the Pacific coast only as far as Wrangell, Alaska, then spend four days on a paddlewheeler going up the Stikine River to Glenora, British Columbia, where passengers like Faith Fenton disembarked to hike 150 gruelling miles to Teslin. There they boarded boats that took them to Fort Selkirk via the Teslin River, to the Yukon River, which carried them to Dawson. It was a long way round compared with the Chilkoot, and just as hard going, owing to the swamps and dense bush.

The longest journey of all was the Edmonton route, with a trail just as bad but more than ten times as long, from 1,500 to 2,500 miles depending on how lost the travellers became. This was considered the route for the poor. It took almost two years to reach the destination of Dawson. Only half of the 1,600 stampeders that set out on this trail made it to the goldfields, and then they were too late for the choice claims. Some died of scurvy or starvation. Many turned back. All wreaked havoc on the lands of the First Nations, carelessly starting forest fires, trashing traplines, taxing the populations of game animals.

*An unbroken line of stampeders climbs the Golden Staircase at Chilkoot Pass.*

The most popular way in was the Overland Trail, which included the legendary Chilkoot Pass and its alternative, the White Pass. This was the famous trail immortalized in the photographs of Eric Hegg and Frank LaRoche and in the ballads of Robert Service, the trail that tested the mettle of the stampeders, its perils too much for some. Basically, the route runs from Skagway, Alaska to lakes in the Yukon Territory, where boats or rafts were built for the rest of the journey down the Yukon River to Dawson City. There were a few different ways to traverse this territory. A stampeder could travel up the Pacific coast by steamship and disembark in Skagway, either hiking the 40 miles to Lake Bennett over the White Pass or taking the Skagway Trail until it joined the Dyea Trail. Or he or she could stay on board until the boat landed in Dyea and take the Dyea Trail the 26 miles over the Chilkoot Pass to Lake Lindeman, then another seven miles to Lake Bennett. Once on the Yukon River, the gold seekers had to find the treacherous Miles Canyon and Five Fingers Rapids before days more of river travel brought them to Dawson City.

Some turned back as soon as Skagway (a corruption of *skaguay*, "home of the north wind" in Tlingit), then a lawless, riotous frontier town ruled by criminal gang boss Soapy Smith. Soapy was a charismatic character who courted the town by donating to Christian charities, starting a campaign to feed stray dogs, and being unfailingly considerate of women and children. At the same time, he was a notorious outlaw who'd barely escaped imprisonment or execution in Denver, Cripple Creek, and Mexico. Backed by the proceeds of his crooked casino and saloon, he and his gang of grifters, thugs, and murderers ran the town and fleeced every sucker they could find. Innocent stampeders staying over in one of the fleabag hotels would have their sleep interrupted by dogfights, brawls, and gunshots at all hours—some just letting off steam in the street, others intentionally resulting in suicide or murder. Soapy was finally killed by a vigilante mob in July 1889.

It must have been a relief, at least initially, for those who chose to cross the White Pass to head out into the great outdoors. This trail didn't have the excruciating incline of the Summit of the Chilkoot Pass, but it was longer. The terrain was just as impassable in severe weather conditions, and the mandatory load of a year's supplies still applied. The trail took the lives of around 2,500 horses, victims of overwork, rough treatment and neglect. Most stampeders chose the faster Chilkoot Pass in their race to get the gold. By 1899 the White Pass and Yukon Railway

*Trouser-clad "actresses" defying the law on the Chilkoot Trail in 1897.*

was up and running, and the White Pass and Chilkoot Pass trails both
became obsolete.

Those stampeders that went on to Dyea (a corruption of the Tlingit
name for the river, Taiya) found a bustling shantytown where they could
buy feed for dogs and horses, hire the services of packers or prostitutes,
get freshly baked bread, even use a telephone. By the end of 1899, Dyea
was a ghost town, a casualty of the White Pass and Yukon Railway.

Up to thirty thousand people headed out of Dyea and across the
Chilkoot Pass between 1897 and 1898. Those that couldn't afford packers had to cross many times to haul the one to two thousand pounds of
supplies required. Since the average person could only carry 70 pounds at
a time, this meant as many as 30 trips back and forth, which could take

almost three months. Not only was the trail so crowded with stampeders that they made an almost unbroken line from start to finish, but caches of supplies and abandoned items deemed too onerous—stoves, canoes, trunks—littered the sides of the path. Over the winter, stashes of goods accumulated in over seven separate layers under snow 70 feet deep, their pole markers buried.

Those who could afford it hired packers. Since the opening of the Chilkoot Pass to the newcomers, packing had replaced trading as the local First Nations' main economic activity. The Tlingit (including the Chilkoot and Chilkat) and Tagish were shrewd bargainers who received as much as a hundred dollars a day for packing, or even one dollar a pound, prices changing with supply, demand, and weather conditions. They had a strong sense of their worth and would strike for higher pay. Whole families worked on the trail, the women and children packing around 75 pounds each and the men up to 200 pounds. In 1886, a horse pack-train began cutting into their business, as did a tram set up in 1898 to haul goods up the last lag of the Summit. In 1900, the White Pass and Yukon Railway put them right out of packing, but until that time the Tlingits and Tagish worked their Pass as no one else could.

For the first 14 miles of the Chilkoot Trail the rocky terrain rises steeply, levelling out only occasionally, and passes through dense brush, swampy patches, and streams. Along the way, stopovers like Canyon City offered opportunities to grab a simple meal or to overnight in a crowded tent. At the base of the Summit was Sheep Camp, a busy hive of canvas shelters, cookfires, and caches. Horses had to be left behind here, as they couldn't make the rest of the climb. Dogs had to be carried over on their owners' backs in winter. The next six miles up over the almost impossibly steep Summit—a 3,739-foot elevation—pass by snowfields, even in summer. The melting of the edges of these fields make the rough ground slippery in the warm season, and some found it easier to cross in winter, when the Golden Stairs were carved into snow.

This was treacherous territory. Health risks included snow blindness, pneumonia, spinal meningitis, and injuries from accidents. Floods and avalanches presented fatal dangers. Heavy rains during the summer of 1897 had created a big pool on the eastern glacier, and in September the ice dam broke, unleashing a torrent of water 20 feet high on Sheep Camp, hurtling the massive boulder called Stone House a quarter of a mile down the slope, sweeping up people and tents in its wake. Luckily, only one man died.

In the spring of 1898, heavy snows let up briefly but another blizzard hit in late March. Then April began with a warm southern wind. The Tlingit packers saw the danger signs and refused to work. No one but old hands listened to their warnings. On the morning of April 3, Palm Sunday, a deafening roar announced the massive avalanche that buried around a hundred people in its monstrous descent down the Scales of the Pass. Shouts of victims under the snow faded away to silence. It took until April 15 to recover and identify 50 of the estimated 70 bodies buried under the snow. One tall tale has it that a sturdy female packer by the name of Vernie Woodward found her suitor laid out with the dead and worked on him for hours until he miraculously came back to life.

Despite these natural perils, the trail was safer than those of previous gold rushes in the United States. On the Canadian side of the trail, the North West Mounted Police were posted, under the legendary Sam Steele, to keep order, and for the most part people were law-abiding and helpful to one another. The NWMP had a checkpoint at the Summit where they checked everyone moving through, refusing entrance to those without the requisite year's worth of provisions. After this, the descent was almost as demanding as the climb, and many stumbled and fell on their way to the lakes.

While some stampeders built their boats or rafts at Lake Lindeman, the first lake, most trekked on to Lake Bennett, where timber was more plentiful and they could avoid navigating the rapids between the two lakes. Emma Kelly, a reporter for the Kansas City *Star,* and Alice Crane, an ethnologist, were thrilled by their wild rides through these churning waters.

Few stampeders were able to build their boats in time to travel the river before freeze-up. Travel by sled in the winter was generally considered too difficult. Overland, travellers would have to break trail through thick forest. The river sometimes froze in great ten-foot-high blocks of ice that were insurmountable. Many stampeders were forced to spend the winter in the tent town of Lake Bennett. More than ten thousand people were lodging there by the spring of 1898, finishing their boats and waiting for breakup. Not until May 29, 1898, did the ice break and then seven thousand boats deserted Bennett for Dawson City, leaving the surrounding forests decimated.

Switching from land to river travel had its own hazards. First there was Miles Canyon, where the river raced headlong through a narrow passage between hundred-foot walls of rock then spun into a sucking whirlpool. Almost two hundred people died during the Gold Rush shooting these and the Whitehorse Rapids. Enough victims had already been claimed by this vortex that the NWMP immediately made it illegal for women or children to travel in boats through either set of rapids. They were expected to portage for miles along the banks or face a hundred-dollar fine. Many women, including Klondike Kate, defiantly faced the terror of the canyon and rapids despite the law. Few regretted doing so, emerging from the challenge wildly exhilarated. One or two— like Emma Kelly—even went back to do it again!

If the boat survived Miles Canyon, it immediately had to wrestle with the Whitehorse Rapids. Coming so closely together, the two rapids were a kind of one-two punch that left passengers thrilled but unsteady when they landed in Whitehorse, the future capital city of the Yukon Territory. Because the river was wide and deep enough past this point, large steamboats began to travel up and down the Yukon River between Whitehorse and Dawson. These boats often left their passengers stranded after running aground or wrecking. First Nations people all along the river sold wood to fuel the boilers and fish and game to feed the passengers. Some worked on board as deckhands.

Most people kept going with their own small boats, camping on the shores of Lake Laberge, then farther along the banks of the Yukon River. There was only one remaining hurdle: the turbulence of the Five Finger Rapids, so called because they are created by five islands spaced across the river like spread fingers, a site of immeasurable beauty but treacherous for steamboat and raft alike. Southern Tutchone people were often hired to guide boats through the mysterious currents. After this it was smooth sailing for days downriver to Dawson City, with perhaps a stopover in Fort Selkirk, where the Northern Tutchone traded fur and meat to the newcomers.

By land and by water, such were the hardships and extreme dangers of the Chilkoot Pass and the Yukon River route—enough to daunt any man. Women had to climb the Summit in the voluminous skirts and restricting corsets of the day, often labouring harder than the menfolk, as gathering firewood, cooking, repairing clothes torn en route, and most camp chores fell to the so-called delicately nurtured. And yet many a woman not only braved this trail in all seasons, but found triumph in it. As many as 1,500 women are on the North West Mounted Police and steamer passenger lists that record stampeders who hit the Yukon River from the Overland Trail.

When the stampeders arrived in Dawson City in 1896, they found a large mud flat where the Klondike River empties into the Yukon River, and already it was overflowing with tents. A seasoned Yukoner named Joe Ladue had staked the area as a townsite, naming it Dawson after Canadian geologist George Dawson, and built a sawmill. His investment paid off in spades. All late summer and fall the boats poured in. The sawmill, a saloon, and a warehouse were soon up and running, and lots were selling faster than the leaves fell from the trees. Almost two thousand people were living there by spring 1897, and thousands more poured in after the river broke.

Shelters precariously perched almost all the way up the steep sides of the surrounding mountains. Hastily built and false-fronted saloons, gambling halls, and dance halls were packed tight together along Front Street, facing the Yukon River, which thronged with makeshift wharves and boats. Stores and laundries ran out of tents and prices were insanely high, four times what they'd been in the fall. During the summer's midnight sun, the townspeople laboured and caroused all day and all night.

After freeze-up in the fall, rations were dangerously low, as were steadily declining temperatures. The town would be entirely cut off from the rest of the world until spring. Starvation threatened and many succumbed to pneumonia, diptheria, smallpox. The situation was dire but by helping each other almost everyone survived.

After breakup in the spring of 1898, Dawson was swarmed by the biggest bevy of stampeders yet, bringing news and fresh supplies. Scarce commodities commanded outrageous prices and made instant fortunes for their purveyors: one orange could cost a dollar. The population rose to thirty thousand—about 40 per cent Canadian, 40 per cent American and 20 per cent from overseas—and the town became a city, wooden shacks, houses, storefronts, churches, theatres, and banks. Electricity came to town, newspapers started up, and a telephone line was installed, thanks to Belinda Mulrooney. The North West Mounted Police were renamed the Royal Canadian Mounted Police, and they kept Dawson in pretty much perfect order, coming down hard on serious crime—like carrying a weapon, assault, and extortion—and letting socially acceptable infractions—like drinking, gambling, and prostitution—slide. Dawson was a much safer community than most cities of its size at the time, making it unique among Gold Rush town.

Of course, the best claims had all been staked by this time, so the new batch of cheechakos had to wrest gold from the miners by selling them supplies or offering entertainment. A class system was in place from the beginning. High-level government appointees, judges, lawyers, company presidents, accountants, ministers, and bankers were at the top. The next level belonged to managers and owners of businesses. The third level encompassed most people: labourers, shopkeepers, blackjack dealers, barbers, waiters, miners, RCMP officers. The bottom rung on the

*Dawson City prostitutes pose for a whimsical souvenir shot entitled "Ladies' Drinking Bee."*

social ladder was reserved for the demimonde: gamblers, pimps, ne'er-do-wells. First Nations were excluded altogether.

It was a male-dominated environment—only 12 per cent women—but even these few women had their own hierarchy. First were the wives of men considered important. Second were the extremely successful women entrepreneurs. Third were female professionals: journalists, teachers, nurses, nuns. Fourth were the skilled labourers: seamstresses, laundresses, cooks, waitresses, and so on. Fifth were domestic workers. Sixth were dance hall girls. On the bottom rung were the prostitutes, socially invisible but accepted as an unfortunate necessity.

By 1900 the boom town had evolved with meteoric speed into a cosmopolitan city—"Paris of the North"—the size of San Francisco. The number of single female residents rose steadily. More families also came to town. Highbrow entertainment was offered at the theatre. Social standards became less accepting. A public school was established for children. The prostitutes were moved out of "The Row," the town's red-light district and across the Klondike River into Lousetown.

At the same time, the city began to shrink in size as gold seekers headed to new rushes in Nome, Alaska and Atlin, British Columbia. Large mining companies snapped up huge blocks of claims and began expensive dredge mining, putting many individual miners out of business. Dawson City was busting, not booming. Within a year, a third of the population had left. But the big companies stabilized the city into an established mining town of about ten thousand people in 1901.

This new city had been the summer fishing grounds of the local Han people, the Tr'ondëk Hwëch'in, whose village was on the site that became Klondike City/Lousetown. Largely due to the urging of Chief Isaac, who wished to avoid the miners and their dominating culture, the Tr'ondëk Hwëch'in had moved three miles away to Moosehide before the Rush. This caused a deeper segregation between the First

*The Tr'ondëk Hwëch'in of the Dawson City area*
*moved to Moosehide Creek when the stampeders flooded in.*

Nations and the newcomers who had peremptorily taken over their territory. Moosehide was also an unsanitary location. Downriver from Dawson, it received all the town's waste. Consequently, more disease wracked the First Nations community. Game was scarce due to the encroaching hordes of miners, and the fish weirs were destroyed by river traffic. The Han people continued to trade fish, meat and fur. The men worked in Dawson as carpenters and mechanics, earning two dollars less an hour than the newcomers. The women made and sold clothing and worked as seamstresses, laundresses, and cooks. However, as more and more newcomers needed work, the Han found jobs hard to come by.

While the First Nations of the Yukon pressed for their rights over their land, the Government of Canada stalled treaty negotiations in anticipation of further gold discoveries. Prior to the Gold Rush, the ratio of First Nations people to non-First Nations people in the Yukon had been four to one. By 1901, it was one to eight. In five years, the First Nations had been effectively overrun. This would have a profound effect on the lives of First Nations women in the Yukon Territory, as the life of Shaaw Tláa, or Kate Carmack, sadly demonstrates.

*A First Nations ceremonial dance performed on May 24, 1901, in the Alaska Commercial Company yard off Front St. in Dawson City.*

# 3

*Shaaw Tláa*
# KATE CARMACK

*A California studio portrait of Kate Carmack wearing her famous gold nugget necklace, 1898.*

*She is a stout woman now. The long hair in a braid down her back is grey. Her face is rounder, a softer frame for her intent brown eyes. Her mouth at rest turns down at the corners. They say the emotions of a lifetime are what shape an aged face. If this is true, this woman has had to be strong; this woman has fought battles; this woman has lost too much.*

*But she carries her weight with the grace of surety, sweeping up the slope in a long, plain brown skirt, her feet light in their summer moccasins. She takes the birch basket out of her sack, lifts the lid, quilled with the design of a ptarmigan. Her fingers nimble and fast in the brambles, her fingertips gentle in their plucking, she picks the wild blueberries, their juices staining her skin violet.*

*When the basket is full, she puts the lid on and tucks it away in her sack, hoisting the load, still light, over her back. She stretches, looks out at the grey mountains ringing her like colossal waves, looks down at the green valley and its thick blue stripe of river. This beauty does not strike her with awe. It is not savage or mysterious or grand to her. It is part of her, a wealth she carries always, the way the world should look.*

*Slowly, she zigzags down the slope, pausing to note a cluster of herbs or the tracks of a fox. She weaves back into the weft of spruce and birch trees, stopping to check a snare she'd set. The rabbit is dead and fresh, its eyes open and staring. She stoops to loosen the snare and slip it off the head of the rabbit. As she bends, what is around her neck swings forward and bumps her chin. Her famous necklace of solid gold nuggets strung like beads.*

Her name was Shaaw Tláa, meaning "older than old," although she was known outside her First Nations community as Kate Carmack, and she may have been the one to discover the gold that turned the trickle into a rush.

No one knows the year of her birth. There is no way of knowing the actual events of Shaaw Tláa's life, nor how she truly experienced them. What is known is that the discovery she was part of unleashed a tsunami of colonization that would swallow up the land of her people and sweep tens of thousands of newcomers off their feet.

In the days of Shaaw Tláa's Tagish and Tlingit grandmothers, her people were nomadic hunter-gatherers, following the natural cycles of nature. In the spring and summer, families converged in large groups on the river to prepare for and then fish the salmon that would swim upriver in teeming waves to their spawning grounds. Elders say you could walk across the river on the backs of the fish as they were that abundant. Celebrations with feasts, songs, and games were just as plentiful. In the fall and winter, the people moved back into the woods to hunt moose and caribou, dispersing into small family groups and spreading out to cover more territory.

Women played integral roles in the survival of their people and were teachers, storytellers, shamans, and, on occasion, chiefs. Descent was matrilineal, and husbands were expected to move in with their wives' families and be responsible for taking care of her aged parents. Marriages were usually arranged to strengthen trading alliances and took place between the ages of 16 and 20. The Tlingit and Tagish each had two clans: Crow and Wolf. Crow must marry Wolf and Wolf must marry Crow.

Most clothing, tools, equipment, and shelter were fashioned immediately for use out of available materials (hides, bark, wood, stone, bone) and discarded. Even trade goods were practical: fur, eulachon oil, dried fish, and cedar bark baskets. The Tlingits (Chilkoot, Chilkat, and Taku) had a monopoly controlling the southern Yukon and traded with both the Coastal Tlingits and the nearby Athapaskans (Tagish, Tutchone, Kaska).

But life was beginning to change as the Tlingits allowed the first white fur traders and missionaries into the territory.

By the time of Shaaw Tláa's parents, the appointing of trading chiefs gave chiefs more power. Trapping and fishing became more important than hunting. With the fur trade came guns, dog teams, and gill nets. Guns made solo hunting more effective. Using dog teams for travel made traplines more efficient but took time away from hunting. The dogs also

needed fish for food, necessitating more fishing. Gill nets caught more
fish. More reliance on fishing and trapping meant spending more time
by the river, close to the trading posts. Many of her people began living
in permanent settlements along the river.

Epidemics of smallpox, polio, whooping cough, influenza, and
tuberculosis decimated entire families because the people had no
immunity to these foreign contagions. In an oral tradition, these dev-
astating losses kill culture as well as kin. Traditional knowledge is
passed down by elders through songs, stories, and dances. This knowledge is the exclusive domain of the elder who possesses it. The recipi-
ent must earn this knowledge and the elder will transmit it only when
he or she has determined that the receiver will use it wisely. When the
elders die before having transmitted all their knowledge, parts of the
culture die with them. Thus the people of the First Nations struggled
not only with personal grief, but also with retaining their culture as a
result of these epidemics.

So much death. So much loss. So much change. Contact with the
newcomers would irrevocably alter the course of Shaaw Tláa's life, putting
her at the centre of one of the greatest historic events of the century—and
breaking her heart.

Shaaw Tláa's mother was Gus'dutéen, a Tagish woman of the
Dakl'aweidí (Wolf) clan. Her father was Kaachgaawáa, a Tlingit man of
the Deisheetaan (Crow) clan. They had eight children. Shaaw Tláa had
five sisters and two brothers; one, Keish, would go down in history as
Skookum Jim. Both brothers and three sisters married into Coastal
Tlingit clans.

Shaaw Tláa's elder brother, Tlákwshaan, died in the early 1890s of
influenza. The eldest sister also died of influenza soon after marrying. It
was the custom, because these were as much trading alliances as marriages, for a dead wife to be replaced by one of her sisters. Second sister
Aagé was then sent to marry the eldest sister's husband, replacing the

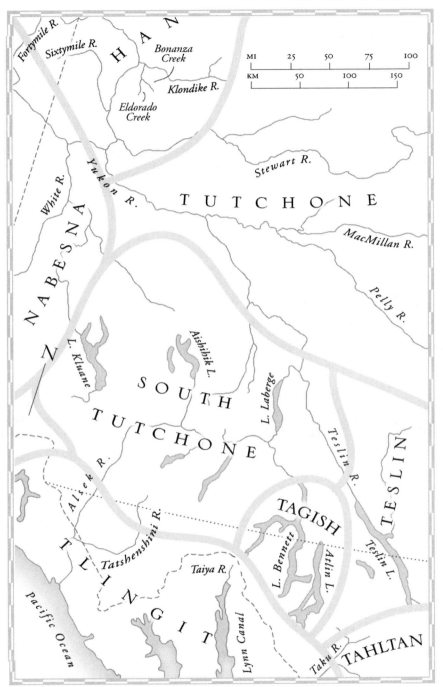

*First Nations language groups of the Yukon.*

woman they all grieved. Then this husband also died, so Aagé married his nephew, since he had no brother. Then this husband, too, died, killed in a dispute with another clan over which had exclusive rights to work as packers over the Chilkoot Pass. Aagé, pregnant with her second child, was allowed to return to her clan as long as her first child, Susie, remained with her in-laws. She then left her baby, Louise, with her mother and went off with a prospector named Mr. Wilson. Perhaps she left her children because it was easier than waiting for them to be taken by disease. Perhaps it was easier than watching them grow into reminders of those she had lost. Perhaps she thought she could cheat death this one time by taking the hand of the white man who was immune to influenza, immune to the fate of her people.

Shaaw Tláa was the third sister. She too would marry a Coastal Tlingit man and bear a daughter. She too would learn to grieve. She too would take the hand of a white man and follow him down the Yukon River in search of gold. But she would find it.

The women of the Yukon First Nations were trained to survive anything. When her first blood came, Shaaw Tláa would have been celebrated in a feast given by her father. Her mother and aunts would then have led her to a special shelter made for her about a mile from camp. She would have been secluded there for up to a year. Her mother would have brought her prepared food to eat and sewing to do, using these visits to instruct her in traditional knowledge. She would not have been allowed to eat fresh meat, as she was to train her body to withstand long periods of privation to increase the chances of her survival in hard times. All year she would have to wear a hide hood that restricted her vision. A bone would have been sewn inside the hood to relieve itchiness, because scratching her head would give her grey hair early. When she'd completed the full period of the rite, she would have attained full status as a grown woman and been able to marry.

In this way, Shaaw Tláa would be prepared to be alone.

She went to the Coastal Tlingit clan and married the man to whom her parents had promised her. She accustomed herself to the ways of her new family, bore her child far from her own mother, in the arms of the women who now possessed her. Then the influenza epidemic took both her husband and her daughter. No matter how strong her grief might have been, it could not be stronger than her duty. According to custom, like her elder sister, she was to marry one of her husband's close relatives.

Instead, her bereft mother pleaded for her return. A fourth sister had married a white man, George Carmack, but had also died of influenza. Shaaw Tláa's mother used this to argue that he was now owed a wife and so Shaaw Tláa was needed back home for this purpose. Another sister, Nadagaat' Tláa, died on the Chilkoot Pass with her daughter in her arms when they were caught in a sudden blizzard. And the last sister, Kooyáy, married a local man and stayed close to home. Shaaw Tláa was allowed back to marry Carmack.

This white man did not seem like the others, the traders who looked her up and down like an artifact, or past her like a shadow. Perhaps that made her love him, if she did love him. Perhaps she was already past love, the way it could sicken and die and go irrevocably from her. Perhaps it was something else she felt, something that could last, a sense of duty that mapped her place in the world, giving her a place to stand on both feet. Perhaps she simply craved something to take her past the suffering of her people.

George Carmack had made friends with Shaaw Tláa's brother Keish, when they both worked as packers on the Chilkoot Pass in 1886. George was known—and despised by some—for his acceptance of First Nations people and their culture, a respect that was unusual for the times. When Keish invited him back to the Tagish village, George went gladly and became one of the community. He learned the language, participated in rituals, wore Tagish clothing, learned to make snowshoes and set traps, hunted with the men, and slept on the floor with the family in the communal house, where Kate—the name he gave her—also slept.

They were married in a Tagish ceremony. George would use this fact later to disown her, saying that they'd never been married, but at the time, he was well satisfied. To have this beauty by his side. To have her strength match his own. To have a wife who could be his equal partner on the river and in the bush, in the First Nations tradition. As elder Kitty Smith put it: "He's got wife. He's all right! She does EVERYTHING, that Indian woman, you know—hunts, just like nothing, sets snares for rabbits. That's what they eat."[1]

Shaaw Tláa joined George, Keish (who came to be known as Skookum Jim) and her cousin Káa Goox (who came to be known as Dawson Charley), packing from Dyea in May 1887 for Dominion Lands Surveyor William Ogilvie. Many times she crossed the Chilkoot Pass, hiking alongside her menfolk, on the paths her ancestors had traversed for centuries. When the season ended, Keish and Káa Goox helped George build a cabin in Dyea to winter in. George wanted his wife to himself. How strange it must have been for her to leave the communal hearth and live as only two, to shoulder alone the burdens of women's work without a sister-in-law or aunt to share stories with, to learn an intimacy so foreign to her.

Keish and Káa Goox returned in the spring to sell their furs and go prospecting down the Yukon River with George. It was an unsuccessful trip. In September, George and Shaaw Tláa settled back in the Tagish village, in a separate cabin this time. Shaaw Tláa rechinked the log walls while George mended the sod roof.

The village was on the shores of the channel running between Lake Marsh and Lake Tagish, north of Lake Bennett. About 12 log cabins were scattered around two community houses. George and Shaaw Tláa lived a traditional Tagish lifestyle. Shaaw Tláa gathered kindling, bucked wood, and kept the fire going, hauling water or melting snow. She tanned hides and sewed mitts, moccasins and mukluks to sell. She picked salmonberries and blueberries, roots and herbs. She caught grayling and salmon, snared ptarmigans and rabbits, was known as a good hunter. She made bone butter and bannock. Her skills and knowledge enabled the pair to live off the land so that George did not need the supplies other prospectors had to buy and pack around.

When news of the Fortymile gold trickle came to the village in 1889, George was wild to go. Keish and Káa Goox decided to stay closer to home. In June, George and Shaaw Tláa went to Fortymile without them. This was a different kind of hunting. Together they dug down to bedrock, sluiced and panned at their claim. They didn't find any gold. It was too late in the year for travel back to the Tagish village so they went trapping on the Porcupine for the winter.

In 1890, after selling their furs in spring, they staked another claim near Fortymile. This time they found gold. They were forced to live in a tent all winter, as they'd been too busy mining to build a cabin. In 1891, they had a good yield but 1892 found the claim depleted. Because Shaaw Tláa wanted to be closer to her family, they went back up the Yukon River and started a trading post near the Five Finger Rapids.

Shaaw Tláa ran the post alone while pregnant. Her lessons in solitude served her well. George was away for the summer, constructing St. Andrew's Church in Fort Selkirk. They moved there for the winter. In this town, far from her family, Shaaw Tláa gave birth to their daughter, whom George named Graphie Grace, on January 11, 1893. Graphie was baptized by the missionary at St. Andrew's, the first claim that George staked for the culture he came from.

They returned to the trading post until May of 1896, when George got itchy feet and took them back to Fortymile, where he could prospect again. In June, legend has it he had an unforgettable dream of an encounter in the river with two salmon: "In place of scales they were armoured in gold nuggets and their eyes were twenty-dollar gold pieces."[2] He decided they should go fishing. They travelled to the Tr'ondëk Hwëch'in fish camp at the mouth of the Klondike River and made nets and a weir together, the Han welcoming Shaaw Tláa as one of their own.

This was where brother Keish, cousin Káa Goox and Káa Goox's youngest brother, Koolseen (whom George dubbed Patsy Henderson) met up with the couple. The family had lost one brother and three sisters, and two of the remaining sisters had been gone for two years with white prospectors. Keish was responsible for looking after his sisters' welfare and he was worried they might be lost. Communally, the clan decided that Keish, Káa Goox and Koolseen should ensure that the sisters were safe. Family concern for Shaaw Tláa, not greed for gold, is what brought the party to the Han fishing village where the Klondike met the Yukon River, and thus to the bonanza.

All the First Nations elders emphasize that gold meant nothing to their people at the time. That they had always known it was there but hadn't bothered about it. Maybe it had come to mean something to Shaaw Tláa and her family, because of George's interest in it. Or maybe it was George who meant something to them, as kin, and so they humoured him on his quests. They had no need of a shiny metal too soft to be any good or of money and what it could buy, but they had great need of a husband, a brother-in-law, a cousin—so many were gone.

Because it had been a bad summer for fish, they cut down trees and sold logs to Ladue's sawmill to earn their grubstake, the financing that would allow them to store provisions and take care of expenses while prospecting or mining. They ran into fellow prospector Bob Henderson, who was staking Gold Bottom and told them outright, in no uncertain terms, that people of the First Nations were not welcome there as far as he was concerned. George was incensed and didn't want to be anywhere near a man of such low opinions. Instead, the party explored the territory further up the Klondike River, especially all the surrounding creeks. And on one of these creeks, they made the discovery that was to galvanize the greed of people all over the world.

There are so many different accounts of this epic moment that we can never know what really happened. At first, George said Kate found the gold, then he said he found it. Skookum Jim later said he'd found the gold himself. Dominion Lands Surveyor William Ogilvie, who had interviewed all of the party shortly after they registered their claims, also gave Skookum Jim credit for the find.

The account of Émilie Tremblay has the menfolk gathering wood to make a cookfire for the bull moose they'd just shot and Shaaw Tláa going to the creek to get water. She carries her cedar bark basket down through the woods and kneels on the bank, as she's probably done already several times that day. But this time there is a flash of sun in the shadows. Gold nuggets gleam at her in the shallow water. She scoops them up, feels their rough shapes, their ominous weight. She takes them back to camp. She tells George to open his hand and, to his wondering eyes, deposits the gold in his palm. He asks her over and over how she found the nuggets and has her lead him to the spot on the creek. They find more and more gold and he shouts, resplendent with triumph, that they are all rich now.

But what does "rich" mean when you have everything you know to need in the land at your feet? When trinkets are burdens slowing canoe or sled? Camping in this gold-rich area, it is likely that Shaaw Tláa found the ore while washing dishes, that Skookum Jim and Dawson Charley found nuggets while getting a drink from the stream, but maybe none would have made a big fuss about the discovery. I can imagine Shaaw Tláa saying: Let my husband claim to be the one to find what he searches so hard for, this yellow stuff he thinks so special; let him find his specialness like that.

But she was savvy, too. She'd run the trading post, she'd mined at Fortymile, she'd sat with the white prospectors and heard their talk. Maybe the gold was something she sought as well, not knowing where the find would lead her.

*Kate, Graphie and George Carmack in front of their Bonanza Creek cabin, 1897.*

Kate, Graphie, George, Skookum Jim, Dawson Charley and Patsy—
the names the world would soon know them by—set up camp at
Bonanza and started sluicing. By fall, they had 88 ounces of gold worth
$1,400. Because none of the men could work their claim alone, they
agreed to work them together and share all the gold equally. They went
to register their claims with the commissioner. George registered the
Discovery Claim and No. 1 Below as his. Skookum Jim signed with an
X for No. 1 Above, as did Dawson Charley for No. 2 Below. It is possible that George got two claims because one represented Kate's share.
That would seem only fair to her brother and cousins, experienced bargainers in the Tagish-Tlingit tradition. Once the registration was secure,
George went to Fortymile with a bullet casing full of gold and boasted
to every soul he could find. The news tore through the territory like a
herd of caribou and the stampede was on.

As cheechakos swarmed the area, the Discovery group spent the next
two winters working their claims. Skookum Jim bought furs from the
Moosehide Han that Kate used to make mitts. She made and sold bread

as well. Some say she took in laundry, others that she refused to. In any case, she added to the coffers, sometimes bringing in more gold than George did. George wrote his family about his success, adding the disingenuous postscript: "My wife is Irish and speaks very broad English, but I have the prettiest little daughter you ever saw."[3]

The spring cleanup of 1898 produced untold wealth: a profit of $150,000. George made good copy as a bombastic media darling. Virgil Moore, writing for the *Klondike News* described him as "a handsome specimen of typical frontiersman, over six feet tall, with broad shoulders and a handsome face" and said that Carmack was going to build his own boat and sail to the Paris Exhibition of 1900, then to the South Sea Islands, Japan, China, the Suez Canal, the Arab and European Mediterranean countries, and across the Atlantic back to North America.[4] Whatever the hyperbole, Carmack had wanderlust and the means to satisfy it.

George convinced Kate and her family to go Outside with him; he wanted to see his sister in California. With money no object, the party travelled in style. On August 30, 1898, the *Roanoke* landed them in Seattle and they checked into the Seattle Hotel, amid a flurry of publicity. Carmack proudly proclaimed to the *Seattle Post-Intelligencer* that he intended to see the 1900 Paris Exposition with his First Nations family as he "would not care to go to Paris and see all the sights knowing that they were missing it all."[5] Carmack signed the register at the hotel including Kate as his legal wife, and he had a jeweller make her the famous nugget necklace.

Kate was now laced tightly into the corset of Victorian society. Outside, she could not be George's equal partner. All her strength, her knowledge, her skills honed through millennia of women before her meant nothing in this new, noisy world. The Tagish family was profoundly unsettled by the crowded city with its streetcars and tall buildings. Out of place in a culture that made little sense to them, they turned to alcohol to ease their alienation and perhaps a horror at what their world might become because of their discovery.

In the fall, they all went to George's sister Rose's ranch near San Francisco. A teetotaler, Rose was offended by Skookum Jim and Dawson Charley's drinking and George asked them to leave. They headed back to the Yukon. Meanwhile, the Carmacks settled in for the winter. Rose was shocked by her sister-in-law. Irish would have been bad enough, but Tagish was too much. Kate especially liked spearing frogs and shooting the heads off rattlesnakes, wearing her gold-nugget necklace all the while.

*George, Kate and Graphie in California, 1898.*

In the spring of 1899, George and Kate returned to Dawson to do spring cleanup, leaving Graphie with Rose and her husband, James. They came back to Seattle in the summer. Kate's sister Aagé, now called Mary Wilson, had died in 1895, so Kate and George brought her eight-year-old daughter (also called Mary) with them as a companion for Graphie. They arrived on June 23 and checked into the luxurious Brunswick Hotel. Two days before, Skookum Jim and Dawson Charley had checked into the Seattle Hotel with their wives and Skookum Jim's daughter.

George left for a short business trip. Kate went to visit her family and, according to the *Seattle Post-Intelligencer*, all hell broke loose. They had all been drinking with Skookum Jim's new gambling friends, and Kate got into a smash-up fight with Skookum Jim's wife. Skookum Jim threw her out of the room and she began breaking into other rooms, convinced that she would find George in one of them. She was arrested "while executing an aboriginal Yukon war dance in the second floor corridor of the Seattle Hotel"[6] and charged with disturbing the peace and being drunk and disorderly. She spent the night in jail with Skookum Jim, who was picked up hours later for being drunk, but apparently not disorderly. The *Seattle Times* followed the story up the next day:

> Mrs. George W. Carmack, the Indian wife of the discoverer of the Klondike, who is probably the richest Indian woman in the world, was fined $3.60 by Judge Cann this morning for drunkenness. Mrs. Carmack loaded up on champagne last night, and in company with some Indian friends, made Rome howl in the Hotel Seattle. Officer Grant gathered her in, and prosecuted her this morning. She refused to tell who furnished her with champagne.[7]

Only days later, Dawson Charley was also arrested for being drunk and disorderly. The papers ate it up, embellishing the facts and even including unsubstantiated anecdotes about previous offences.

George was disgusted. The bad publicity damaged his reputation in the local business community and endangered his investments. He wrote his sister that he was furious, ready to write them all off, and wished he could send Kate back to where she came from. In the spring of 1900, he left Kate and Graphie with Rose and returned to Dawson alone.

At a dinner party in June, he met Marguerite Laimee—a cigar store owner and veteran of mining camps in Australia and South Africa who had a string of aliases—and asked her to marry him that same night. She said yes, sold her cigar store and went with George to Seattle. George wrote his sister: "I can't ever live with Kate again; it is simply a misery for me. You may tell Kate so if you like."[8] He dissolved his business partnership with Skookum Jim and Dawson Charley.

Kate and Graphie stayed on with Rose, though unwelcome there. Rose took a house in the nearby town of Holister and brought Graphie and Mary with her, leaving Kate at the ranch. Kate came to town and rented the house next door. She tried to sue for divorce, charging adultery, but could not produce legal registration of the marriage. Meanwhile, George legally wed Marguerite in Olympia, Washington on October 30, 1899. Kate then tried to sue Rose for kidnapping her girls. But, bewildered by the unfamiliar legal system, and unable to produce documentation for her cases, Kate soon dropped the suits. Graphie and Mary were given back to her. Then, in January, Kate tried to sue George for separate maintenance. By July, she'd given up on that tack as well and returned to the Yukon, penniless, with her girls.

Her Tagish village had been displaced by the White Pass and Yukon Railway. Most of the former villagers, including Skookum Jim and Dawson Charley, had moved to the new railway town of Caribou Crossing (now named Carcross). Skookum Jim built her a cabin and helped out financially. She did beadwork and posed for pictures, earning a little money from tourist trade.

Graphie went to the Bompas mission school. Once Graphie and two friends snuck on board the train and made it to Whitehorse, where they were caught by an RCMP officer and forced to spend the night in headquarters before being sent home on the next train. She got up to more hijinks when living with the Reverend and Mrs. Stringer in Whitehorse and attending their mission school. She convinced their daughter to explore the red-light district with her, and the two girls delighted the women working there. The prostitutes showered these surprise visitors with gifts of candy, hair ribbons, even hats. Mrs. Stringer tossed the booty into the fire to punish the girls when they came home.

George, who had never contributed to his daughter's support, managed to contact Graphie at the Stringers' mission school and convince her to move to Seattle, where he and his new wife were living. He did this behind Kate's back, depriving her of her Tagish right to keep her children within her, the mother's, clan. Sixteen-year-old Graphie was seduced by white society, and by her stepmother's brother, a 32-year-old man, whom she married when she was 17. Neither Kate nor her family would ever see Graphie again. Kate had lost another husband and daughter.

Skookum Jim and Dawson Charley had new, large houses filled with valuable furniture, but they struggled with alcohol problems. Dawson Charley died the morning after Christmas 1908, by falling off the railway bridge into the river, where he drowned. Skookum Jim was arrested often for being drunk and his wife left him in 1905. He sold his claims to a large mining company for $65,000 and set up the Skookum Jim Indian Trust Fund of $20,000 for his daughter and other First Nations people of the Yukon. Then he spent the next decade unsuccessfully prospecting in the southeastern Yukon. He was 60 years old when he died on July 11, 1916. He left one thousand dollars to Kate.

Kate continued drinking heavily, especially after George took Graphie away, and her weight ballooned. The newspapers still sought her out on occasion and printed accounts of the gold discovery that said that Kate was not only present but was the true discoverer. She still made mitts and mukluks for sale and lived off the land in a traditional way, satisfied to be back in her culture with her people, but she was bitter about George's desertion, his denial of their marriage, his failure to share their wealth. She grieved for her daughter and for the world of her people.

On March 29, 1920, she died of pneumonia, a victim of the global influenza epidemic. Her obituary in the Whitehorse *Weekly Star* gives her, tentatively, "the credit of finding the dull yellow nuggets in the riffle in the bed of Bonanza creek" and states that "she soon tired of the ways of the whites and the never-ending noise and turmoil of the city,"[9] and so deserted George Carmack to return to her land and people. She might have been 50 or 60 years old, no one knew. As with much of her life, this detail was not recorded.

*Shaaw Tl'áa/Kate Carmack selling her handicrafts.*

What was recorded was George's version of the discovery. And he was a known liar. In fact, long before the Bonanza find, the miners at Fortymile nicknamed him "Lying George" as he bragged of gold discoveries he hadn't made. His stories changed radically after he'd turned his back on his First Nations friends and wife. In his earliest accounts, Kate found the gold; in his later ones, she wasn't even there. He first proclaimed her as his wife; he later claimed they'd never been married. The memoir he wrote, privately published by Marguerite Carmack, erases all traces of Kate from his story. This overblown tale was written solely to dispute newspaper articles that mocked him for camping on gold-laden ground for so long before finding any nuggets.

First Nations stories say that gold was found with the guidance of spirit helpers. They recount that once Keish had helped a frog out of a hole. That spirit returned as a woman with a gold-tipped walking stick. She pointed the stick down the Yukon River and told Keish that that's where he would find gold. On the journey, Keish and his cousins heard the wail of Wealth Woman—Tl'anaxéedakw—and chased the cry around

the lake but never saw her. Because they couldn't catch her, the legend goes, they couldn't keep their riches from running through their fingers.

They also lost their families because of this swift-running wealth. Shaaw Tláa, Keish, and Káa Goox all developed problems with alcohol, were left by their spouses, and died too soon. This version of Shaaw Tláa's life casts the Gold Rush in a different light, revealing the less glorious legacy of the newcomers' quest for gold: the destruction of the First Nations. Unlike Jennie Bosco Harper Alexander, who left her white husband to return to her First Nations family, or Katherine McQuesten, who

*Shaaw Tláa/Kate Carmack, sister of Keish/Skookum Jim and wife of George Carmack.*

was part Russian and able to fit into white society as a wealthy Gold Rush widow, Shaaw Tláa came to fit a common stereotype of the Native person struggling with alcoholism, poverty, and a broken family. Perhaps her decline came about because she had already lost so much before she even met George. Because George took what she had left away from her. Because she felt responsible for what she unearthed, a rush of white fortune seekers that poured over her people in their own land, erasing them.

She is not the end of the story, though she was the beginning. The First Nations people of the Yukon ultimately managed not only to survive this onslaught, but even succeeded in preserving their culture and eventually regaining much of their sovereignty as they fought to settle their land claims a hundred years after the Gold Rush.

While Shaaw Tláa's story was gradually eclipsed by those of the brave white women who followed her footsteps into the goldfields, it is she who played the most vital role in the Gold Rush, and it is her life that most strongly challenges the mythology of the white man's frontier.

# 4

*Émilie Fortin Tremblay*

## THE MOTHER OF THE PRIESTS

*Émilie Tremblay in front of her cabin in Miller Creek, outside Fortymile.*

*Curled up within the warm, flannelled arms of her husband, the 26-year-old French-Canadian woman sleeps gratefully on the bunk, knowing that nights of hard ground are to follow. If she hears the tremendous roar tearing down the mountain, it stays within her dreams. The couple wake instead to the screams.*

*They'd slept in their clothes and so do not need to pause as they rush headlong out of the four-room shack of a hotel and in the direction of the disaster. All the survivors converge at the site of the avalanche that has just killed over 70 men on the Chilkoot Pass on Palm Sunday, 1898.*

*She darts among the other rescuers, listening for buried cries, scrambling to unearth the victims from layers and layers of snow. Sometimes they are too late, and the frigid body, still running in place, is claimed only to join a pile on one of the many sleds filling with corpses. Sometimes they are in the nick of time and she breathes warm, gentle life back into the bearded mouths. She joins Dr. Brown and his assistants as they rub a frozen patient with snow and mustard. The doctor commands them to prick the man's skin with sewing needles, and this she does, her usually gentle fingers poking fiercely and relentlessly until the man jumps up with pain and life, as if only startled from a deep snooze.*

*Her husband comes to tell her that their nephews and cousin are safe, and she pauses to let her small shoulders sag with relief before returning to the toil of rescue attempts, the reconnaissance of human remains, the removal of mounds and hills and turrets of snow. So much snow. Wagonloads, shacks full, castles full.*

*It reminds her of the first time she crossed the Chilkoot five years ago, a bride of 22 on her honeymoon. How Jack had to go back for forgotten parcels and she spent the night alone in their tent on the Dyea Trail. How she had woken in the morning with the sides and roof pressing in on her and their dogs. How she was unable to move much and the dogs barked with fear as the air grew thin. She had ripped a hole in the tent. The dogs had escaped to tear around the rest of the party and bring help back to her. They had dug her out in no time. It had seemed like an adventure. Never would she have let herself imagine the immensity of this slide. She had been a cheechako then, proud to be considered the first white woman to cross the Pass. Now she was a sourdough, tried and true, and she never wanted to see a sight like this again.*

Émilie Tremblay was born Marie-Émilie Fortin on January 4, 1872. French Canadian and Catholic, she was delivered into the arms of nuns in St-Joseph-d'Alma in the Lac-St-Jean area of Quebec and then into the bosom of her poor pioneer family. When she was six months old, her father, Cléophas Fortin, moved them to Chicoutimi, where her mother found work as a schoolteacher. It was there that Émilie spent her childhood and received the only formal education she would get: grammar school at the convent of the Sisters of the Congregation of St-Roch.

The family emigrated to New York State when she was 15, settling into the town of Cohoes. That is where, in the fall of 1893, Pierre-Nolasque Tremblay chanced upon Émilie in his travels. He was originally from the same region of Quebec as she but had left home at 21 to find his fortune. And he found it—$10,000—on his claim at Miller Creek, a tributary of the Sixtymile River. Having been in the Yukon since 1886, he decided to go back to Quebec for a visit with his family. Somehow he wound up in Cohoes and this 33-year-old man immediately became smitten with 22-year-old Émilie. She was spirited yet serene, lively yet dignified, playful yet sincere. He knew his heart would be safe in her hands.

In turn, Émilie was entranced by him, his easygoing, friendly nature, kindly ways and solid strength. She was also enthralled by his tales of the Klondike; it seemed such a wild, free place, a place beyond all ken. Just hearing about it made wings beat in her chest.

After a whirlwind courtship, she accepted his proposal of marriage, against the objections of her family and friends. They had nothing against Tremblay personally but were appalled at the thought of their Émilie venturing into such dangerous territory, so far from home, from them. Émilie's mother was ill and feared she would never see her daughter again. Émilie would brook no opposition, and so they relented after securing a promise that she would return in a year if the claim was successful.

On December 11, 1893, Émilie Fortin married Pierre-Nolasque Tremblay in the local Catholic church. Word got out and the town was in an uproar. No one thought a petite young woman like Émilie should be allowed to gallivant off to the treacherous North. Nevertheless, crowds of well-wishers saw the newlyweds off at the train station, giving Émilie a pang of regret in leaving her loved ones and community for the lure of the unknown.

After a wedding tour to family in Montreal, Quebec City, Chicoutimi, and Pierre's hometown of Sainte-Anne, on March 5, 1894 they set off for the Klondike, a journey of more than five thousand miles. Crossing the country by rail, they then sailed on the S.S. *Topeka* up the Pacific coast to Juneau, Alaska, where they loaded up on supplies. In the small city, Émilie was a figure of interest, as few could believe a white woman would survive the trip into the Yukon. The Sisters of St. Ann visited and invited her to drop by their mission on the Lower Yukon River when she was in that area.

With their business concluded, they boarded the *Rustler* and travelled the Lynn Canal to Wilson Post over calm waters. Then they hired three First Nations packers at Dyea and started the trail to the Chilkoot Pass, joined by three Canadian prospectors. Because they had so many supplies, including tent and stove, their expedition included three dogs and a sled. Neither Émilie, at 125 pounds, or her husband, at 225 pounds, carried a pack. Instead, the two would get far ahead of their party, no doubt stealing time to be honeymooners, and would wait at the next camp for the others to catch up. The newlyweds were inseparable.

Then Jack, as Pierre was called in the Klondike, realized that they'd forgotten some of their gear in Wilson Post. He had to go back. That was the night, her first one alone since her wedding, that Émilie became snowed in with the dogs until rescued. She took it all with composure and was still raring to go when Jack returned. Even without a pack, the steep trail up the Chilkoot was a trial, but Émilie concentrated on the majesty that surrounded them: the rings of grand mountains, the length of the Taiya River Valley, the thick forests ending at the timberline of each peak, all seamlessly blanketed by white. It snowed on the climb up to the Summit and was slippery on the way down. Jack asked Émilie if she was scared and she said no, "If you can get down that steep hill, so can I."[1]

She drew her skirts together, plunked herself down and slid the last two hundred feet behind the sled, her laughter echoing up to the sky, Jack and the others tumbling behind.

That night, they camped early. Émilie played with the dogs and basked in the glory of the March sun tinting the landscape gold and

*Men and women building boats on the shore of Lake Bennett in 1898.*

peach and violet. Jack hunted addled white ptarmigans for dinner. A couple of days later they were at Lake Bennett. For two months, the men worked on building two boats, hunted bear and ptarmigan and grouse, fished for grayling, while Émilie cooked and waited for the boats to be ready, the ice to break up, the long river journey to her new home to begin.

They set off across the lake in mid-May. In rough waters at Windy Arm, a rambunctious dog almost capsized their boat, and Jack was forced to toss him overboard to ensure their safety. Amazingly, this dog turned up again in Fortymile, accompanying a prospector who'd picked him up along the way.

Émilie thrived on this outdoor life, rising early to row all day, cooking quick lunches at rest stops and more substantial meals at camp as the men pitched tents. She took pride in her culinary arts—once making omelettes and then cookies out of fresh seagull eggs—unfazed by the lack of proper equipment and ingredients.

But she was daunted by the rapids at Miles Canyon and Whitehorse. Although there was not yet a NWMP law against women riding through, when her husband set down his own law, Émilie did not protest. She portaged along the bank, anxiously watching Jack, and all their worldly goods, escape the roiling currents without incident.

Other near escapes farther along the river took her breath from her corseted chest. Once, an ice floe almost overtook them. Fortunately, miners on the shore came to their aid, wading into the water and grabbing the line the Tremblays had flung out, pulling them to safety. Another time, they ran aground on a sandbar and spent a night in the rain. But mostly they went gracefully with the current, delighted with each other's company, taking in the beauty of their surroundings. Émilie was later to claim that "this first trip down the Yukon River remains in my memory, full of romance, joy and love. There was nothing like it in all the world."[2]

*Five Finger Rapids*

They reached Fortymile on June 16, 1894 and were welcomed by all its 20 miners, including Jack and Katherine McQuesten. Émilie was an object of curiosity for the First Nations women, and they made her uneasy by the way they touched her and her clothes: "They wouldn't sit down but stared curiously as if I were a caged animal."[3] While later she would become more familiar with Han women, she never came to count them as friends.

After two weeks, they were ready to embark on the last and hardest stage of their trip. It was summer now, July, which brought black swarms of mosquitoes. Émilie sweated in her layers of protective clothing, the hot sun beating down for almost 20 hours a day. Even though packers bore the brunt of their expedition, the course was arduous. They had to pole the boat 20 miles up the Fortymile River, sometimes having to walk along the shore, pulling the boat with towlines. Then they had to hike ten miles up the valley at Moose Creek and a further 20 miles over steep mountains, through swamps, across muskeg. At one point, Émilie fearlessly jumped across a deep creek, to the admiration of all the men. At another, her foot slipped into a wet hole. The parched party drank the muddy water at the hole's bottom.

Rather than finding comfort at the end of the journey, Émilie was faced with a rough one-room log cabin with a sod roof, glass bottles for window panes, and a pole in the middle of the floor encrusted with layers of black tobacco spit from the miners who had bunked here. Her new home was small, dark, and filthy. She may have wanted to throw up her hands in dismay, but she rolled up her sleeves instead and got to work. For the next few days, Jack helped her clean the cabin, assemble makeshift furniture, and install their stove. She had the fortitude for the frontier: "I needed a lot of courage to face and endure that kind of life. But, thank God, I had it and I was never homesick or downhearted."[4]

In fact, she was often joyous, thrilled by the exotic sights around her, glimpses of caribou, moose, bear. To curtail her sense of isolation from being not only the only white woman in the area but also a unilingual French Canadian, she studied English grammar books and soon learned well enough to converse with the Anglo miners.

Jack had men helping him placer mine. They stayed in their own cabin but were fed by Émilie. And the miners on surrounding claims would come visit, bringing fresh fruit from a rare steamer that had passed. For Christmas, Émilie sent out invitations written on birch bark and concocted a feast of stuffed rabbit, roast caribou, sardines, evaporated potatoes, sourdough bread and scones, prune pudding and cake, all prepared in a small stove with a six-inch-wide oven. She cut up one of her long skirts to make a tablecloth. The invitation requested that the miners bring their own dishes and cutlery as the married couple had only two of everything. Two days before Christmas, one of the miners had disappeared and it turned out he'd walked 30 miles and back to bring a bottle of rum to the merry feast.

An occasional guest was Father Munroe of the Catholic Mission in Fortymile, whom Émilie spoiled with sweetened prunes. During her years in the North, Émilie would be visited by every priest in the area, earning her the sobriquet "Mother of the Priests."

Other than the occasional company of prospectors and priests, Émilie was quite alone. While she had an affectionate marriage, she had no one to banter with besides her husband. At this time, there were fewer than 30 white women in the entire Yukon, and none near Miller Creek. She was far from both female companionship and her family. When a miner finally brought her mail in the fall of 1894, she was so overwhelmed that she botched a batch of bread. She wouldn't see her family again until the fall of 1895.

Both the claim and the garden Émilie had planted on the sod roof produced well. A family by the name of Day had also come to Miller Creek. The Tremblays decided it was a good time for the trip home they'd promised Émilie's parents. They packed up their gold and left the Days to look after their cabin in exchange for one of Jack's claims.

The way out was almost as hard as the way in. In August, they set off for Fortymile and by September were aboard the S.S. *Yukon,* travelling down the Yukon River to St. Michael, Alaska. Once, the steamer got stuck on a sandbar for three days. Later, the captain stopped so that Émilie could visit the Sisters of St. Ann in the mission of Holy Cross. In Alaska, they took the S.S. *Bertha* across the Bering Strait to Unalaska, and then the *Dory* to Sitka, a stormy crossing that left all passengers seasick. The inclement weather also tossed around the S.S. *WallaWalla* on it way down to Seattle. The journey so far had taken 38 days. After boarding a cross-country train, Émilie and Jack arrived in Cohoes in November 1985.

After a visit of a couple weeks, they travelled again to Montreal and Quebec City, then spent the winter holidays with Jack's family in

Sainte-Anne. Everyone was overjoyed to see the pair again, and the married couple strew gold nuggets about and enjoyed sharing their success with their loved ones

By February 1896, they were back in Cohoes and, despite their wishes, here they would stay for the next two years. Émilie's mother was increasingly ill and demanded that Émilie stay with her. The doctor said she could die at any time so Émilie complied. Changing bedpans, giving sponge baths, administering medicine, breathing the stale decay of her mother's sickroom and watching the withering of the body that had birthed her, how Émilie must have longed for the tangy scent of spruce and unbounded life of the North. Forced to remain in New York State, she and Jack almost went mad hearing the media frenzy about the Klondike Gold Rush. As soon as Émilie's mother died, they rushed back to the Yukon.

They left in March 1898 and for the second time Émilie crossed the Chilkoot Pass. This time they had even more supplies, enough for 18 months or more, hauled by 22 huskies. As sourdoughs, they anticipated shortages and were bringing goods to trade with the new prospectors. They were also joined by cousin Joe Fortin, and nephews Onésime Gravel and Edmond Tremblay. Émilie was amazed at how crowded the territory had become, with its unbroken line of stampeders across the Trail of '98. What bustle and hustle. A hive vibrating with impatience and exhilaration, the banks of snow honeycombed with the hurried tracks of gold seekers, horses, dogs, sleds.

Then the deafening roar as the snow hurtled down the mountain on the morning of Palm Sunday, tossing tents and shacks and caches in its mad rush down, burying cheechako and sourdough alike. Imagine waking to an unimaginable force of white, pressing cold and blindness all around you, muffling your shocked breath as you are heaved and tumbled and twisted into a world without air, without gravity, without up or down, only whiteness, silent and still as a tomb, heavy as a mountain, as you try to be heard through all the layers of your white doom.

Émilie must have felt her heart break and slide a hundred times that day as she went from one buried scream to the next, digging for life. The tragedy of the Palm Sunday avalanche filled the unscathed party with horror and purpose as they stayed on to save what victims they could and recover the dead.

Then the party was further delayed by more personal tragedy. Onésime and Edmond fell ill but survived with Émilie's careful nursing. Poor Joe was not so lucky. A lung infection killed him. They buried him at Lake Lindeman, sinking their roots even deeper into this dire land.

Beyond this keen loss, they were two years too late to stake one of the richest claims. Had they not gone to visit family, they could have been among the kings and queens of the Klondike.

They settled in Bonanza. Jack would continue to prospect from 1898 to 1913, buying claims at No. 14 Above on Émilie's advice, and working as a foreman at No. 17 Above. The Tremblays lived well enough, even in the costly North, but would never be rich.

The first Christmas at Bonanza was celebrated with a midnight mass given by visiting priest Father Desmarais in a large tent with wooden benches. He and attending priest Father Corbeil were touched that Jack had made a crèche out of birch sticks. The first wedding was performed here in June 1900. Nephew Onésime Gravel's fiancée, Émilie's sister Mary Fortin, arrived on the summer solstice, the bride's face lit by the sun for almost the entire day and night. On June 25, Father Desmarais married the couple in the tent that Émilie had bedecked in garlands of wildflowers. Eighty men attended the ceremony, and one played the wedding march on his harmonica. All the guests celebrated with a feast at Émilie's. The two sisters, as the only women in that region, kept open house for visiting miners, and of course, priests.

Émilie knew Fathers Corbeil, Gendreau, Lefebvre, Desmarais, Shulte, Lebert, Godfrey, Eichelsbacher, Allerd, Lewis, Plamondon, Gagné, River, and Leray and played hostess to Bishops Breynat, Grouard, Langevin,

Bunoz, and Courdet. She worked tirelessly to collect for Christian charities, and no doubt came to know Nellie Cashman, since both women toiled devotedly for Catholic causes and played nurse to the ill. While caring for sick miners, Émilie also acted as midwife for many local women, including First Nations women. Childless herself, she was godmother to 26 children, many of Han mothers, and she even baptized some of these new souls.

If she was saddened not to have sons or daughters of her own, she never showed it. Perhaps she was happy to have her skirts swishing free of clinging hands, her beloved Jack hers alone. Perhaps the hurt was so

*View of Dawson City from the Dome peak looking south,*
*taken at midnight with the sun still shining, June 21, 1899.*

heavy that it took all her quiet courage to carry it. Perhaps her abiding faith allowed her to be thankful enough for all her blessings that one less could not deflate her joy.

In 1902, she was honoured in the *Dawson News Clean-Up Edition* as a "brave and beautiful French mademoiselle" who'd been "not only willing but anxious to brave all the hardships" of her husband's Yukon and whose kindness and courtesy had won the hearts of the frontier men. In telling the story of both the Tremblays and the Gravels, the newspaper said of Émilie that "no queen was ever treated with greater kindness and courtesy by loyal subjects than she by these rough miners."

Loyal as she was to the Klondike, by 1906 Émilie needed a change of scene. She and Jack had been saving up for a big trip and they decided on a four-month tour of Europe. The spunky small-town French-Canadian girl had grown up to scale the highest heights of the northern wilderness and now she would be conquering the Continent. Their trip was highlighted by the hospitality of those who had made their fortunes in the Klondike. On the transatlantic crossing, the Baron de Silance invited them to the captain's table on the S.S. *La Provence.* In Chartres, they stayed at the castle bought by their old friends the Auberts with Yukon gold. Jack would hunt larks with M. Aubert while Émilie walked the formal gardens, admiring fountains and lime trees. In Paris, they saw the opera and in Rome they received the blessing of Pope Pius X. After seeing the sights, they paid a visit to their families in Quebec, returning like royalty, full of glamorous stories of mountain passes and majestic palaces. Then they went home to the Yukon, Émilie relishing the familiar hospitality of the northern miners, whom she esteemed above the members of the elite.

On her trip to the family, Émilie adopted her six-year-old niece, whose mother had been widowed with nine children. The girl went to school in New York, later marrying down South. As Madame Poirier she returned to Dawson with her husband to raise their three children.

After a few more years of mining, it was time for Jack to retire. It was hard now for an individual prospector to compete against the big mining companies. The Tremblays' claims hadn't come through. Jack was beginning to feel his age. In 1913, they moved to Dawson, buying a two-storey building at the corner of King Street and Third Avenue for $3,000. Here Émilie opened Madame Tremblay's, a ladies dry goods shop that sold accessories and novelties, today the site of my brother's office. They lived in the apartment above. The store was in a prime location and became immensely popular. From the bay windows of the apartment, you can watch much of the goings-on in town. After all the years of solitude out on the creeks, living in the centre of town must have given her a renewed lease on life.

Jack carved the prehistoric mastodon ivory that is still plentiful in these parts, making souvenirs to sell in the store and even a chess set that came to be prized by a New York collector. The first year, Émilie ordered couture gowns and goods from Paris, but World War I interfered with such imports, and the dwindling population of Dawson made the idea less profitable. While running her store, Émilie still kept a toehold in mining activities. It was her signature, not Jack's that graced placer mining grant applications for claims near Sixtymile, signed on April 18, 1914 and May 27, 1914.[5]

Émilie was also very active in the community. Having long been president of the Christmas Tree Association, she was now made the organizer for the St. Mary's Catholic Church Bazaar and Banquet. She was renowned for knitting 263 pairs of socks for the soldiers in the war. She founded the Society of the Ladies of the Golden North in 1922 and was elected as the first president. She received a gold medal for community service. And she became president of the Yukon Order of Pioneers Auxiliary in 1927 (protest marches were still being held in the 1980s because women were not allowed to be members of the Order). Émilie also was honoured with a lifetime membership in her friend Martha

Black's pet society, the Imperial Order of the Daughters of the Empire. In 1937, at the coronation of King George VI, Émilie received another commemorative medal. As a mining woman, prominent business-woman, and active member of the community in Dawson, Émilie was closely associated with and esteemed by the other women profiled in this book, especially Ethel Berry, Nellie Cashman, and Martha Black.

Her return to Bonanza for a brief visit in 1921 was reported as a big event in the *Dawson Daily News,* which markedly noted the hospitality extended to her by all and her appreciation of the changes that had been made since she'd lived there. She had been invited to stay at the Chateau Lehman in Grand Forks while treading her old stomping grounds, at the behest of owner Harry Lehman. She is quoted saying that the "Chateau Lehman is certainly as comfortable a little roadhouse as one could wish to find in any mining centre and the new proprietor has certainly gone eto [sic] much time and trouble in making this hotel one that is not only a comfortable stopping place but a very cheery home for the miners and others in the vicinity of upper Bonanza and Eldorado."[6] It seems it might have been a publicity move on his part to have a *grande dame* of Dawson recommend his hotel.

For 30 years she ran her store and did not leave the Yukon. Then, on July 16, 1935, her dear husband Jack died, at 75. His funeral was that of a beloved and prominent citizen. His obituary in the *Dawson Daily News* celebrated him as the "Grand Old Man of the Yukon."

This was the man who had held her hand as she climbed every strange peak and valley on her journeys, sharing her frolicsome laughter. For a year, she mourned him deeply; then she was ready to be brave again.

Alone, she boarded her first plane, flying from Dawson to Whitehorse over the terrain that she had crossed by foot and boat on so many adventures with her husband. Then she took the White Pass and Yukon Railway, the ease of the journey almost shocking after the trials of the Chilkoot Pass. In Skagway, she boarded the S.S. *Nora* for Vancouver, where she spent Christmas, dining with old friends, including Martha Black's husband, George.

She visited sourdoughs in Seattle, the *Alaska Weekly* reporting the welcome received by "this woman whose charms and vivacity have not been lessened by the years and whose face, with its sparkling eyes, is adorned with silky white curls."[7] She was also guest of honour at a Ladies of the Golden North meeting.

She went on, with old pals, to Portland, Oregon, near where Klondike Kate had her homestead, Santa Rosa, and to San Francisco. Then she returned to Seattle and Vancouver, toured Lake Louise and Banff, and took the train to Montreal. She visited her sister Mary, who had long survived her husband, Onésime, and was interviewed by a historian of the Saguenay, Abbé Victor Tremblay. She stayed at the Chateau Frontenac in Quebec City and was the guest of honour at an Imperial Order of the Daughters of the Empire reception. She made a devout pilgrimage to the shrine at Ste-Anne-de-Beaupré.

In Saratoga, New York, family gave Émilie a surprise party. She then reunited with another sister and spent two months in Schenectady and more weeks in Cohoes, Troy and New York City, which stunned her with its frantic energy. She spent the summer holidays travelling with family to lake resorts in New York State. On August 14, she was ready to begin the long journey home, stopping in Vancouver and Prince Rupert before travelling down the Yukon River on the S.S. *Casca*, back to the place she considered her true home.

Everywhere she went, with Jack or without him, she was feted as a courageous woman of the Klondike, this kindly, tireless woman who was ever taking a step toward adventure.

She resumed business at her store and lived alone for a few years, only moving from the store in 1938. A surprise housewarming party was thrown for her, attended by Martha Black and all the doyennes of Dawson, and "a beautiful bridge lamp was presented to her."[8] In the same year, Émilie was honoured when the Historical Society of Chicoutimi accepted her donation of all her medals and placed them in their archive collection.

After a couple more years on her own, Émilie married fellow sourdough Louis Lagrois on September 23, 1940. Once again she moved into a log cabin as a bride. The couple settled down at the Forks, where Bonanza Creek meets Eldorado Creek, and where Belinda Mulrooney had a hotel in the heyday of the Gold Rush. They were only half a mile away from where Kate Carmack's husband, brother, and cousin had made the big discovery. Émilie was delighted to be in the great outdoors again, and her relationship with Louis was teasing and friendly. They welcomed many visitors and kept a place in Dawson so as to visit their many friends there.

In August 1946, Émilie attended the Sourdough Convention of the Alaska and Yukon Pioneers in San Francisco, her presence singled out and noted by the *Alaska Weekly:* "Among [the mining veterans] were Madame Émilie Tremblay-Lagrois, the first white woman to cross the Chilkoot Pass."[9]

Long has been the controversy over who was the first white woman to cross the Chilkoot. Émilie believed it was herself. Certainly all the miners at Fortymile when she arrived believed she was the first and often told her so. Martha Black would also name Émilie as the first in her writings. As Émilie understood it, the other major contender for this honour was a prostitute named Dutch Kate, whom she was told had turned back before reaching the Summit. Émilie was determined to hold this distinction. Indeed, she claimed it as a *French-Canadian* woman, in an effort to commend French Canadians in the face of prejudice.

But a 1924 report in the *Dawson Daily News* had caused a brouhaha when it printed verbatim a *San Francisco Bulletin* article in which Anna DeGraf was quoted saying she was the first white woman to cross the Chilkoot. Émilie then made a statement to the press that Anna DeGraf's claim was false. From San Francisco, Anna DeGraf wrote to defend herself to the paper, saying that she had never made this statement, that Mme Tremblay had misquoted the article, and that there was conflicting evidence supporting many claimants to this honour. She asks the paper to "relieve Mme Tremblay and her friends of the misapprehension under which they are labouring."[10]

In the same edition, a lengthy letter from E. Valentine is reprinted from Juneau's *Stroller's Weekly*. E. Valentine wrote that he knew both Émilie and Dutch Kate in their early days in the Klondike and that Dutch Kate had been the first white woman to complete the Dyea Trail to Lake Bennett in 1887; a Mrs. Healey had been second in 1888; someone named Viola was third in 1889; and that first Anna DeGraf and then Émilie Tremblay had come long after these other women had left. Local historian Sam Holloway names a Mrs. Beaumont as crossing in 1892 and posits the likelihood of white prostitutes crossing earlier with miners. It is a measure of the respect and goodwill that Émilie had earned in the Yukon that the Sourdough Convention ignored the evidence and upheld her position as the first white woman to cross the Chilkoot. The debate firmly entered the life of Émilie Tremblay into the public record and it revealed that these brave women of the Klondike knew each other, that they supported one another and quarrelled with each other, and shared a sense of specialness from all being sourdoughs.

After returning from the convention, Émilie had only one more year in the territory that had claimed her heart. At age 75, with her 80-year-old husband, Émilie moved to a boarding house in Victoria. She began a hard battle with cancer, a fight she lost in 1949 at 77 years of age. Louis lived on until 1956. Her obituary in the *Whitehorse Star* named her "first white woman settler."[11]

Émilie Fortin Tremblay may not be able to lay absolute claim to any firsts, but she was an intrepid woman who ventured into remote territory and lived a pioneer life with aplomb, persistence, and grace. And she was just as eager as her husband to do so: "Thanks to God," Father Bobillier quotes her as saying, "the profession of explorers has not been, even in the North, the lot of men alone."

Like most of the women in this book, Émilie Tremblay loved the North and served it well, becoming an example to all of the kind of spirit that does reach the Summit. Today, she remains an important figure in the history of the Gold Rush and an inspiration to the French-Canadian community in the North, who named the French First Language program in the Yukon École Émilie-Tremblay.

*Anna DeGraf, Lake Laberge, 1897.*

# 5

*Anna DeGraf*
## THE SAMARITAN

On the shores of frozen Lake Laberge, an old woman sits on a large boulder, leaning on a neat pile of rough rocks. She is hungrily gnawing on hardtack moistened with melting snow. A heavy scarf swathes her grey hair and is knotted under her chin. Her hands are covered in enormous moosehide mitts, like worn tan flippers. Her coat and skirt sport ballooning pleats of coarse, thick fabric in autumn colours. Her feet are wrapped in wide strips of sacking, as if in casts. Looking at these tattered bundles, you can guess that this is a woman who has almost lost her feet to frostbite, who has almost died breaking through the ice of the river, who has fought off dangerous men with just her courage and a loaded six-shooter.

The photographer snaps her picture, freezing forever an image of those steady eyes, that wry mouth and strong chin, that expression of archetypal strength and earthy humour. One eyebrow is raised archly. She is an icon of the wise old crone. She is a souvenir of the Gold Rush. She is a symbol of the North—its hard, rough beauty, the strength of its mettle.

*Years later, in a distant city, the stooped great-grandmother stops in shock before a photo parlour window. There is her image, not reflected in the glass but framed, showcased inside. She stares bemusedly, then shrugs. She has never needed anything to show her who she is.*

Anna DeGraf was born Anna Lötsch in 1839 in the tiny nation of Saxony. Details of her life before going to Alaska and the Yukon are both sketchy and heartbreaking. While growing up, she lived through the terrors of the 1848 revolution and the Austro-Prussian war of 1866. She married a man named Girndt and their first baby died of illness; she and their second child barely survived cholera. Her husband emigrated to the United States and fought in the Civil War.

In 1867 Anna, at age 26, and her child made the Atlantic crossing from Germany to New York through violently stormy seas. Reunited with her husband, Anna had at least one more child. Then the Panic of 1873 ruined them. Anna and her children were left homeless in New York City when her husband went prospecting in Yakima, Washington.

Such was the promise of the New World.

Mysteriously, Anna changed her name to DeGraf and set out West with her children only to find that her husband had been murdered. She laboured to establish a home dressmaking business in Seattle, but everything she owned was consumed by the flames of the 1889 Seattle Fire. She rebuilt her business while suffering from a broken leg, and perhaps saw her daughter married, only to have her beloved son disappear into thin air in July 1892.

George DeGraf kissed his mother goodbye, assuring her that he'd return in 14 days. Anna anxiously waited for the 23-year-old for three weeks. Then a stranger from Juneau said that George, or someone of that name, had been seen in a party of young men in that town. She wrote for and received confirmation of this rumour. Anna was wild to go and

*Anna (standing) in her workshop with her employees.*

find him. She had watched helplessly as her first child had struggled out a last breath. She had missed the last heartbeat of her husband. She refused to stand by as one more loved one was lost to her.

At 53, she sold her business, packed up her sewing machine, and headed North, confident she could earn her way in a place where women and their sewing skills would be in short supply, while she searched Juneau for her son. Little did she know how far this quest would take her.

The steamship trip up the Pacific coast passed without incident and ended at a small mining town of about a thousand people, largely men, beneath the imposing bulk of Mount Juneau. Along Front Street, a dance hall, saloons, and stores paraded loud signs. The beach and the hillside clamoured with makeshift cabins. The settlement was bookended by two Koyukuk villages. Juneau was rough and lawless and violent. The editor of the newspaper was shot in the back because he'd criticized one of the men involved in a dispute over who was the best volunteer fireman.

There were settlers who were trying to create order in their community, and these good people gave Anna a warm welcome and helped her tour the mining claims, looking for her son. She became confidante to the young people of the town and ended up matchmaking quite a few marriages. Because women were so rare in these parts, they were showered with proposals the second they got off the boat, and it was not uncommon to be married before the week was over.

For two years, Anna plied her trade in Juneau, hearing no news of her son. Then Joe Ladue, later founder of Dawson City, came to town from his sawmill near Sixtymile. He claimed that a boy named DeGraf had stopped into his mill one day, on his way through the territory with a pack of lads. Frantic to catch up to her son, Anna rushed around trying to find a party travelling in that direction. One of the customs officers, a miner named Montana, and a baker and his wife were headed to Sixtymile and agreed that Anna could come along.

It was July 1894 when they headed out to the Chilkoot Pass. Anna packed her trusty sewing machine and the feather bed that she'd brought with her from Germany and kept with her through stormy seas and raging fires. The journey began with a tugboat ride to the little ranch belonging to a white man and his First Nations wife that would become Skagway in a few years. A rowboat then brought the travellers to Dyea. Setting up camp, Anna was pleased to run into a woman she'd known years ago when she'd spent time in Montana. This old acquaintance had no news of Anna's son but fed her dinner, gave her a horse to ride to Sheep Camp, and a hired man to escort her and bring the horse back.

Everywhere she went, she was torn between rushing and lingering. Her son might be just beyond the next mountain pass, the next bend in the river. Or he might be circling back right to where she sat by the fire.

Anna was using a crutch for her broken leg that hadn't healed properly, but she still packed 30 pounds and made it up the Scales to the Summit, where she was struck immobile by the intense beauty of the sun gleaming across seven glaciers, exclaiming: "My God, how beautiful you have made the world!"[1] Despite the others' impatience, Anna insisted that they camp the night there.

The next day, her co-travellers were less patient with Anna's disability and penchant for scenery, and she found herself left behind and lost, with wolves howling all around. A young First Nations girl showed her the rest of the way to Lake Lindeman. Anna's party did not wish to waste time building their own boat so they asked to join a pair of men who were almost finished a large rowboat. The Dutchman agreed but the Frenchman screamed no, not even for money. He said he didn't like his partner and proceeded to smash up his stove with a hammer, cut the boat into two with his saw, throw half the gear to the Dutchman, and tear off into the woods, leaving his own half of the gear behind.

The Dutchman joined Anna's party, and they built another boat, rowing through a storm on Lake Bennett, passing the broken hulls of other boats at Windy Arm. Only one man remained in the boat through Miles Canyon and its Devil's Hole whirlpool. The others watched anxiously from the steep bank as he lay flat on the heavy stores of provisions and let himself be sucked in and spit out the other side. As they joined him, another boat capsized coming through, so they threw out a rope and rescued the hapless souls. Shaken, they portaged their boat and all their supplies past the Whitehorse Rapids. Without further incident, they made it through the Five Finger Rapids and all the way down to Sixtymile.

Joe Ladue wasn't at home but his First Nations wife affirmed that the young men Anna sought had been there. As Anna's heart leapt, the woman said she didn't know whether they had gone upriver or down. Hope and frustration swelled in her breast as she determined then to go on to Circle City, Alaska, a new mining camp that was attracting many prospectors. Despite the lateness of the season, she carried on down the river, stopping at Fortymile to ask fruitlessly about the whereabouts of her son, with the first ice floes dangerously careening by the boat. They arrived in Circle City in October 1894, in the middle of a blizzard, just in the nick of time before the river froze the next day. The entire camp rushed to the shore to welcome them. With Anna and the baker's wife, there would be eight, instead of six, non-Native women in town for the winter, and fewer than 30 First Nations women, among about 650 male miners.

Anna was immediately taken under the wing of two white women who ran their own restaurant. She stayed with them until taking a job nursing a sick girl, making $300 in three weeks as her charge recovered. Anna was amazed to be paid with a poke of gold dust.

She was then hired by Jack McQuesten of the Northern Commercial Company as a seamstress and moved into her own cabin behind this store, the largest in town. McQuesten taught her how to weigh gold dust and even gave her her own scales. She became friendly with his wife, Satejdenalno, called Kate, a Russian-Koyukuk woman. Kate McQuesten surprised Anna by giving birth to her ninth child in a little tent in front of Anna's door. Anna asked why she didn't just go in the cabin but Kate told her that First Nations babies had to be born in the fresh air. Anna viewed the newborn daughter with amazement, then watched as Kate carried her child home, her female attendants packing up the tent and following behind.

Anna became well acquainted with the First Nations community and would sit in their cabins admiring the swiftness and deftness of the women's fingers as they created beautiful beadwork designs on the moccasins and mukluks they made. She hired a young First Nations man named Charlie to do occasional work and was impressed at how he would work even in the most extreme cold. After she gave him ribbons and candy for his family, he brought her a large hunk of moose meat, saying she was the only white person to share in the bounty from the First Nations hunting party.

Anna made everything from shirts to tents for the company and did sewing after hours for the general public. She had a lot of extra work for the New Year's Pioneer Dance, when the men paid to have her make party dresses for their First Nations wives. Anna also did these women's hair and makeup and then went to the dance herself, on the arm of Judge Metlock, who had drawn lots to get her. There was a 14-piece orchestra at the Opera House and a feast of potatoes, cabbages, moose, blueberry sauce, and beer. The men were slicked up as best as possible in their regular clothes—two men wore ill-fitting dress suits—and danced with each other when they couldn't cut in to dance with one of the few women. They had such a good time that they convinced all the ladies to stay dancing until noon the next day, bribing them by cooking their breakfast.

There were some bad eggs in Circle, though. One night a hulking brute came into Anna's cabin and tried to take the tent she was sewing right out of her hands. He locked her in with him after grabbing her by the shoulders and sat down to wait for her to finish the tent. She convinced him that she needed wood for the stove then cocked him hard across the face with a small log from the woodpile. He let out a pained howl. Men came running and the thief fled with Anna calling after him: "Now, you go back to the creek and tell the miners that the dressmaker gave you a licking for not behaving yourself."[2]

The company manager gave Anna a six-shooter and carte blanche to defend herself however she saw fit. Another night, a dance hall girl ran to Anna for help. She'd been badly burned on a cookstove when six men had broken into her cabin and tried to molest her. These men then surrounded Anna's cabin and demanded that she give them the young woman she was harbouring. Anna refused, so they started to break down the door. After giving fair warning, Anna fired off three shots and scared them away. These incidents prompted a miners' meeting, and it was agreed that signs would be put up stating that bad behaviour would get you run out of town, to face almost certain exposure and starvation.

This warning did not have the intended effect immediately. Hearing a rumour that some men had targeted her for revenge, Anna had a company officer hide in her room one night. Two men who came in to rob her were caught in the act. After a night under guard, they were booted out of Circle and this action served as the needed deterrent to others.

Still not having heard news of her son, Anna became anxious to go home to her daughter. But that summer the company boat arrived too late to return to St. Michael and the steamship south. She was stuck one more winter. A bevy of dance hall girls had come into town the summer of 1895, and Anna had heaps more work. She would sew all day for the company then most of the night for the entertainers. She also organized a bake sale to raise funds to establish a school for the local children. It was such a success that Washington soon sent up a teacher.

When the ice broke and the company boat came, Anna sold her sewing machine to a First Nations woman and cruised down the Yukon River to St. Michael with joy and relief. The ocean voyage to San Francisco was a marked contrast to the pleasure of that river cruise. For six weeks the waves swelled and churned through storm after storm, buffeting the ship about like a bay leaf in a bubbling stew. Anna was overjoyed to reunite with her daughter, although disheartened that her son was still missing. She took her $1200 worth of gold dust to the mint and exchanged it for gold coins; with these substantial savings, she rented a rooming house to run and resolved to stay put.

Then news of the Klondike Bonanza spread gold fever from Seattle to San Francisco and throughout the world. Anna had been pining for both her son and the North. In 1898, she leapt into action, outfitting herself with dressmaking supplies, fabric, and another sewing machine.

She booked passage to Skagway, hoping against hope that her son would be at the thick of it in Dawson.

On the steamship, the wealthy New York Vanderbilts invited her to their elegant table to tell them tales of the land of the midnight sun. Her stories gave them much amusement, but they abandoned their own journey when faced with the Chilkoot. Anna's troubles started before the Pass. The steamship had left a load of freight, including all of Anna's worldly goods, behind on the wharf in Seattle. The captain let her stay on board until the ship had to depart again in three days. Then a woman from Juneau let Anna earn room and board working at her café and tent camp for the two weeks it would take for the next steamer to bring Anna's supplies. Skagway was under the brutal control of Soapy Smith and his band of thugs, but Anna was prepared. When a hand crept under her tent flap, she stomped on it with all her weight, thwarting the would-be thief.

When her ship came in, bearing 3,000 pounds of provisions, Anna hired some young white men as packers. It took six weeks to relay all those goods just one day's hike. Once again, Anna made the Summit, but on the other side she realized her feet were getting frostbitten. After being turned away by a man in one tent, she was taken in by a man in another, who quickly got her fixed up with a pan of snow that saved her feet. She treated the gunshot wound in his foot, in turn, before falling asleep, blanketless, in the cold. When she woke, she saw seven men in a circle around a single candle, asleep with their heads on the table. Not one wore a coat. She looked down and discovered that each had laid his coat on her to keep her warm. They woke, made her breakfast, and called her "Mother," a nickname that stuck throughout her days in Dawson.

To avoid paying duty at the customs house at Windy Arm, Anna and her boys serenaded the NWMP with a rousing rendition of "God Save the King." The ploy worked. The officers gave them lunch and waved them on their way without a word about duty charges.

At Lake Laberge, Anna's packers got into a wild drinking party at a First Nations camp. She threatened to leave them there and they dared her to. She brandished her revolver and said she'd shoot anyone who tried to stop her. They left with her. At the next NWMP station, she told commanding officer Major Strickland about how the young men were acting up, and he advised her to take them with the party he'd organized to bring supplies to Hootalinqua. At the Thirtymile River, the NWMP ignored Anna's advice to stay to the right of the whirlpools. Anna and her packers threw out ropes when the police boat was hit by an ice floe but were only able to save the captain. By the time they reached Hootalinqua, the river had frozen over.

For six weeks, Anna cooled her heels in the station, but she couldn't bear the thought of being stuck there for six months until the river broke. Six months without her daughter or any sign of her son. She sold her supplies to the NWMP, who'd lost theirs in the boat wreck, and turned back, armed with a letter instructing all police stations to feed and shelter her for her services to the men at Hootalinqua. She had to travel 20 miles a day to make it from post to post in the brief daylight of bone-chilling winter. She walked the whole way, her packers pulling the one small sled laden with essentials. Often she had to push the young men on when they were ready to give up. They were warmly welcomed again at Windy Arm and had a New Year's celebration there.

At Lake Lindeman Anna broke through the ice. Thrashing in the frigid water and screaming, she thought her day had come. The packers didn't hear her and continued on ahead in the distance. Just when she was about to succumb to hypothermia and drown, the NWMP came running and saved her life.

It was shortly after this episode that the famous photograph of Anna was taken as she sat on a rock at Lake Laberge, her feet wrapped in rags. She had no idea the shot had been taken and was startled years later by this picture hanging in a photo parlour window in Seattle.

Again she crossed the Pass, this time in a blizzard, sliding back down the side she'd climbed up so many weeks before. Dyea, Seattle, and she was home in San Francisco, determined to make the attempt again, convinced that Dawson was where her son would be found.

In the spring of 1899, Anna succeeded in bringing her sewing machine and stock to Dawson City. No sooner than she had set up shop in a little cabin than, on April 26, the hotel next door burst into flames and the fire spread to her domain. The next morning she was found stunned and shivering, incongruously perched on a chair right in the middle of the street. She'd saved her feather bed. Anna was taken in by the Alaska Commercial Company, which gave her a job sewing furs, including those on the NWMP uniforms.

As in Juneau and Circle, Anna worked days for the company and nights for the dance hall girls, then used any spare time to visit nearby mining camps, looking for her son. She lost almost everything to fire a second time but persevered. The summers were glorious, and she revelled in nature walks and the bounty of riotous wildflowers and berries. But the winters were gruelling, minus 40 to minus 60 degrees Celsius, daylight lasting only four or five hours a day. As with all the women under the Spell of the Yukon, a hardy fortitude kept her going:

> My mother used to say, "You must howl with the wolves, when you
> are with the wolves," and so I made the best of things up there. Many
> times my heart did bump—I was so frightened—but I pretended I
> was the bravest thing in the world, and got through all right.[3]

She kept others going as well. On the trail, the boys called her "Mother" but in Dawson she was known as "The Samaritan," especially for her maternal protection of the dance hall girls. These young women brought her not only their dresses to sew, but their secrets to keep and their hearts to mend. Anna gave them advice, helped hide their affairs from jealous wives, and fished them out of the ditch, getting them sobered up for good.

Once, when delivering a dress before a show, Anna found a dance hall girl in bed with boot prints on her chest and side, the vicious marks of a drunken man she'd tried to bar from her room. Anna arranged for a government matron to nurse the young woman and get her out on the first spring boat, but the dancer died of her injuries six months later.

Another time Anna arrived too late to help at all. She had been hired to make matching blue dresses for a pair of dance hall girls, a blonde and a brunette. When she delivered them to the girls' room, the brunette burst into tears and led her to the bed where the blonde lay dead, a suicide. The man who had cheated on her came in, stared, turned, lit a cigarette, and left. Another young woman took the dress and the show went on.

On top of her company job, freelance work for the dance hall girls, and kindness to all, Anna was soon to add another responsibility to her heavy load. When Klondike Kate and Alexander Pantages opened their

*Anna in San Francisco, circa 1900, with her two grandchildren, daughter and son-in-law.*

vaudeville house, they wanted whole costume changes every week and hired Anna for the job.

Anna took a break after seven straight years in Dawson and went South in 1906 to see her family. No longer did she have to go by foot as there were now regular steamers along the Yukon River and the White Pass and Yukon Railway to Skagway. She was amazed to land in Seattle and find a Pantages theatre. The next day she ran into some of the performers she'd known in Dawson and they took her to the show. Alex himself gave her a box seat and invited her to dine with his new wife while she was in town. The actors paid homage to Anna by cracking in-jokes during the play and even pausing to call out questions to her. After this visit, Anna made sure to take a trip Outside every two years.

Back in Dawson, Anna would sometimes get tips for mining claims that she'd stake herself, often in the middle of the night so she could beat out the competition. Because she frequently made trips Outside, she lost many of these ventures. The rule was that you had to work your claim every year and pay for an assessment. She couldn't do this when she was in San Francisco with her daughter, so others legally jumped her claims.

But it wasn't the gold or the cold that fired Anna's devotion to the North. What she sought was her son. What she loved in the seeking was the beauty of the wilderness, the chance to test herself, and the camaraderie that developed in a remote area where people needed to help each other, a social leveller that created a democratic culture. When Yukon Commissioner George Black and his wife Martha invited her to a reception at the Government House, she was impressed that they had included everyone, not just the elite. Anna was honoured by Martha Black's announcing her as "the oldest pioneer in the Yukon"[4] and giving her two girls as attendants for the dinner and dance. Anna also loved the frequent Pioneer dances and musicales, kicking up her heels and even entertaining marriage proposals from young men. She always declined, considering a husband a luxury she did not need. She was well enough on her own: "To one who loves to study human nature, this big, overgrown, raw mining town of Dawson was a source of never ending interest."[5]

A sociable and fun-loving old soul, Anna had many friends to keep her company. A particular friend was a widowed storekeeper. Anna and she became part of a theosophist reading group that met on Sundays, a gathering of educated men, including a librarian, a miner, a manager at Standard Oil, and the engineer who was the widow's fiancé. The women loved to spoil these men, who lived so plainly. For Christmas, they snuck into the miner and librarian's cabin and decorated it with new curtains, spruce boughs, and toys. The men were delighted, whirling the women around the room as the miner lay on the floor blowing a toy horn and kicking his heels together. Then the women tied aprons on the men so they could finish cooking the feast.

These companions looked out for Anna. At one of the weekly reading groups, her friends said she should go Outside for a year for her own protection. When she asked what they meant, they commented on how hard she worked and how she'd been feeling a little poorly over the winter. Later she would learn that they'd overheard two men planning to murder her in order to get one of her claims. The blackguards were going to drop a heavy object on her through the skylight of her shop had she not left town.

The recommended trip South started late and badly. The river froze up around the boat and grounded it a day out of Dawson. First Nations men took the passengers back to the city, where they had to wait two weeks for the stage. But the stage driver was drunk and crashed the coach twice. Then the train broke down. Thus the party from Dawson missed their boat and went on a small fishing craft instead, which was so slow that they didn't get to Seattle until Christmas. Anna was ecstatic to arrive in San Francisco the next day and embrace her family. She ate all the vegetables she could and saw the opera every night.

*A 1924 portrait of Anna in San Francisco.*

She stayed only six weeks then headed North again, arriving so early that she had to stay in Whitehorse for almost a month before travel was possible on the Yukon River. While she was there, the Whitehorse Hotel caught fire, burning Anna out of her room next door. This time, not even the feather bed survived. All her stock was gone and destitution forced her to work as a seamstress in Whitehorse until she could save money to get back to her family. In a year, she had sufficient funds to make a trip to Skagway then Juneau, following the lure of more work and a last-ditch attempt to find her son.

It was in this newly cosmopolitan city, in 1917, that Anna heard of the birth of her great-granddaughter. It was time to let go of the son she'd lost, leave the home she'd found in the Yukon, and reach toward the new generation. She left the North forever, moving to San Francisco to be near her family. She continued to miss Dawson City even as she loved her life in California. In 1924, the *Dawson Daily News* printed this short article about her:

Mrs. Anna de Graff [sic], noted pioneer woman of the Yukon camps of Circle, Fortymile and Dawson, is living at the Ventura Hotel, 1039 Mission Street, San Francisco, and, although over 80 years of age, continues her daily work with the Chicago Fur Store, and is as energetic as ever, and hopeful of again visiting the Yukon. She is planning, she writes, to go into the movies.[6]

Never an idle woman, Anna also worked at the Pantages Theatre as the wardrobe lady until she was 90 years old. A year later, in 1930, she died of pneumonia, her son's whereabouts still a mystery.

While the search for her missing son was ostensibly what drew Anna DeGraf to Alaska and the Yukon, she stayed on many years in Dawson City because she had fallen under the famous Spell of the North. While much older than the other Gold Rush women in this book, she had their same lively, indomitable spirit.

# 6

*Belinda Mulrooney*
## THE MOGUL

A studio portrait of Belinda Mulrooney.

*She paces the worn carpet of the Seattle hotel room, her ire rising with every step. Two men hover near the door. And then it comes, the knock she's been waiting for. She nods at the men. One throws the door open, the other grabs the surprised visitor. The door is locked. There is a tussle, but the two henchmen soon have the tall man held firmly between them. They wait for her instructions.*

*She is only five feet, three inches tall. A severely pulled bun of dark hair and spectacles give her a no-nonsense look, as do her plain, dark clothes. Her mouth twists into an expression of hardness. She looks like a stern schoolmistress. She has the men strip off the man's jacket, then his shirt, so the victim is presenting his back to her. Then she takes out the horsewhip. The first lashes are revenge for what he has done to her and her sister. Then there are more, for the gold-digging husband, for the law that always stands in her way, for the hired men who ignored her orders, for the teacher that whipped her, for the parents who left her behind. The man's back is lacerated with the red stripes of her rage. The marks on her are deeper, layered over many years, all under the skin.*

*Her motions, as she cracks the horsewhip, seem purposeful and businesslike. She knows how to get a job done. She is one of the entrepreneurs that made the town of Dawson a city, the richest woman of the Klondike Gold Rush.*

Belinda Agnes Mulrooney was born on May 16, 1872 in Carns, County Sligo, Ireland to John and Maria Connor Mulrooney, on her grandparents' small tenant farm. She was the first-born, her parents having married on January 21, 1871. Immediately after her birth, her father crossed the Atlantic for the coal mines of Archbald, Pennsylvania, and her mother followed a couple years later, leaving Belinda behind with her grandparents to be raised with her young uncles.

A donkey was born on the same day as Belinda and raffled off as a prize to raise money for the church. A ticket was bought for the newborn baby girl and she won, but there was a dispute over the draw. Another raffle was held and she won again. Nothing in life would come easy for Belinda, and she would always be having to beat the odds.

The donkey became her best childhood friend; she, too, was stubborn, independent, with skin as thick as hide. With the donkey kicking all the fear out of her and her uncles brawling with her, Belinda became a tomboy and a scrapper. This education would serve her in the Klondike.

> Seriously, what I learned from my uncles was useful later in Alaska. Never to expect any favors. To know that a woman around men who couldn't do her share was a nuisance and was left behind. So that is why I tried to be in front always, to lead.[1]

She certainly wasn't afraid of authority. At school, she got whipped for a subterfuge and lost her temper in her first week. Each student was required to bring two sods of turf for heating fuel. When Belinda rode her donkey across the river, one of her sods fell in and was carried away. She tried to cover up by breaking the remaining sod in half, but the teacher was not fooled. He called her to the carpet in front of the whole class and

> [he] gave me a good wallop. That darn rod thing, when it spread, it felt as though it were a bushel of them. I looked up, and I saw my uncle with fire in his eye. I was stunned, but I wouldn't cry. I saw he expected something. I picked up the sod and let it fly. It struck that teacher above the glasses and knocked 'em off! I was frozen for a minute, but there was nothing left but to fly. The teacher started up and dropped his stick. His game leg wouldn't work. He could only shuffle along without his stick. By that time I was on the donkey and beating it for home.[2]

It would be months before her family could convince Belinda to return to the classroom. Her uncles helped her with her studies and tried to keep her out of trouble. Then three of the uncles emigrated to join her parents in the coal mines.

Belinda, at nine, went to work doing odd jobs whenever she could sneak the time from farm chores and school. Proudly, she gave her grandmother the first oil lamp seen in the village. She didn't have friends, but her greatest satisfaction came from working hard and proving herself. Not an affectionate girl, she was nevertheless quite attached to her uncles and grandmother.

At 13, she was ripped away from her home. Her parents had had more children in the States and needed her to help care for them. They'd had a son, Patrick, in 1879 and another daughter, Helen, in 1884. When the baby, called Nellie, was one year old, and Belinda was 12, her parents sent money to bring her over to Pennsylvania. Belinda didn't want to go. The parents who had rejected her now wanted her to give up the only home she knew to be a free nursemaid to siblings who were strangers to her. Her departure was wrenching: "Leaving my uncles was bad. Leaving my grandmother was worse. But leaving the donkey—I threw my arms around his neck. And cried for hours and hours after I left him."[3]

It was on the deck of the ship that young Belinda discovered her spirit: "A flying fish came up once and knocked me silly. There was something in my blood, something the storm appealed to [in] me."[4]

Whatever it was—will, rage, greed or passion—she would need it in Archbald. She hated the town, her family, the coal dust. Instead of being the youngest child, she had the new responsibility of being the eldest. Instead of the green spaces and familiar faces of her home in Ireland, Belinda was packed into the close quarters of the Irish mining settlement with virtual strangers. Her only thought was to get enough money to escape.

What she escaped first was the school where she fought and won 30 fights a day. Usually she could restrain herself during the other children's teasing until after school, when she would wallop them. But one day she lost it. Excited to have been asked by the teacher to do a recitation for the class play, she devoted herself to learning the piece, determined to show everyone what she could do. During her recitation, her classmates dissolved into helpless laughter over her Irish brogue. This time she couldn't wait. She sucker-punched the first one she saw in the hall, and not for love or money would she darken the school's doors again.

It was just as well. In April 1886, sister Margaret Ann was born, followed by Agnes in 1887. Belinda's hands were full taking care of her siblings and trying to earn the money to get back to Ireland. She was ingenious at finding jobs. While many of the children picked huckleberries for eight cents a quart, Belinda would go alone into the dreaded snake-infested bushes to get the best berries, waiting until rattler after rattler was coiled to strike her before attacking and snapping off their heads.

Covertly, young Belinda also became one of the mule drivers for the coal mine, when it was illegal for women to do so. The man in charge kept her secret because she was the best in the business. Instead of putting her earnings into the family pot, as was expected, Belinda hoarded hers in a buried coffee can.

When it was full enough, she campaigned, at age 17, for a visit to her aunt in Philadelphia, secretly intending this to be her escape for good. Permission was granted, and finally Belinda was free.

Living with her mother's sister, Bridget Agnes, and her husband, Belinda pounded the pavement. Soon she was moving into the prosperous Cummings estate as a nursemaid for their baby, Jack. Belinda was in her element. She didn't have to hide her dreams here. Mrs. Belle Cummings took a real interest in her, teaching her how to use a bank, encouraging her to use their large library, including her in the family. Belle's father was the artist John George Brown, and he painted Belinda and Jack into his painting *The Sidewalk Dance.*

Then this kind family lost all their money. Belinda sweetly and naively tried to give them her savings and offered to sell the paintings for them. When they gently turned her down, she said that their son didn't need her anymore, so she was going to Chicago to start a business at the World's Fair of 1893.

True to her word, at 20 years of age, Belinda bought a lot in a key location at the Fair, hired a contractor to put up a building, and sold it at a profit–a highly unusual activity for a woman at the time. She then bought a restaurant close to the Midway and hired another woman to help her feed the masses hot dogs. Nearby was the Women's Building, where socialite Martha Black was helping with the International Women's Congress, where journalist Faith Fenton spoke, where suffragettes campaigned for the vote.

In one of her sidelines, Belinda was selling bread to a teeming mob when she was surprised by Belle Cummings. Belinda greeted her warmly and took her back to her restaurant, very proud and pleased with Mrs. Cummings' amazement at how much she'd achieved.

After the Fair closed, Belinda rented a restaurant and rooming house in San Francisco during the Midwinter International Exposition of 1894 but it was destroyed by fire. Belle Cummings then set her up with a job as a steamship stewardess aboard the *City of Topeka,* which ran to Alaska with both freight and passengers.

Northern tourism was in its infancy so Belinda's duties were unclear, but she soon learned to take orders and serve, making a lower crew member act as busboy while she sassed the customers. Once she told some miners who had requested that she polish their boots: "Listen, and this goes for every man on board who needs a little valuable lesson-learning quick. Go clean them and polish them yourself. Anybody who leaves boots at my office will find them filled with sea water."[5] She also had a retail business on the side, bringing up desired merchandise—like a cow and a canary—to the Alaskans. There's a rumour that she was smuggling whisky, "bringing untaxed bottles into Canada in specially sewn pouches in the lining of her fur coat."[6] At any rate, the shipping company saw that she was not cut out for service positions and decided to use her talents elsewhere.

On July 15, 1896, she opened up their Juneau store, but found being a manager unchallenging. When news of the gold strike hit, she was wild to go mine the prospectors. Her first attempt to cross the Chilkoot failed. She went to Seattle to get better equipment and a trail wardrobe. She replaced the corset with a boned skirt, adding layers of long underwear, a thick shirt, a denim and fur hooded parka, boots and snowshoes. Her sleeping bag was a sourdough's dream: red fox fur, lined inside with eiderdown and outside with silk, oiled for rainproofing.

From March to April 1897, she travelled back to Dyea with a full load of supplies and merchandise. She had a large party to pack her goods 30 or so trips across the Chilkoot, including a couple with three children. She put saddlebags and booties on the dogs. The people pushed and pulled sleds over the snow, with Belinda insistent on pulling her own weight. She also hired First Nations packers, who hiked with the gear strapped to their backs.

The going was gruelling and many gave up, Belinda snapping up their supplies at a bargain. She was always on the make, keeping close-mouthed about her doings while pumping others for useful information. She was derisive of almost everyone, but especially of anyone who was not white. Above all, she wanted to best everyone.

That she did. Not content to wait for Lake Bennett to break up, she had her boats full of supplies put on sleds and pulled to the river, which had just broken up. Unfazed by the turbulent rapids, Belinda fell in love with the North on this trip: "The beauty of Alaska [actually, it was mostly the Yukon]—you can't possibly overdo it. It seems to me that every day and every night is different. You just feast on it. You become quite religious, seem to get inspiration. Or it might be the electricity of the air. You are filled with it, ready to go."[7]

She was featured in a story in the *Klondike News*, entitled "Women in the Klondike: Where Strong Men Turn Back Before Hardships, Brave Women Continue the Journey."

*Belinda and her party packing her goods through Dyea Canyon in April 1897.*

Miss B. Mulrooney, the subject of this sketch, had no big brother or husband to rely upon, but she believed that if a woman could grace almost any business or profession at home she could be a successful trailblazer.[8]

By the time she'd blazed her way to Dawson on June 1897, Belinda was down to her last quarter. With bravado, she hurled her last cent into the Yukon River.

Dawson was little more than a scattering of tents with a couple blocks of hastily built buildings on Front Street, facing the Yukon River. Belinda used the boats to build a house, then started her store and hired new friend Esther Duffie, a prostitute, to run it. Women flocked to buy fine silk underclothes. Esther taught Belinda how to weigh and assign value to the piles of gold dust they were raking in. In less than a month, she had enough to start a restaurant with cook Mrs. Lizzie Geise. Belinda was still quick to take offence in a service role—she forcibly threw one customer out for joking that she was swiping extra gold dust—so she hired popular Sadie O'Hara as waitress. Belinda was aloof and reserved and liked to keep herself to herself, spending most of her leisure time with her pet St. Bernard, Nero.

She then bought a block of property on Front Street, bought up the rafts that were bringing more stampeders in, and had log cabins built from the logs. They went like hotcakes even as she kept raising the prices. She hired people to make furnishings and even started having a scenery painter from the theatre paint murals on the canvas walls. Dawson was no longer just a mass of shacks and tents. As gold poured in from the creeks, everyone wanted to catch its flow. Outrageous fortunes could be gained and lost in the space of a day. At 25, Belinda owned a store, a restaurant, and prime lots on Front Street and Second Avenue.

It was in July 1897 that she saw her first gold mines out at Bonanza Creek. Her eyes lit up, not at the sight of gold but at the perfect spot for a roadhouse—the Forks, where Eldorado Creek meets Bonanza, the centre of all the mines around. The idea produced much amusement among the men, who believed that Dawson was the only right place for a hotel. When she asked some pointed questions about the length of the walk into town from the mines, they changed their tune and told her that, with her head for business, she'd end up owning the Klondike.

With one mule, she hauled logs to the site and commenced building, impatient to get everything accomplished before the animal gave out. The Grand Forks Hotel was completed in August 1897, with two floors and large windows. There were even kennels for the sled dogs. Soon a town sprang up around it to serve the miners in the nearby creeks, taking its name from her hotel.

Looking for peace and privacy, Belinda moved into her own cabin up the hill behind the bustling hotel, also taking in Sadie O'Hara. Here were the space and beauty she had longed for, and no one could send her away. Her independence and industry had given her a security that she'd never known and she guarded her gains closely.

As winter froze Dawson in and food shortages in the Klondike hit a crisis point, Belinda was forced to share her large stores, which made it hard to run the hotel. With ever an eye to the main chance, she seized on a steamer full of provisions that had run aground. She got "Big Alex" MacDonald, then the largest mine owner in the Klondike, in on a deal to get the goods cheap, hoping to supply her hotel, but he took all the food to feed his miners. When she pointed out that she had a hotel to run, he dismissed her concern, saying that she couldn't run a hotel anyway, a girl like her. Belinda vowed revenge.

The hotel was booming, acting as trading post, bank, and claim brokerage house for the miners. MacDonald offered ten grand to buy it, she said a hundred grand or no deal. Appalled, he tried to make a deal to use her house for his freight and headquarters. She said he should build his own place. It was payback time. She bought up all the gumboots and candles around and charged him double for them when he came in to supply his men.

By now, Belinda was a familiar figure going back and forth between Dawson and the Forks.

Miss Mulrooney is a modest, refined and prepossessing young woman, a brilliant conversationalist, and a bright business woman. She makes the 18-mile-trip to Dawson in a basket sleigh drawn by her faithful dog Nero, a noble animal of the St. Bernard breed and the largest dog in the Northwest. The trip is made in less than three hours.

So reported the *Klondike News* on April Fool's Day, 1898. But Belinda was tired of making this trek. She was dying for a telephone to save her some of these business trips. She founded the Yukon Telegraph and Telephone Syndicate, once again giving MacDonald a dig, as she wouldn't let him put in a bigger investment than the other mine owners. She had the equipment brought in from Outside over the Chilkoot and provided the poles herself. She put Tom O'Brien in charge of running the company and had her own telephone—before most small cities down South were on the line!

With the news and tips coming over the wires and through her hotel, she grubstaked miners for a share and started doing her own staking out at Dominion Creek. She was a partner in the lucrative Eldorado-Bonanza Quartz and Placer Mining Company, along with Alex MacDonald and the Berry brothers. In the spring of 1898, she added two more buildings to the hotel. In one short year, she'd become the richest woman in the Klondike and one of the moguls that made Dawson a city.

Using her position to speak her mind, Belinda went head-to-head in community meetings, a force to be reckoned with when it came to the bad-inage of insults common to the mining folk. It was sharp-tongued Belinda that Inspector of Mines Captain H. H. Norwood went to for advice. Always, she held to her own opinions, sneaking $20,000 in donations from the dance hall girls and prostitutes into the charity pot for the new hospital.

Ever the entrepreneur, Belinda was not satisfied with all that she'd accumulated. She had yet another dream: to build the *best* hotel in Dawson, as grand as any in San Francisco. There was a shortage of lumber and nails in the spring of 1898, so Belinda had men prying nails out of old boats and foresting logs in the bush and floating them downriver to Dawson. Then she cleverly and audaciously placed a bet of $10,000 that she'd get her hotel built by summer. Miners are gamblers at heart, and they all rushed to get in on this wager. Her workers bet their wages that she would do it and worked long hours on the construction, even through the flood that followed breakup the end of May.

On July 27, 1898, she opened the newly built three-storey Fairview Hotel at the corner of Front and Princess Streets, with a fine view of the Yukon River. She won all the bets, even the ones from the men in town who'd said she'd never be able to heat the place with so many storeys. She'd gotten a local to redesign a boiler so that she could. Even though it was not quite completed—glass for the windows hadn't yet arrived—

*The hotel that Belinda built at Princess and Front streets.*
*She may be one of the women on the balcony.*

the hotel was a smashing success. The *Dawson Daily News* called it "a first-class hotel in every sense of the word."[9] Mumm's champagne and oysters were served on the house at the opening and an orchestra played for dancing. The hotel offered a saloon, a gourmet restaurant, and private rooms with electric lights, lace curtains, and Brussels carpets. The third floor was for the sourdoughs from the creeks and the second floor was for society folks. The Fairview hosted regular dances and events and ran the town telephone switchboard. Next Belinda opened a bathhouse adjacent to the hotel. There was nothing else like it in the whole Yukon. The entire operation was not only her pride and joy, all of Dawson saw it as a monument to the city it was becoming.

It was in her hotel that Belinda met the man who would later become her husband, Count Charles Eugène Carbonneau. At this first meeting, she was less than enamoured when he claimed he was being overcharged for the wine. When she exasperatedly said he could have it on the house, he insisted on paying for it. He approached her again to convince her he wasn't cheap. Finally he tried to impress her with his title. Belinda didn't have the time of day for such nonsense. She had more important worries.

She wanted to get the windows installed before winter. Carrying $30,000, she took a small boat upriver to Whitehorse, then set out towards Skagway in a canoe with hired helpers Jenny and Jack, a First Nations couple that Belinda respected and liked. The canoe tipped over at Lake Bennett amid the torrents of floundering cheechakos who had been lured by news of the Rush. Belinda, dripping wet, asked a pair of old-timers whether her party could dry off in their tent. They had that famous bush hospitality and wouldn't let her pay for food.

A young packer named George was stopping there as well. He had stashed his money with two brothers in the next tent. The following morning, the camp was in an uproar. Sometime in the night, someone had hit one of the brothers on the head and stolen George's grubstake. Belinda told him not to worry, he would be taken care of as part of her party. In her account, she adds a description that may explain this generosity: "He was in condition, that youngster, I tell you. He had the finest physique I ever laid eyes on."[10] She also went to the Mounted Police.

Meanwhile, the injured man sported a head bandage and required nursing from his brother. But Belinda noticed the two were quite restless when a Mountie visited her. She went straight to RCMP commanding officer Major Wood with her suspicions and he offered to send an officer back with her. She suggested that the Mountie impersonate a doctor and examine the injured man. Sure enough, there was no wound under the bandage, and there was a stash of cash under the pillow. The grateful George became one of her most devoted employees.

Ordering 14 boats to be ready for her return, Belinda continued on to Skagway, which was busy with the construction of the White Pass and Yukon Railway. She got her furnishings and building materials, but it was already September and she needed to get everything all the way to Dawson before freeze-up. She paid Joe Brooks a large sum—40 cents a pound—under a contract specifying that the goods reach Bennett within three days. A reformed gambler named Broad joined her party. They watched Brooks head off with 22 mules loaded with her goods. Belinda raced to Bennett to check that the boats she'd ordered would be ready. Then Broad came with bad news: Brooks had dumped everything of hers at the Summit and left on a more lucrative whisky-hauling contract. Goaded, and wanting to avoid the derision of the miners when she failed to bring home the goods, Belinda cooked up a scheme to get her own back.

She and Broad borrowed a pair of horses and headed back to the Summit. She hired a crew of tough, weary packers eager for excitement. They had to ambush Brooks and his men on the American side so as to avoid the Mounties. In the afternoon, they cornered their quarry. Belinda stopped Brooks in his tracks, barring the trail on horseback. She ordered him to read the contract. He said paper meant nothing to him.

She informed him that there was a clause allowing her to take possession of his mules. Like hell she would, he said. Her men tensed.

Belinda whipped out a pistol and held it under the belt of the fore-man, saying he'd better get off the mule. Later she'd say: "Did you think I was going to take that mule train with a bunch of roses?"[11]

Then her men took him and roughed him up so he could save face at conceding to Belinda. Belinda and her gang offered jobs to Brooks's men. They not only joined her, they gave her Brooks's own fine saddle horse. She and her posse also took off with his mules and his foreman.

She got the whole kit and caboodle to Bennett, only to wrangle with another charlatan. It was an anxious time for all stampeders, trying to get to Dawson before freeze-up. The doctor hired to do inspections for the Mounties had a great scheme going: quarantine the more prosperous travellers with invented diseases until they'd bribe him with vast sums to be allowed to continue their journey. One look at Belinda's posse and he knew he had a live one. He declared typhoid and quarantined her when she didn't even have a touch of fever. She pretended to comply, disappointing him with a complete lack of protest, even seeming eager to rest there all winter.

Meanwhile, she had arranged for her men to load the boats, distract the doctor, and signal her when ready. The next morning they burst into her cabin and yelled for her to run. They had sent the doctor out on a false call to an imaginary accident in the canyon. He figured out the ruse just in time to see the fleet pulling away from the shore.

The last big hurdle was the rapids. Belinda held her breath the whole way through the churning turmoil. Her description betrays a certain soupçon of eroticism: "It was a beautiful sight to see those men on the White Horse rapids, every muscle in their arms showing, stripped down to undershirts and pants . . ."[12] When they came through, they had to rub their eyes and look again at the bank. Everywhere were ticking alarm clocks. They burst out laughing.

Then Belinda performed a requested kindness for her friend Ella Card, who had buried a baby nearby. She found the grave and piled boulders on it so it would be safe from animals. She grieved for both mother and child. This fierce and vengeful woman harboured sentiments that few suspected.

Their arrival in Dawson was followed by the return of Charles Carbonneau, who had hauled almost eight tons of provisions over the trail from Skagway with a team of 33 dogs, in temperatures down to 40 below. He was a bearer of world news, having been in Paris, and he cut a dashing figure to boot, in his spats and all slicked up. Belinda noticed his heavy mustache; his large, sleepy eyes; and his five-foot-ten, 210-pound physique. But what impressed her was that he had the best dogs she'd ever seen. She didn't know that a newspaper article, based on the word of eyewitnesses, had accused him of being cruel to his dogs on the trail—a cardinal sin in the Yukon.

Carbonneau wasn't respected by the miners, who resented his cosmopolitan airs and love of luxury. The dislike was mutual. He was quoted as saying he wished they'd shave sometimes. Belinda was attracted to his worldliness and understood his ambitiousness, but she hated his taste for opulence. On one of his frequent jaunts to Europe, he enraged her by bringing her back a whole wardrobe of frills and furbelows.

Their romance progressed in fits and starts. Charles was in and out of town on his own business for a French mining company and Belinda was going gangbusters with her concerns. So established was she by now that the Yukon Order of Pioneers (known as YOOP), although notorious for excluding women, made her an honourary member. She now had a lively social life. She appeared in blackface for a charity minstrel show, and she went to a masquerade ball, taking her housekeeper as a date. The two women were costumed as a married couple, with Belinda as the husband.

She also started another business. In 1898, unsanitary conditions had led to epidemics of typhoid and other diseases. That winter Belinda founded the Yukon Hygeia Water Supply Company to supply the town with clean water. She and her partners were granted a monopoly as competition grew. Once again, her ideas not only made her money, they made Dawson more of a metropolis.

Belinda made the rounds of her mining claims in the winter, using the expertise she'd gained in mining operations to implement improvements, like the tram she used to pick up water at French Hill. In an interview she claimed to hire foremen only for show—she was the real manager of her mines. Stories abound of her tyranny, especially from male employees.

By 1899, she was 27 and had begun to want children. Carbonneau proposed, but Belinda realized she had no idea how to be a wife, nor was she willing to dismantle all her business partnerships in accordance with laws that assigned a married woman's property to the control of her husband. She would be able to hold property in her name but could not sell without her spouse's consent. Her legal rights in terms of contract and suits would also be compromised. These laws were in flux at the time, having been strongly contested by women, and there was no knowing exactly how matters would stand. Belinda and Charles kept their engagement a secret so as not to disrupt her business dealings.

During their engagement, there was a rapacious fire in Dawson that consumed over a hundred buildings and caused half a million dollars in damage. Belinda's most pressing concern was for the dance hall girls, whose cabins behind the saloons were in flames. When she came to their aid, the women were running out into the snow in scant apparel. Belinda and others wrapped them in coats, had their frostbitten feet attended to by a doctor, and allowed them to sleep on the dining room tables in her hotel. When the manager objected, Belinda dryly said she'd be boss that night.

The Fairview escaped harm, and served as a shelter for those who'd lost everything. Belinda continued to improve the hotel and to develop all her mines and concerns. But, because of the laws regarding married women's property, she was also preparing to divest her empire in order to marry Carbonneau. She had taken him on as a partner in her hotel out at the Forks when he built an annex onto it, but she soon sold the Grand Forks for about $45,000 to Anton F. Standor and his wife, Violet Raymond. It was renamed the Gold Hill Hotel and later sold to Max Endelman and his partners.

Carbonneau also mortgaged some of his claims to Belinda and others, apparently needing cash to finance his next trip Outside. Some suggest that the claims weren't Carbonneau's to mortgage. The claims were owned by the Anglo-French Klondike Syndicate, and Charles was only manager and promoter. There is evidence that a power of attorney existed prohibiting Charles from mortgaging the claims, but this document was destroyed in a fire. If the mortgages were a scam, Charles hid this fact from Belinda. The intricate financial dealings between the couple suggest a growing trust on Belinda's part. Encouraging such trust by creating financial ties was part of Charles's strategy to overcome Belinda's ambivalence about their marriage. That this ambivalence remained is clear in her reaction to his departure. When Charles left for his trip Outside, in June of 1899, he kissed Belinda publicly, which shocked, embarrassed, and angered her. The news was out on their engagement.

Belinda was angry that Charles would jeopardize her financial dealings by exposing their relationship. Other concerns cast doubts on Charles's character. Gossip in town fuelled by the local newspaper deemed Carbonneau to be a French-Canadian barber from Montreal, not a French count. Unbeknownst to Belinda, when he arrived in Vancouver, Charles was rolled for over three grand by a woman he'd spent the night with, an incident reported in the *Province*. The woman was arrested and sent to jail for a year and a half, leaving three children on their own. Captain Norwood, the government mining inspector, and many of Belinda's male friends were worried about her and did not approve of the match.

Norwood and Belinda had recently gone trough a trying time. Fellow entrepreneur and mine claim owner Nellie Cashman had brought a bribery charge against Norwood, naming Belinda as his accomplice. Nellie then recanted her charge, claiming that she had been misled by Belinda. According to Nellie, Belinda had suggested that Norwood would be more likely to support Nellie in certain claim disputes if Nellie gave Belinda an interest in one of her claims. Belinda's version was that Nellie had handed her a deed, worth 25 per cent of a Cashman claim, which she then tossed into a safe without recording it. The case remains unresolved.

As the Gold Rush began to wind down, Belinda held on to her many claims, but in 1899 she put the Fairview Hotel up for sale. Her affairs in order, she went on the road in October, waiting to board her old steamship, the *City of Topeka*, on the first leg of a journey that would take her back to Ireland. She had a wonderful reunion on board with her former shipmates, and was thronged by mobs in Seattle, where she stayed at the same hotel as George and Kate Carmack. Then she went home to Pennsylvania and visited her parents after a decade away. By coincidence, she ran into her old benefactress, Belle Cummings, in New York at a furrier's, where she had brought her family on a shopping spree.

That winter she had all the glory of coming back to Ireland a success, and the satisfaction of using her money to spoil her beloved grandmother and uncles. On a visit in London, she had a chance meeting with Charles Carbonneau, who thought she was still in Ireland. He took her and her grandmother to the theatre, and she wore a purple gown trimmed with rare orange marten fur, and a string of pearls. He was in his element in this glittery world and she was impressed by the kindness with which he seemed to treat everyone. He went to Paris and she returned her grandmother to Carns then went back North again, to her real home, with a grand sense of achievement.

Belinda arrived in Dawson in the spring of 1900 and was greeted by a tangle of business matters. She came to blows with a foreman named J.B. Fields. According to a news report, "Miss Mulrooney and Fields had a dispute which ended in the latter being utterly vanquished for the time, the woman striking him over the head with a club, knocking him out in the first round and causing bright red blood to freely flow."[13]

In the midst of this kerfuffle and other complications with claim holdings and mortgages, Charles returned from Europe and they set a date for their wedding. Belinda's attitude was not quite that of the swooning bride:

> I had to get rid of the pest somehow, so we were going to get married in October, 1900. About my trousseau? I wasn't anxious to get at it, as I was too busy thinking how I could postpone the wedding until we could get affairs straightened up, clean up, and buy a place somewhere and retire. I wanted to be through with Alaska.[14]

Although not devout, Belinda was an Irish Catholic and began arrangements with her priest. He advised against the marriage but she didn't listen. Most of the couple's circle saw that she just wanted children and he just wanted her money. Some friends refused to attend the wedding, so strongly did they object to the marriage. Belinda persisted. She tried on her wedding dress with its full sleeves in front of Charles, clowning around, pretending to be bowlegged, and making everyone who watched almost sick with laughter.

The wedding, on October 1, 1900, was a massive affair, notable for both elegance and inebriation. A prankster turned out the lights as 28-year-old Belinda walked down the aisle on the arm of a friend. At the Fairview two hundred and fifty guests danced to the orchestra hired for the reception. Here another joke was played. Inflatable rubber disks had been put under some of the plates so that they danced when a bulb was squeezed. Belinda appreciated these efforts to keep the whole shindig from being too stiff. The all-night party exhausted her, and she settled down to a quiet life after that.

After the wedding, the couple continued to buy, sell, and manage their

*Charles Eugène and Belinda Mulrooney Carbonneau, newlyweds.*
*A studio portrait possibly taken on a trip to Europe, circa 1900.*

claims. While Belinda's improvements to her mining operation succeeded, Charles failed with his attempts to work his mines and he was often sued. Belinda had her father John up for his first visit in June 1901, and she used this opportunity to protect her holdings, signing over all her property to him. Her father stayed on for a year, and was available to sign documents while Belinda continued to do her own wheeling and dealing.

After their first anniversary, Belinda and Charles began a habit of going abroad to Europe for months, renting the second floor of an opulent house around the Champs Élysées in Paris, because Charles didn't want to be considered a tourist. They had much company, entertaining royalty with four of Belinda's younger brothers and sisters, whom she'd enrolled in Parisian schools, underfoot. They had a full staff, including a valet, a butler, and a footman.

Back in Dawson in the spring of 1902, the couple formed the Gold Run Mining Company to consolidate their many claims in this lucrative area. They incorporated in October, declaring capital of $2 million. Charles was appointed managing director and received huge sums for negotiating the deal. After a lawsuit over this deal, he left for Paris and seems never to have returned to the Yukon. Belinda took charge and whipped the workforce of hundreds into shape, establishing the town of Gold Run to house and serve the employees working on the mines, and forbidding gambling and prostitution on the property. She continued to purchase mining claims and kept pace with the transition to large-scale operations. She then left for her winter in Paris, with trips to Monte Carlo and Nice.

Meanwhile, Charles had used her money to form a shipping company, which was failing. Belinda realized that she'd been married for her fortune and began squirrelling away assets and working to distinguish herself as separate from Carbonneau. At Gold Run, she instituted bonuses and production quotas and got peak efficiency from the men. Nonetheless, one of the directors disagreed with her strategy and was suspicious of her connection to Carbonneau. The company shareholders and directors took away her power of attorney and her managerial position in August. They also launched lawsuits against Charles and Belinda. The suit against Belinda was eventually dismissed. Belinda sold the Fairview to a company owned by Charles and a man named Schneider, just before the hotel would be appropriated to settle another lawsuit brought against the Carbonneaus by two former associates, Letourneau and Bernier. These men, who had been their laymen at No. 12 Gold Run, held a disputed mortgage on the claim and won their suit on appeal in the Supreme Court of Canada on September 7, 1904.

At 32, Belinda moved to Fairbanks, Alaska in 1904 for a fresh start, bankrolled with money held for her by her father. Her first venture, a mining partnership with two women, ended when the women launched a suit against her that would continue for years.

Then another lawsuit damaged her reputation back in Dawson. Early in February 1905, the Canadian Bank of Commerce sued the Carbonneaus and other major shareholders in the Gold Run Mining Company for over half a million dollars. Charles was also being sued and convicted in all manner of swindling and embezzlement cases in France. Belinda's bonanza went bust and her empire crumbled. The claims she lost would end up yielding some of the greatest hauls of gold in the Klondike, producing right into the 1990s.

Lawsuits would only multiply as Belinda tried to rebuild her fortune in Alaska with untrustworthy partners. Her life had always been a battle but the never-ending litigation of her future business dealings would keep her fighting until she died.

Joined by her sisters Margaret and Nellie, whom she brought to Fairbanks, Belinda switched tack and started the Dome City Bank in 1906. But the Mulrooney women were out of luck with both men and money. Also in 1906, Belinda filed for a divorce from Charles, prompting the *Yukon World* to announce "Belinda Gives Up Her Title."[15] Glad as she was to be rid of the charming con man, with him went her dream of being a mother (as a Catholic, she could not marry again). She had yet to see the last of the scoundrel, though. In the fall, he kidnapped Belinda's sister Agnes, who was in convent school in Philadelphia, grabbing her off the street, throwing her in his car, and confining her in his room at the Bellevue-Stratford Hotel. Caught by the police, he smooth-talked his way into an acquittal with a tall tale about saving Agnes from the inappropriate embrace of a suitor. On December 10, 1906, Belinda received her divorce from Carbonneau.

Meanwhile, sister Nellie had married Belinda's Dome City bank partner, Jesse Noble, who was soon to squeak out of charges of gold robbery and pistol-whipping arising out of his overzealous repossession practices. In 1907, Belinda evicted him by hurling his trunk out the window. He criminally charged and sued the two sisters for fraud, claiming they were keeping his assets. When an official search turned up the relevant documents, he dropped the charges and bought the sisters out of the bank. Meanwhile, Nellie had his son, named Robert, on November 29, 1907. The boy was lovingly raised by all three Mulrooney sisters.

To escape all the trouble in the North, on December 27, 1908, Belinda bought acreage in Yakima, Washington for $25,000. She had 20 acres of fruit orchards to develop, but first she would build the immense fortress-like house—with not one, but *two* towers—that is still known today as Carbonneau Castle. Belinda filled its many rooms—including a ballroom and a billiards room—with her treasures from Europe. She once entertained President Taft, whose bulk wouldn't fit in her chairs, causing her to have a grand Chinese seat fetched from her Aunt Agnes's home.

Soon Belinda had gathered almost the entirety of her family—including her parents, siblings, in-laws, nieces, and nephews—around her and was concentrating on the orchards: irrigating, pruning, harvesting. A large warehouse housed the apples awaiting shipment. It was a good living, but lawsuits would gradually drain away her profits.

Soon after Belinda's move to Yakima, when Margaret was starting the Yakima and Alaska Investment Company, Jesse Noble and his new partner, August Ruser, sued both Belinda and Margaret for alleged embezzlement during their days at the bank. Although their chances of winning were slight, Noble and Ruser were using the suit to damage Margaret's reputation and threaten her new business. Frustrated by so many lawsuits, and fiercely protective of her little sister, Belinda exploded with violence.

Ruser was lured to a Seattle hotel room, where 39-year-old Belinda horsewhipped him soundly, shoving a towel into his mouth to stifle his cries, and leaving him bruised and bleeding from skin-breaking lashes. She was arrested and pleaded guilty for a fine of $150, freely admitting that she'd whipped him and contending that she was perfectly justified in doing so. The only lie she told was to protect the two men who'd helped her. She said that she, five-foot-three and 135 pounds, had been completely on her own as she beat the six-foot Ruser, and that his story of two accomplices was a lie.

Belinda won the suit after a three-year battle but otherwise her luck was running out. Throughout her forties, there were other suits with mining partners up North, the Yakima real estate prospects were dimming, her orchards were failing, and she was continuing to support her large family. At the end of the First World War, she tried to sell Carbonneau Castle but no one wanted to buy it.

In the 1920s, Belinda was reduced to becoming a housekeeper to tenants in her own home. Eventually, she took out a mortgage on the Castle to buy a modest home in Seattle, where she moved with her parents in 1925. Finally, she sold the Castle and the orchards. She bought another house in Seattle and converted it to apartments for her family and tenants. During the Depression, she worked as a seamstress for the Work Projects Administration and cared for her aged mother. During the Second World War, in her sunset years, she worked scraping rust from steel used to make minesweepers. At 85, in 1957, Belinda moved into a nursing home, where Margaret joined her within three months. There she enjoyed a shot of whisky and two cigarettes a day.

She died at 95, on September 3, 1967, of pneumonia and a hip fracture. As a final irony, her death certificate identifies this intrepid entrepreneur as a "housewife."

While her professional reputation lay in tatters, the other stampeders of the Klondike would always honour her as a figurehead. She was one of the charter members of the Pioneer Women of Alaska, and writer Harry Leon Wilson immortalized her as the character Ma Pettengill in his books.

Belinda spent her life cursing and kicking, a fierce and unrelenting fighter, determined to have her own way. She fought most of all to prove she was someone to be reckoned with, not someone to be passed by or left behind. Although her forceful nature at times erupted into violence, she was the epitome of the clever, resourceful, and willful entrepreneur. With her restaurants, the Grand Forks and Fairview Hotels, the telephone company, the water business, and all her gold claims, she made the shantytown of Dawson into a city and herself into an icon. Vengeful, greedy, industrious, loyal, with brilliant business acumen, Belinda was one of the Klondike's most complex and fascinating women.

*An Atlantic City, New Jersey studio portrait of Belinda wearing a
bathing costume and displaying her wedding ring.*

# 7

*Martha Louise Black*
# FIRST LADY OF THE YUKON

*Martha Louise Munger Purdy Black, socialite and outdoorswoman.*

Her first memory is of fire. Red sky, black clouds, flaming winds. Her face soot-stained and eyes stinging on the frantic flight to the lake. All around the wagon, horses stampeding and people running, bearing *crying children, bundles of belongings, even occupied stretchers, their fear filling the suffocating air as the fire consumes their homes. She is five years old. It is October 9, 1871, the second day of the Great Chicago Fire, and along with almost one hundred thousand others, her family has lost everything.*

*When asked what he would save should his house be on fire, French writer Jean Cocteau replied, "The fire." The child Martha might agree. Her sympathy for those suffering does not dampen the excitement of that wild ride. Sleeping on the shore for three nights, she revels in the out-door life she's dreamt of, baking potatoes over a hissing campfire and waking to the waves lapping. When they move into tents because of the cold, she is stirred by the adventure of beginning life anew, the whole world flipped topsy-turvy.*

*She is, after all, safe in the arms of loving parents, with the confi-dence an impressive family tree bears. Those that fortune favours will always walk through fire unscathed.*

Martha Louise Munger was born into the ninth generation of Mungers in America since her forebear Nicholas had arrived in 1645. Her family had fought in the American Revolution, the War of 1812, and the Civil War. It was during this last war that her parents met. Her father, George, fought for the North and was recovering from the battle of Seven Pines in Cincinnati. Her mother, Susan Owens, was visiting relatives in Cincinnati after the death of her own father, a wealthy plantation owner. Her forebears had founded Owensville, Kentucky and Cumminsville, Ohio. Neither family welcomed the match of a 28-year-old Yankee man and a 16-year-old Southern woman, but they married, moved near Chicago, and on February 24, 1866, had Martha and a twin sister who died hours after birth. George was frankly disappointed Martha was not a son. Susan had five more children in four years; all died in infancy. Martha would later be followed by a brother, George Merrick Munger, and apparently by other siblings as well, although they go largely unmentioned in her recollections.

Martha expressed pride in her lineage as a Governor's Daughter, Colonial Dame, and Daughter of the American Revolution. But her experience after the Great Fire was also to give her a lifelong affinity for people of all classes and a hatred of snobbery.

Chicago built houses for the homeless, and the Mungers went from the ashes of their own substantial home on West Van Buren to living seven in one room of a four-room shanty on Wapense Avenue, quickly nicknamed "Poverty Flats." Used to the regard accorded to privilege, Martha was furious at local children who shunned the shanty kids. Her chief pleasure in the new clothes and toys given by wealthy relatives was to give these children their comeuppance.

Soon, with the substantial help of family affluence, George rebuilt his laundry business and their fortunes flourished again. He would eventually own 72 laundries around the country, a sugar plantation in the West Indies, and a 2000-acre ranch bordering both Oklahoma and Kansas. They moved into a house befitting their station and Martha, called Mattie, was again subject to the Victorian propriety required of her sex and station.

In her memoir, *My Ninety Years,* Martha says her father was irritated by smart women. He was kind, though, and conceded graciously when she outsmarted him. As a child, she declared she could find a hundred four-leaf clovers. He said he didn't believe her and would pay her a dollar for each one she found, hoping to teach her the error of hyperbole. In two days, she delivered 50. He paid her the fabulous sum and asked to be let out of the contract, saying that he now had a lifetime of good luck.

Mattie was a little scamp. When her paternal grandparents took her to the circus, they forbid her going up in a balloon. Instead, they gave her a quarter for the merry-go-round. A few minutes later, she was excitedly shouting and waving a flag at them from the sky.

Occasionally she was outsmarted. When she was 14, an uncle gave her diamond earrings. She begged her mother for permission to pierce her ears. Grandfather Munger seemed to come to her rescue and offered to pierce her ears himself. For days he'd set out barbarous instruments and ask if she had time for the operation, taking into consideration two days of painful recovery. Eventually he suggested that since she was too busy to get her ears pierced, she might have the earrings made into a brooch.

This familial love helped reconcile spirited young Mattie to the strictures of decorum imposed upon her. And her love of finery—pages of *My Ninety Years* are devoted to descriptions of outfits—seems to have offered consolation as well. Still, sometimes she just had to bust out wild and free. Never aggressively defiant, she was removed from the Lake Forest Select Seminary for Young Ladies for the frequency of her good-natured escapades.

She was sent to St. Mary's of Notre Dame, Indiana and, despite the discipline demanded by the convent tradition, thrived in the freedom and beauty offered by its gardens, woods, and river. Hers was the education of a lady: watercolour painting, needlework, tennis, ballroom dancing, fitting her only for the life of a wealthy socialite. Her main subjects were deportment, elocution, and botany, all of which would serve her in surprising ways in later years. She graduated in June 1886. She was voted class poet, awarded medals for essay writing and elocution, and distinguished herself by having the best herbarium. She also was crowned with the only green wreath for poor conduct—all other heads bore gold or silver.

Her father took her West to visit his sister as he arranged to buy his retirement ranch. Her aunt, the first woman elected to the Denver School Board, was a progressive woman, friends with woman's rights activist and abolitionist Susan B. Anthony—Martha's idol—and Frances E. Willard, a former university dean of women who founded the Women's Christian Temperance Union. Meeting these women provided awestruck Martha with role models for being her own woman.

In the fall of 1885, Martha had her debut at her family's 20-room Chicago home. She loved being young and rich and pretty. She delighted in wearing her first evening gown: a frilled, flounced, lacy pink silk concoction.

In her school years, Martha was befriended by Will Purdy, a handsome military academy student and son of the president of Chicago Rock Island and Pacific Railway Company. After her debutante season, they became engaged and she spent months going to the dressmakers for her trousseau and doing the fancywork for her hope chest—pyrographically ornamenting furniture, monogramming linen, embroidering cushions, painting china. They were married in August 1887 and settled into the house that her father had given them and their relations had furnished.

The life of a young society matron suited Martha in many ways. She adored her two sons, Warren and Donald, and was devoted to their care. Having servants, she had plenty of time to help out at a kindergarten, the Women's Building at the World's Fair, and Hull House (headquarters of famed social worker Jane Addams). She wrote poetry, which was published in the Chicago papers and sometimes reprinted elsewhere. She had her "at-home" the last Thursday of every month, belonged to a cycling club, attended formal dinners, and saw performances by the celebrated actresses of the day, such as Ellen Terry and Lillian Russell. In short, Martha Munger Purdy's life was all that her elite background and upbringing had groomed her for: ease, good works, and cultural pleasures. But in the fall of 1897, she attended a reception that was to spell out a very different destiny.

The famous fortune teller Cheiro selected Martha from the glittering crowd and traced the lines of her palm with a gold snake, emerald-headed and ruby-eyed. He said, "You are leaving this country within the year. You will travel far. You will face danger, privation and sorrow. Although you are going to a foreign land you will be among

English-speaking people and will never have to learn to speak another language. You will have another child, a girl, or an unusually devoted son."[1] She scoffed. The next summer she was struggling over the Chilkoot Pass on her way to the goldfields, her husband and sons left far behind her, not yet aware that she was pregnant.

Originally it had been her husband Will who had been struck by the gold fever sweeping the country. Will partnered his friend Eli Gage and bought five boats to form a company offering passage to the Klondike. Martha wanted to go, too. After ten years of marriage, she was bored and unhappy. Her boys were in school and Will was away on business much of the time. She needed something to awaken her from her high-society slumber. Two things made her involvement possible. Her parents agreed to take care of her sons, and a man named Lambert commissioned her to be his agent in the collection of the $1 million in gold dust willed to him from his uncle who'd died in the goldfields.

Martha and Will outfitted themselves in Denver then landed in bustling Seattle with Martha's brother George. They were joined by companions Captain Treat, Captain Spencer, and his son, Ed. Will was unexpectedly called to San Francisco on business by Eli Gage. There he heard about the trials of the trail ahead and telegrammed Martha that he'd changed his mind, he now wanted to go to the Sandwich Islands (Hawaii).

Martha was not impressed. She had her ticket and $1 million in gold dust waiting for her. She wrote her husband that she was going to the Klondike without him and that she wanted nothing further to do with him. She never saw him again.

Martha convinced her brother to let her continue with the party, keeping Will's defection a secret from their parents: "It was the pivotal point of my life—my destiny. The North Star, my lodestar, beckoned me. It lured me onward. My whole being cried out to follow it. Miserable and heartbroken as I was, I could not turn back."[2]

When Martha boarded her steamer to Skagway from Seattle in June 1898, she was surprised to find her expensive private room occupied by a notorious prostitute, a gambler, and his girlfriend. She had no choice but to share. The wildness aboard unsettled her. In the end her roommates won her over with their kindness, bringing her morning coffee and fruit, and making her feel at home among so many disreputable strangers. She marveled at the 20 hours of daylight.

Martha reached Skagway in its last days of the despotic rule of Soapy Smith, who was killed ten days after she arrived. It was still his town, utterly lawless. The night was filled with wild yelling and bottles smashing as drunks were rolled for their grubstakes, prostitutes were taken in alleys, and poker games turned into shootouts. After unloading, the steamer carried Martha on to Dyea, a tent town a bit closer to the Chilkoot.

As she watched the steamer retreat, Martha was hit by the realization of just what she'd done.

Briefly, her resolve faltered. But the call of the North carried the day. A generous man donated his shack to her, and her brother George set himself up in a tent. For two weeks they got their bearings, resting, fishing, picking wildflowers, and hiking to prepare for the climb. They hired packers to haul their tons of gear for $900, an extravagant sum only the wealthy could afford, but cheap as wages for traversing the long, dangerous trail and transferring baggage from steamer to wagon, to horse, to man, to sled, and to horse again to reach Lake Bennett.

While crossing the Chilkoot in summer might seem like a walk in the park compared with the harsh winter journeys other women made, the sun brought its own dangers. The First Nations said anyone who tried the climb in summer was cursed. The snow began to melt in the warmth of the midnight sun. Instead of gently trickling away, Yukon snow breaks off in huge chunks and tumbles downhill like a herd of white elephants. Almost a hundred gold seekers had been trampled to death by the time Martha made her attempt.

They set out at noon on July 12, 1898. Martha wore the latest fashion: high leather boots, a brown velvet corduroy and silk skirt five yards around that shockingly showed her ankles, a high-collared blouse, a pleated jacket, long underwear, enormous brown silk bloomers and petticoats, and a corset laced tightly enough to make her waist measure 18 inches. She would make the entire journey thus encumbered, while George carried her straw sailor hat on a stick.

The first six miles over a wagon road were easy; the four-mile climb over huge boulders in a rocky valley was more taxing. They stopped for a cup of tea at a trailside cabin before pushing on. The trail to Sheep Camp was lined with miners' caches, heaps of dead horses, an odd shack that hadn't saved its inhabitants from dying of exposure—all evidence of how unprepared most stampeders were for the extreme hardships of this rough country.

Their first sights at Sheep Camp were the gleaming glacier ahead and the pile of ice, snow, and rocks in front of them, left by the spring avalanche that had taken many lives. Their first news was that more bodies had been unearthed that day.

They slept in the Grand Pacific Hotel, a misnomer as, far from being grand, it resembled a woodshed in which Martha received a cubicle as the only private room. She was glad for the rare feather pillow and filling breakfast provided.

The next morning they joined the chain of stampeders going up for 3,000 feet of treacherous trail, an unbroken line of men with heavy packs, laden horses, even an ox cart driven by a woman. The beginning of the hike traversed the spring slide. Martha was panting too hard to enjoy the scenery as she carefully stepped on fragile ice coating streams and slippery rocks beside sharp drops. Sweating in the unrelenting sun and her voluminous fashions, she clung to anything that would hold her, trees and rocks rough under her soft hands. The physical strain was almost insupportable.

Mush on . . . Mush on . . . It beat into my brain . . . Cracking of whips. . . .Wild screams of too heavily loaded pack horses which lost their footing and were dashed to the rocks below . . . stumbling . . . staggering . . . crawling . . . God pity me!

Mush on . . . Mush on . . . Another breath! Another step . . . God give me strength. How far away that summit! Can I ever make it?

Mush on . . . Mush on . . . or die![3]

One hundred feet before the Summit, Martha slipped, her leg caught in a crevice, cut by jagged edges. She sat and wept as man after man passed, offering assistance. George finally snapped, "For God's sake, Polly, buck up and be a man!"[4]

Goaded, she rose in fury and made it to the top. George paid five dollars for a fire to warm her, and she nursed her leg before going through Canadian customs.

The way down was far worse than the way up. On shaky legs, her hands scratched and bleeding, with roots tripping her and rocks shredding her boots, she begged the men to go on without her and leave her there to die. George carried her the last mile to Lindeman camp and she lost consciousness on the straw bed in the Tacoma Hotel.

By the next evening she was ready to go again and they quickly walked two miles to the chaotic shantytown of Lake Bennett. Their gear had not arrived, nor could they find any kind of sleeping quarters. They returned to two cabins near Lindeman for two weeks. As they waited for their boat to be built, she learned to make sourdough and scoured the impressive landscape for wildflowers, awed by the fan of mountains mirrored in the gleaming lake. She met many people, including Flora Shaw, the colonial editor for *The Times of London*. All around would gather about the fireplace in Martha's cabin to sing songs in the bright evenings. Martha's scream on being surprised by a mouse provided days of amusement.

Finally Martha and George's boat was finished and loaded with their gear. Part of the ceaseless stream of gold seekers, they crossed Lake Bennett and camped at Caribou Crossing. The next day they reached the post at Lake Tagish. Martha was impressed by the solicitude of her companions as they gave her a seat on two large boxes covered with a fur robe. Later she learned that these were cases of Scotch whisky that her skirts hid from the inspecting officer, who told her she was the 631st woman to pass since May. Their boat was number 14,405.

At Marsh Lake they were warned that there was a hundred-dollar fine for taking a woman through Miles Canyon and the Whitehorse Rapids and that their abundantly laden boat would never make it. Undaunted and unwilling to portage five miles alone, Martha stuck with the men and the boat. They raced through the canyon then were sucked into the mad swirl of the rapids, one of the oars breaking apart with a resounding crack and the boat overturning, saved at the last moment by Captain Spencer's expertise and a spare oar.

Whitehorse was pestilent with bloodthirsty mosquitoes, and the Five Finger Rapids required cool heads and skillful hands on the oars. But the rest of the journey was monotonously idyllic, floating down the Yukon River for eight hours a day, fishing and catching squirrels and picking berries while camping on high banks away from the mosquitoes, sleeping on spruce boughs around the campfire. Two nights before reaching Dawson, Martha named Excelsior Creek, making her first of many marks on the territory. The next day, she and George staked their own claims.

After the 12-day river trip, Dawson was finally in view, a disorderly makeshift town of twenty to thirty thousand newcomers swarming from the riverfront to halfway up King Solomon's Dome, the high rounded hill from which you can see stupendous mountain ranges in every direction, including the majestic Ogilvies. Hastily built buildings, a few with Victorian facades, housed saloons, dance halls, restaurants, hotels. Laundries and supply stores operated out of tents. More tents, shacks, and log cabins were crowded with people and cases of typhoid, malaria, and smallpox were spreading. There was no place left for Martha and her party to squeeze into.

They squatted high above Lousetown, across the Klondike River from Dawson, building a one-room cabin with a small cubicle for Martha. They made furniture from twigs and boxes, and Martha sewed curtains, pillows, and tablecloths, setting out tin cans of flowers with the fine silver and linen she'd brought. Then she went to work to get the $1 million worth of gold dust.

Corruption was rampant in the office of the Gold Commissioner and the post office. In vain, Martha searched for the registration of the claims, the witnesses of the will, Lambert's grave, and the gold dust. Meanwhile, the Lamberts began to suspect Martha of fraud and headed to Dawson by way of St. Michael with a lawyer to help retrieve their stolen $1 million. The lawyer disappeared with a blonde gold digger who fleeced him of every cent he had and the Lamberts' search ended in futility. To this day, the fate of the "Lambert Million" remains a mystery.

But another mystery *was* solved. Martha forced herself reluctantly to admit that the cause of the exhaustion and nausea she'd been experiencing was not stomach flu or travel sickness. She was pregnant, she was trapped, and she was terrified. She could not endure the hardships of the return journey on the verge of winter in her condition. Having separated from her husband, she would have to raise her child alone. Having overspent on the trip up, she would have to bear her child in poverty, ill equipped in a strange, harsh land. Having lost hope, she prayed for death.

Her prayer was answered in the form of renewed faith. She again drew upon pioneer spirit and began sewing baby clothes out of her tablecloths and napkins by candlelight. The days grew so short that soon there was no sign of sun, only rare flashes of the northern lights, swaths of green swirling erratically across the sky. It was a horrendous winter. For a time, temperatures dropped lower than minus 70 degrees, and the dishwater froze as it was tossed out, the crystals forming in mid-air and tinkling to the ground. Diseases swept Dawson and food shortages drove up prices, making starvation a real possibility. Martha lived on cornmeal, molasses, prunes, and tea, going without milk and sugar. She also went without medical care, as the delivery of her baby would have cost one thousand dollars.

A son, Lyman, was born at noon on Tuesday, January 31, 1899. There are different versions of the birth. In her memoir, Martha says she was alone. Late in her life, in a CBC interview with Flo Whyard, she said there were two men at the birth, one with a hook where his hand had been and the other a ship's captain. At the time it would have been considered improper for non-medical men to witness a delivery—even fathers were banned—and Martha already had to endure the stigma of bearing her child with no husband in evidence, so this version raises questions. In her short biography of Martha, Joyce Hayden suggests that she was probably alone and that the later story might have been invented to shock people Martha saw as stuffy, a favourite indulgence. Most likely

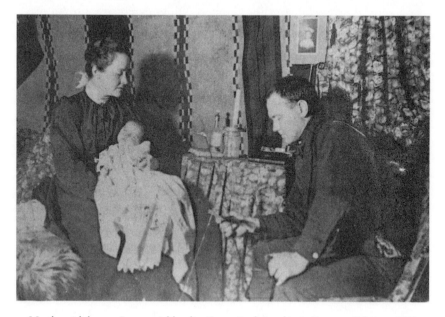

*Martha with her son Lyman and brother George in their cabin in Dawson, February 1899.*

the men *were* there. She was living with her brother George and their party, including two sea captains. And she effuses at length in the memoir about how the local miners and prospectors came with gifts during her confinement and how they all called after to pay respects to the baby, holding him and playing with his tiny fingers and toes. Finally, she was not known for fabrication, possessing enough true unconventionality to shock most people. What is certain is that Martha welcomed her son with delight.

In the spring, Martha again saw flames and clouds of smoke claim the sky. The Dawson fire of April 26, 1899 destroyed half the city and, like the Great Chicago Fire, was thought to have been started by an overturned lamp. Safe above Lousetown, Martha might have seen this parallel as a sign that she was right to claim all that was adventurous in her.

On May 23 she became a sourdough. As she watched the spring breakup—the river heaving up its raucous turmoil of ice—the whole hillside suddenly tumbled down toward her. She raced into the cabin and gathered up her baby. A small circle of trees just above the cabin miraculously stalled then split the landslide. The right side took the two cabins below, the left scooped up her outhouses. Amazed at her own survival, Martha fainted.

In July her father appeared out of the blue to take her home. She made a deal: if her claims on Excelsior made $10,000 by the following year, she would be allowed to return. The voyage south was actually pleasant, owing to the existence of the new railway between Lake Bennett and Skagway. Her parents' ranch was a paradise of plenty and prettiness. The family was kind and welcoming but Martha, feeling like a failure at age 33, descended into a severe depression. She lost weight, diminishing to 90 pounds. She lost interest and finally she lost patience. She realized that she wanted to make something of her life. She knew she had to return to the Klondike: "What I wanted was not shelter and safety, but liberty and opportunity."[5]

Her mines came in above expectations, and she returned alone with her father's blessing. She settled at Gold Hill mining camp and acquired two men as partners and 16 men as crew, rising at five A.M. to cook for all of them. In 1901, her parents and sons arrived, bringing the machinery to set up a sawmill and a quartz mill on the bank of the Klondike River, a hydraulic monitor at Excelsior Creek, and a large lodge to live in. Her parents took her eldest son, Warren, back with them but Donald and Lyman stayed with their mother as she became manager of the mills.

While the Klondike was a place where women were able to live rough, own businesses, and dispense with the fussier feminine proprieties, it was nevertheless a male-dominated world. Men far outnumbered women and set the tone of frontier culture. Martha had to fight harder than any man to prove her mettle.

The difficulty was that men resented working for a woman. The mill hands were sloppy in their work and did not respond to her direction. The foreman announced he wasn't going to be bossed by a woman. An escalating battle over orderliness—the men were deliberately strewing tools around—cumulated in a mutinous walkout led by the foreman. Martha and her son Donald were left doing all the work themselves until word got out and a new crew offered their services. The matter didn't end there. The former foreman snuck back to sabotage the equipment. Martha had the RCMP give him a "blue ticket" to get out of town, and he yelled from his boat that he'd get that "hellcat" someday.

Martha's first claims came in big pay dirt—a mining expression meaning lots of gold among the gravel—but this wealth was lost speculating on more claims and grubstaking other miners. The mill made more than enough, though, to provide her with a housekeeper, fine furniture, and $500 gowns from Paris. By the winter of 1898–99, Martha was enjoying the luxuries that Dawson City could now offer, especially the fashionable clothes—she was infamous for always wearing fancy hats on the camping trips she loved—and the skating parties, ice carnivals, card parties, benefits and balls, refusing marriage proposals every other week.

It was not at such a social event that Martha met her next husband. She needed to consult a lawyer because a mill hand had defrauded her of some expense money, and George Black was recommended. She liked him immediately and invited him home. He was handsome, devoted to serving the Yukon, politically ambitions, an outdoorsman, and a splendid companion for her and her sons. Within two weeks, he asked her to marry him. She had her divorce from Will Purdy but was reluctant to marry again. It took two years for her to accept his proposal. They were married in her home on August 1, 1904.

After her marriage, believing that wives and husbands should be in accord about politics, country, and religion, Martha became a Conservative, an Imperialist, and an Anglican.

Martha was at George's side when he was elected to the Yukon Council three times, where he campaigned to establish Miners' and Woodmens' Lien Ordinances so that wage earners would have the first lien on production. They had a happy life of social events, family camping trips (she shot a bear on one), and meaningful work. Martha organized the George M. Dawson Chapter of the Imperial Order Daughters of the Empire (IODE) for Dawson women and another chapter for girls. She still had her interest in flowers and was invited to give talks on local flora. For illustrations, she pressed and mounted blooms on watercoloured backgrounds, a hobby she called "artistic botany." In 1909 she won the Yukon Government's prize for the best native wild flowers exhibit and her entry was sent to the World's Fair in Seattle.

As the first decade of the twentieth century came to a close, Dawson was in decline. Many had given up on gold or had left for gold strikes in places like Nome, Alaska. Only six thousand of thirty thousand people remained, not enough to support George's law practice.

*Martha (holding a shotgun) loved camping trips.*

The Blacks moved to Vancouver. Martha was commissioned by the Canadian Pacific Railway to prepare an exhibit of the flowers of British Columbia. For the summer she travelled alone all around the province, gathering specimens. She was then offered a three-year job doing the same for the Belgian government but declined because she didn't want to leave her boys.

George was appointed seventh Commissioner of the Yukon Territory in 1912 and the Blacks were eager to return to the North, where they moved into Government House. As chatelaine, Martha shocked some of the prominent townspeople by keeping open house and including one and all in social occasions.

Among the invited guests at one evening reception were C.W.C.
Taber . . . and his wife. It was the presence of the latter that roused
half the town to righteous indignation, for no one could forget that
Mrs. Taber had once been Diamond Tooth Gertie Lovejoy, a popular soubrette famed for the glittering jewel fastened between her
two front teeth.[6]

True to her democratic principles, Martha used her position to change
the cultural climate of Dawson from one of hierarchical exclusion to one
of egalitarian community.

Then came World War I. George resigned as commissioner to form
the Yukon Infantry Company, which Lyman joined. The company left
Dawson on October 16, 1916 with Martha the only woman on board.
Friends saluted her by forming a Martha Munger Black chapter of the
IODE and one of the sergeants read a poem in her honour.

To get permission to go overseas with the troops, Martha went to
Ottawa and then Halifax to petition the military brass. When the general
in charge expressed concern about her being the only woman on board,
she retorted that she'd crossed the Chilkoot with thousands of men without any wanting to elope with her. Once he confirmed that her husband
really did want her along, the general allowed it.

Martha settled in London for the war, holding open house for
Yukoners on leave, working for the Prisoners of War Department, and
giving talks on the Yukon, which led to her being elected a Fellow of the
Royal Geographical Society in July 1917. The Military Cross was awarded
to Lyman by King George V at Buckingham Palace with his mother
watching. In August of 1918, George was injured with a gunshot wound
but was well by November 11, 1918, when the Armistice was signed.

They returned to Vancouver for two years. In 1921 George was chosen to represent the Independent Conservative Party of the Yukon in the
federal election and went North to campaign. He won. After his victory,

*Martha in 1932 as wife of the First Commoner.*

Martha would spend winters in Ottawa and summers in the Yukon (George was re-elected in 1925, 1926 and 1930). He had the Yukon Act amended to allow Yukoners the same rights to jury trials and civil actions that existed in the rest of Canada. In 1930 he was elected Speaker of the House of Commons and First Commoner. Martha acted as his hostess in the Speaker's Chamber and entertained dignitaries such as Lord and Lady Bessborough, Prince and Princess Takamatsu of Japan, and Charles Lindbergh and Anne Morrow. When in London on holiday, Martha was received by the Duchess of York and was amused by young Princess Margaret not wanting to put on her rubber boots.

George had to resign in January 1935 due to a serious illness. (In the dozens of accounts that exist, this illness is spelled out only in one: nervous breakdown.) Martha ran in his stead, a campaign that had to reach 1,805 voters spread over two hundred thousand miles. She won by a 134-vote majority even though the Conservative party was badly defeated overall. She was the first female Member of Parliament for the Yukon and the second woman to be Speaker of the House of Commons. She took her seat two weeks before turning 70.

In interviews and in her memoir, Martha asserts that she was only keeping the seat warm for George, would rather have been at home with her family, and had to think of the Klondike motto—Mush on!—to have the courage to speak. When asked why more women were not in politics, Martha answered: "Marriage is to man a thing in part . . . a woman's whole existence."[7] She went on to wonder why women would want the drudgery of campaigning and dealing with dry, dusty statistics. She added: "Women's chief mission is not administering artificial respiration to a dying world, nor working perspiringly in forward movements. Into the life of every woman that is well-ordered come those years of child-bearing and child-rearing. For this reason, most women must defer activity in politics until middle life."[8] This from a woman who left her husband and children to climb the treacherous Chilkoot on a quest for gold! No doubt such assertions of her domestic femininity were politic. For a woman of such independent spirit, ambitious to make something of her life even if she had to defy convention, her achievements must have brought a deep sense of fulfillment.

She was greatly concerned for George and felt the many miles between them keenly. Then, on February 27, 1937, she was struck one of the worst blows of her life. Her diary entry for that day reads:

> We expected Lyman up for the weekend. He was motoring up with Bob Mimes. About three o'clock and a little later, Aimee commenced to be a little anxious as she felt Bob Mimes . . . was a very careless driver. About half past four, Mary Scott, wife of Col. Clyde Scott, military secretary to the Minister, called and meeting Aimee on the stairs, said, "Come with me. There has been an accident."— After a little conversation I took Mary Scott aside and said, "So Lyman's dead." She replied, "Yes, he was killed instantly just outside Brockville." We were stunned—beyond words—it was all *too* dreadful—Aimee's husband, my boy, the very light of our lives . . . [9]

Despite her own grief, Martha's main concern was for Lyman's young wife Aimee: "I have lost a dearly beloved son—but I am an old woman now with but comparatively few years left—while Aimee with her life before her will be lonely beyond words . . . my heart aches for her. She is brave. Another day gone—the world moves on no matter *what* happens."[10]

That was not to be the only blow. On August 17, 1937, her oldest son, Warren, died; the cause of death is not known. Then on February 1, 1938, Martha learned that her cherished brother George had died of tuberculosis in Oregon. The old adage about death coming in threes was proving true. Her diary shows that she was often bowed, even broken, by these tragedies but continued to meet all her responsibilities in the House, believing that it would never do to fall apart. Her fortitude in the face of such painful personal losses disproved notions of the day about women being too weak and affected by sentiment to be involved in public affairs.

Martha was a superb MP: a charismatic personality and a strong and popular speaker, willing to trust her own instincts and defy party lines. Outspoken and passionate about her independent beliefs, Martha was not afraid to comment on world affairs or to tweak noses. In an extensive interview with an American newspaper, she explained the superiority of the Canadian legal system, adding: "Canadians, sure that the law will be enforced, do not require screaming headlines of the execution of criminals to make them law abiding."[11] Not that she was nationalistic, in fact, she thought that "all nationalism is an obsession born of fear,"[12] and that it produced the barbarism of war, which women would not tolerate.

Despite this belief, she was fiercely loyal to the British Empire, and especially to the Yukon. Always fighting in the House of Commons for the interests of her riding, she protested vigorously when British Columbia was allowed to annex the Yukon, an agreement that was immediately dissolved. In a 1939 reply to the Speech from the Throne, Martha praised her territory:

The Yukon is a good country; it is a cruel country; it is a kind country. It is a country that you can love; it is a country that you can hate, depending on your attitude. I have lived there for forty years; I have travelled from one end of Canada to the other, as well as across the United States; I have travelled overseas; but I have never in my life seen a country that thrills me as does the Yukon."[13]

Martha was still in office at the beginning of the Second World War, her term ending in 1940, when George was re-elected and they returned to their old routine. Martha continued the writing she'd done since her first marriage; she was even a member of the Canadian Authors Association. By now she had completed her memoir, *My Ninety Years;* booklets in the series *Yukon Wildflowers;* and many published articles on various subjects.

The population of Dawson had meanwhile diminished to fewer than five hundred people. In 1944, the Blacks moved to Whitehorse, which was made the capital in 1953.

Martha had one more encounter with fire, but this time she got burned. She was alone in the Whitehorse house—George didn't retire from law until she was 90—and making toast when flames shot from the toaster then scrambled up the kitchen curtains. Martha frantically beat at the blaze with whatever came to hand and suffered serious burns as the fire raged out of control. For several weeks she repaired to the Regina Hotel to convalesce while her house was reconstructed. For once, her strength had failed her

But she still had an eager curiosity about the world and the people in it, which made her resilient and lively up to the end. Catching a friend looking through her photographs, Martha said, "Having a gander? Well, never be ashamed of it—half the world are too dead to see what's there in front of them."[14]

Several falls, a fractured hip, and arthritis confined Martha to a wheelchair for her last years, but this did not stop her from being the vibrant centre of a social whirl. Yukoners are known as hard drinkers, and Martha would insist her nurse begin her shift by drinking a large glass of straight liquor. At 90, she especially relished shocking the governor-general by swearing—and she always could curse like a sailor.

She died at 91, on October 31, 1957. At her insistence, both the American and Canadian flags draped her coffin. One newspaper said: "All Canada looked to the Yukon with a bow when Martha Black died."[15] A Canadian Navy icebreaker was named for her and her visage graced a postage stamp. She had made something of her life all right—she had made history.

Those early lessons in deportment, elocution and botany that Martha had thought so uselessly trivial had served her well in unexpected ways. Her career as a miner, mill manager, writer, "artistic botanist," lecturer, and politician earned her the Order of the British Empire in 1948. From the Victorian drawing rooms of Chicago to the shacks of the Yukon and all the way to the bastions of power in Ottawa, Martha was her own woman. She derived equal pleasure from swishing about in the latest fashions in the company of royalty and frying pancakes for grubby prospectors over a campfire in the bush. She combined the sweetness of her trained refinement with the saltiness of her headstrong, adventurous, outspoken frontier spirit and made no apologies for either. It was this spirit that the *Whitehorse Star* mourned the most:

> A blithe spirit has left the Yukon. Martha Louise Black was the unrivalled queen of all that host of men and women who sought the northern magic . . . She, above all, caught and reflected the true spirit of the Yukon and some of it died with her.[16]

# 8

*Klondike Kate Rockwell*

## QUEEN OF THE KLONDIKE

*Klondike Kate would usually autograph these
photos of herself with the phrase "Mush on and Smile!"*

*A woman of flame appears suddenly on the stage, red hair rising from
a black cape beribboned by shifting red, purple, yellow, and green lights.
A hush spreads throughout the hall thronging with miners. Glasses of
beer about to bang and slosh the tables are held suspended, gambling*

*chips are left half-stacked, curses are cut off mid-word. All eyes follow the slide of the cape down that statuesque body to the floor. Faces lift to see the vision thus revealed, her blue eyes burning, the centre of a flame. Sparks fly from the red sequins spangling her curves, the diamonds studding her fingers, the bracelets gilding her wrist. Pink tights blush her shocking legs. She bends to grasp and brandish a wand trailing two hundred yards of red chiffon. And then she begins to turn. Spinning faster and faster within swaths of twirling scarlet, until she combusts, falling to the floor as if consumed by the descending crimson.*

*She rises with the wild applause, the whoops and hollers and stomps. Bags of gold dust and nuggets shower her feet. She responds with bows and blown kisses, disappearing with her bounty, her Flame Dance done.*

*When she returns to the stage, it is in a $1500 Worth gown from Paris, white, trimmed with pearls and rhinestones, and trailing a wide train. Perched on top of her head is a handmade tin crown with its points sprouting 50 lit candles, just in case there's any doubt who the Queen of the Klondike is.*

*Dancing her way through the crowd, she reaches the Silent Swede who has been staring at her all evening. He is really a Norwegian named Johnny Matson. Matson doesn't drink, smoke, gamble, or, it seems, dance. He says he just wants to watch her, she is so beautiful. At the end of the night, he promises to wait for her.*

*It is Christmas Eve, 1900 at the Savoy in Dawson. Thirty-odd years later, he marries her: Klondike Kate, Queen of the Klondike, a legend made not born.*

While Kate Rockwell always promoted Christmas Eve, 1900 as the night the miners of Dawson crowned her Queen of the Klondike, she made a telling slip when she told a reporter years later that "I did the dance wearing a crown of candles for the first time in Juneau. I could have skipped rope and the men there would've been just as appreciative."[1] It seems that she might have crowned herself, but the men came to believe that they'd done it. Yukon writer Sam Holloway calls her "a tremendous liar."[2] He claims that she "told stories of her popularity that were taken from earlier days in the City of Gold, before she had arrived on the scene."[3] The encounter with Matson may well be a fabrication, too, although he was definitely there that night and did remember the sight of her with candles dripping wax into her hair.

Kate was born Kathleen Eloisa Rockwell in Junction City, Kansas on October 4, 1876. Her mother, Martha Alice Murphy, was a waitress 18 years younger than John W. Rockwell, a railway agent and telegraph operator. Both had been married before. Martha had a son, Morris, and John had two sons, Fred and Ralph, and a daughter, Maud. Shortly after Kate was born, the family moved to Oswego, Kansas, where John worked for the Missouri & Western Railroad, with Martha running the station's restaurant.

Kate recalled her mother as a rather helpless woman quite dependent on men. She did not remember much of her father. In November 1881, her mother divorced him. Kate, then called Kitty, was five years old. A year later, Martha married her lawyer, Francis Allison Bettis, his chief attraction being that he was wealthy and successful. He'd been an attorney for the Internal Revenue Service and for the Central Pacific Railroad and was a partner in a prestigious firm in Kansas, serving both on the bench and in the state legislature. He was a loud, straight talker, a showman, and something of a character. Kitty worshipped his brash sense of drama.

The couple moved with Kitty to Spokane Falls, Washington. As a judge, Bettis provided them with a life of prestige and plenty. Kitty was a lively, mischievous tomboy, always rebelling against her governess and rambling with the boys by the river, whittling and fishing, a harum-scarum girl according to locals.[4] While only her controversial husband's money enabled Martha to put up with the social hubbub surrounding him, Kitty thrived on it.

When a fire left more than a hundred neighbours homeless, eight-year-old Kitty impulsively brought them all to stay at the Bettis home. They were camped out all over the floors before her parents knew anything about it. Martha hit the roof, but the judge recognized what this could do for his political position and was entertained by his stepdaughter's derring-do and generosity.

Trying to tame Kitty, the beleaguered parents sent her to a number of convent schools, including those in Osage Mission, Kansas and Sprague, Washington, and to the renowned Snell Seminary in California. She was inevitably expelled from each. At St. Joseph's Academy in St. Paul, Minnesota, the nuns locked her in a bathroom for doing a dance show during study period. Enraged, Kitty clogged the drains with towels and ran out all the hot water. Triumphant, she was sent home.

She had become a boy-crazy teenager, popular with the local young men for her fun-loving impropriety, gaining a reputation for being fast and loose and careless, a restless hussy constantly craving attention and excitement. This desperation grew when the only stable home she'd known fell apart.

Judge Bettis's fortune was wiped out by a stock market crash. Martha refused to face the fact that they were broke and continued to spend extravagantly and speculate foolishly in real estate. The judge kicked her out. Kitty had to go with her, devastated by the loss of not only another father but of a role model she adored and admired. Sour and distant as he'd become, she missed him terribly. She never saw him again. He died in California in 1912.

Martha ran Lewis House, a boarding house on Riverside Avenue, and both she and Kitty felt their comedown keenly. Receiving proceeds of $65,000 from the sale of the Bettis house and the rooming house, Martha decided to splurge on a big trip to visit her son Morris in Chile, sailing down the west coast past Cape Horn to Valparaiso, then ending their journey in New York. Kitty was thrilled to arrive in bustling

Seattle—the fast pace and loose revelry of a big city suited her perfectly. Martha tried to find passage for them without luck. Finally she convinced a skipper named Captain Sauter to sign them on to his British four-master as stewardesses, since the company didn't allow passengers. They were under strict orders not to fraternize with the crew and, when not working, were confined to their cabin and areas reserved for officers. Kitty threw a fit and flounced off to her berth, vowing not to leave it. Martha probably wished this high dudgeon had lasted, for Kitty soon emerged and began a flirtation with one of the young officers. As the 87-day journey wore on, restrictions relaxed and Kitty could roam the ship freely, dancing and singing with the sailors as the sails flapped in the salty breeze and waves sprayed up onto the rocking deck.

Later in life, Kate would love telling a story of mutiny on the high seas, with herself as heroine:

> In Valparaiso the crew went on a terrible bender, and I watched drunken sailors close in on the hated mate. He had his back up against the rail and a belaying-pin in each hand, and he was using them. Then I saw a sailor sneaking up on him with a knife in his fist, and I screamed at the top of my good lungs. The mate took my signal and clipped that sailor with a backhand blow. There were only three men on their feet by the time the captain showed up.[5]

When they landed, Kitty attempted a mutiny of her own, telling her mother that she was engaged to the young ship officer. She was 15. Martha shut her up in the Convent of Sacred Heart, where she would teach kindergarten and never leave the convent walls unchaperoned. After a brief visit with Morris, Martha herself was restless and left for New York to get settled before sending for Kitty to join her. The next thing Kitty knew, her mother was in England. She wrote that she had been hired by the wife of the captain to be her midwife.

That was fine with Kitty. Having figured out how to escape her chaperones, she was no longer impatient to reach New York. Scads of dashing Chilean suitors serenaded her, the only redhead in town. They taught her the trick of rolling a cigarette with one hand, which became her trademark as Queen of the Klondike. Knowing only the word *si,* she was engaged to seven young men until a nun discovered her drawer full of diamond rings and made her return them.

Alerted to her daughter's wanton ways, Martha hightailed it to New York and cabled Kitty to get the first ship out. A luxury square-rigger, the *Willie Rosenfeld,* was ready to go but fully booked. Kitty convinced the first mate to bring her on board posing as his wife, his real wife having decided to stay in Chile at the last minute. Kitty had a wonderful time: she was the only woman on board.

In New York she discovered that her mother had spent all their savings on her adventure in the British Isles. They were down to $87. Martha got a four-dollar-a-week job in a shirt factory but it wasn't enough for both of them to live on. Scouring the classifieds, Kitty went behind her mother's back to answer an ad for chorus girls, no experience necessary. She gave her name as Kitty Phillips.

Mother was, to put it mildly, horrified when I told her I'd signed a contract to work as a chorus girl, but she finally came to reason and trailed along like a Spanish chaperon. I was eighteen, like an opening rosebud, but knew as little about life as the average girl of twelve knows today.

When the show decided to try a stand in Pittsburgh, I went along without telling Mother, who was busy with a job then. That's where the company went broke—flopped. We were all stranded. Another girl, Madeline Garcia, and I went into a church that day and prayed for some way back to New York. Then Madeline thought of sneaking into a boxcar at the railroad yards and stealing a ride back.

The train crew found us, but let us stay on. We got to Jersey City where the ferry ticket-taker accepted our last dime for the ride to New York. We were penniless but had thoughtfully purchased stale doughnuts. I remember we had to walk 183 blocks to get to the room of a girl Madeline knew, so we could fix up to go home looking respectable.

Mother had alerted the New York police to look for me. She was quite disturbed, you might say. She didn't want me to go on stage after that, but I had had a taste of chorus girl life.[6]

Kitty had given a diamond ring to the road manager for security on a loan to keep the show going but he had skipped town with it.

Her mother couldn't say no to the money–and Kitty was now 20 years old—so she was soon on the boards again, at Coney Island: "I was still virgin about life in those days. Mother allowed me so many minutes to get dressed after my last act, and enough to ride home from Coney Island on a street car."[7] She worked her way up from a page who raised the curtain for tableaux with live models to the chorus line in a midway vaudeville house, where she wore tights for four dances a day and got to sing a song or two.

An old schoolmate from Spokane wrote to say there was a job available there in "continuous vaudeville." Kitty arrived out West and was shocked to discover what that meant—getting men to buy drinks in between acts for a commission: "I didn't want to do it, but I owed the advanced money for my railway ticket. I had visions that they'd put me in jail for the rest of my life if I didn't pay it at once. So I went to work . . . The percentage money kept coming in. It grew. I was having a high time, and so I stayed on."[8]

That is, until gold fever hit in 1897. She went to Seattle, where the boats laden with gold from the frozen Klondike had come in to cause the frenzy spreading across the newspapers of the world. She performed at the People's Theatre for two weeks and got her mother settled into the port city. Then she got an offer from the Savoy Theatre in Victoria, British Columbia, where she met Gertie Jackson. Drawn by the excitement of the stampede, she and Gertie teamed up for a sister act and they took it on the road North. Kitty left behind a fiancé, 31-year-old minstrel star Danny Allmon, who promised to join her in Dawson. Soon she was to be completely alone. Frightened by the rough and rowdy frontier town, Gertie jumped ship in Skagway. Kitty kept on.

She joined a few other entertainers and worked the Skagway dance halls briefly to raise the money to go on. Some accounts say she climbed the Chilkoot with a troupe packing a piano in 1899, only to be turned back at the Summit by Mounties forbidding women to risk the dangers still ahead. Still, she arrived in Bennett in 1900 by the new White Pass and Yukon Railway passenger train. Like Gertie in Skagway, her three companions took one look at the shabby tent town and turned tail. Kate stood her ground for two months, starring as the sole singer-dancer in a rough shack with a lone pianist and doing as many as 20 shows a day for little pay. The customers were on their way to find their fortunes and needed to keep a good grip on their grubstakes. Their tributes were not gold nuggets. In keeping with the custom of the times, the prospectors used corks to spell out her new stage name across the ceiling of a hotel: Kate Rockwell. The homage remained there for years.

In June of 1900, Kate made her way to Canyon City and prepared to board a boat going through Miles Canyon and the Whitehorse Rapids. She was stopped by a North West Mounted Police officer who was there to enforce orders that women were not permitted to boat through the treacherous waters but must portage five miles—the fine for noncompliance was one hundred dollars. She tried argument, then charm, but for once the irresistible Kate met an implacable force: "That little whipper-snapper shooed me right off the bank like an old hen."[9] Livid, she went into the town and scrounged some overalls and a flannel shirt, tucking her red locks up into a battered cap. Disguised, she hovered around the landing watching for her chance.

> Well, I was young and didn't give a whoop. So I put on boy's clothing, waited until the scow was about to pull out, and jumped aboard just as the lines were released from the bank.
>
> The Mountie saw me hit the deck. I should say hit the water, but I got a hold and was pulled aboard. He bellowed orders "in the name of the Queen," and he was still fuming when we hit those rapids. That Mountie didn't get his woman.[10]

She stuck out her tongue at him, held on through the hair-raising trip, and made it to Whitehorse scot-free. While she was dancing there, a letter from the Savoy Theatrical Company offered her a soubrette position in a show they were rehearsing in Victoria to storm the stage in Dawson in early spring. Kate was faced with the choice of continuing on her own or retreating down South. Part of her just wanted to get to Dawson and not miss another day of the Gold Rush, but she was anxious not to get stuck in an unrewarding job like those she'd had in Skagway and Bennett. She decided to return in style with the Savoy.

In Whitehorse, the 173 members of the Savoy Theatrical Company took over the first riverboat headed to Dawson after breakup. The whole town gathered at the waterfront to meet the boat—just as today everyone eagerly watches for new arrivals flooding the highway in spring—and a celebratory atmosphere prevailed. Down the planks streamed dancers, comedians, singers, actors, stagehands, prop men, wardrobe ladies, and the musicians of the ragtime orchestra. Kate, insouciant in hiking pants despite the disapproving double takes of passersby, sauntered past the saloon barkers on Front Street. Many of the buildings were new, built after the ashes from the Great Fire of 1899 had been panned for gold. One of the finest was the Savoy saloon with its 50-foot mahogany bar, chandeliers, and notorious paintings of nudes. The attached dance hall was vacant, with two tiers of red damask-curtained balcony boxes.

Billed as Soubrette Extraordinaire, Kate received star treatment: a luxuriously furnished private room upstairs. On opening night she appeared onstage in a pink gown edged with lace and an enormous hat trimmed with ostrich feathers, in the style popularized by Lillian Russell. Singing one of the sentimental songs of the day, she flattered her youthful looks with sweet poses. The scruffy miners ate it up and strewed her wake with gold nuggets.

After the show, she donned a demure white Gibson Girl gown and pearls, Danny Allmon's engagement ring tucked away. Miners—lonesome for loved ones back home, or despondent from having risked all for so little, or heartbroken over being jilted—drank bottle after bottle of champagne at her side, pouring out their woes as she pocketed the corks to get her percentage on the alcohol sales.

Kate Rockwell was one of the most popular dance hall girls of her time. While some, like old-timer Alex Adams, have described her as not particularly pretty and having a horrible voice, others were charmed. Miner Ed Lungs recalled that "she had an appeal and winsomeness that was truly captivating. It was alluring, intangible—something, yes, difficult to describe." He remembered her as "just a bit taller than average; hair, reddish gold; eyes, blue; complexion, like peaches and cream; her voice ranged from velvety soft to musical bells; and yes, she was sweet as honey!"[11]

She could be racy. Her Egyptian number involved spinning to unwrap herself from a long bandage until she was exposed in her pink tights: "If the Mounties weren't watching, a happy miner would hold one end of the bandage to start off her dance."[12]

She looked 15, claimed to be 20 and was actually 24. Her fun-loving flamboyance lightened any load; her good-natured friendliness conquered loneliness; and her sincere sympathy soothed hurt feelings. She

*Klondike Kate wrapped in chiffon.*

talked more than one man out of suicide. In gratitude, one gave her a diamond and gold nugget dog collar and named his next daughter Kathleen in her honour. Within her first four months in Dawson, she'd had a hundred proposals of marriage. But she was not that kind of gold digger; time and again, she stuck with the limelight.

It was hard work, six full nights a week until nine in the morning. Every day there were exercise sessions and rehearsals, and she had to learn new acts constantly—roller-skating numbers, song-and-dance routines, scenes from *Uncle Tom's Cabin* and *Camille*, solos and duets. She designed and made her own costumes and developed her own material as well, writing ballads and skits. One night, she danced 182 times.

But she was richly rewarded, $50 a week base pay and $200 for her famous Flame Dance. On top of this, she got a quarter for every dollar-a-dance, a cut of $7.50 on each $15 bottle of champagne and 25 per cent on single drinks at the bar. Then there were the nuggets and bags of gold dust—worth $16 an ounce at the time—bestowed by the besotted miners. The dance hall girls all wore "percentage" belts made of these nuggets, some having been crudely fashioned into charms, little picks and pans, dog teams and sleds. From these belts hung the bags that collected the percentage chips and corks that would be cashed in the next morning. Kate was soon rolling in it.

Questioning why the men would give their gold for just a sympathetic ear and seductive smile, some townspeople suspected Kate of prostitution. She did not deny it. In fact, she admitted, "sometimes a girl blended now and then."

> I'm not trying to put over the idea that we were vestal virgins. Far from it. We fell head over heels in love and we made mistakes. But, primarily, we were vendors of laughter and music to men who were starved for beauty and gaiety. And we gave good measure for all the gold the miners showered on us.[13]

But in another interview, she recanted: "We weren't fallen women. Sure we worked for percentages on the liquor checks, but it stopped there."[14] It is true that the miners spent rigorous, grim hours grubbing about in dark shafts and that the gold was plentiful. They certainly threw away enough of it at the gaming tables, so why not on the sure return of cheering company?

Kate really felt for these men. She plied her wiles to get the gold but was a soft touch for a sob story or hopeful scheme. She lost a lot of money grubstaking miners or giving much-needed handouts. The men appreciated her as a straight shooter who made no bones about being after their money. They all knew they could trust her. As one logger said to young prospector Bill Walker: "If a miner goes to Dawson for a blowout, he'll head for Kate every time and get her to mind his poke."[15] Sourdough Alex Adams tells this story:

> I remember one time a miner had broken his leg and was walking on crutches. When Kate seen him she asks, "How are you fixed?" Then she hauls up her dress and goes into her stocking and pulls out a $100 bill and gives it to him. "Come back if you need to, there's more where that came from," she said.[16]

Walker also recalled the first time he met her. She and a male companion had ridden from Dawson to Bennett on horseback for a nostalgic jaunt. She stopped to banter with the loggers:

> She opened her saddle bag and tossed out packets of cigarettes, shrieking with laughter as the loggers ran to catch them. Seeing me hanging back, bashful as usual, she pointed at me and then tossed one directly into my hands, causing me to blush and giving the men fodder for months of joshing. Then she rode off down the trail, the sunlight glinting on her auburn hair, turning often to blow kisses as the men cheered and whistled.[17]

Their respect and adulation probably meant as much to her as their gold. What Kate really wanted was to be special—crowned, starred, loved. What she got was Alexander Pantages.

Alexander Pantages was an illiterate jack-of-all-trades who'd left his working-class parents in Greece while still a boy and worked his way around the world, determined to make his fortune. Men didn't like him. Obsequious and servile when it suited his purpose, he was otherwise a cold, insolent, and miserly man without a sense of humour. But he intentionally charmed women and many saw him as a prize, with his dark looks and big muscles. As a waiter at the Savoy, he teamed with Kate to rook the customers, Kate diverting attention as he took the half-full bottles away. This was called "singling out" and was common practice in the boxes.

Kate was smitten. She forgot all about Danny Allmon, who later died of a cerebral hemorrhage in Vancouver on his way up to see her. She fell for Alex's exotic accent and stylish turnout, his stocky, strong body and fierce drive. They seemed to share past, present, and future. Both had travelled and sought adventures, both were working exhaustively to mine the Gold Rush for all it was worth, and both were ambitious. They shared a love of beauty, in nature and in art, poetry, music. They made a good team and their first year together was to be the happiest of Kate's life. Alex even talked of marriage.

A month later he was fired and unable to get another position because the town was mostly closing up for the winter (even today in Dawson the restaurant named for Kate is boarded up for the winter, as are many other venues). He'd also lost the savings he'd invested with dance hall girl Gussie Lamore and others, in a cooperative stock company. Alex was jealous that Kate still brought home the gold when he couldn't get the lowest job and worried that she would leave him for another. He was depressed and desperate to secure her and her money for himself. He seduced her and convinced her to move in with him, promising to marry her when he was ahead again. In Dawson, this arrangement was not considered too shocking:

> Everybody knew that Alex Pantages and I lived together, but it was the custom of the country and nobody thought anything of it. It made no difference in my social standing. Almost every girl in the north had her man. It was a rough, hard country for women at best, and if a girl could get a good, comfortable cabin for the winter, she was lucky.[18]

But some friends didn't approve of Kate's choice. Diamond Tooth Gertie Lovejoy announced that she was "plum crazy to fall so hard for a foreign 'patent-leather kid' who will love her, take her gold and leave her."[19]

Kate not only kept a roof over Alex's head, she supplied money for the luxuries he needed, expensive cigars and silk shirts. She believed in him, though he kept postponing the wedding. When he came to her with a proposal to buy a theatre for them to run as partners, she backed him completely.

Their theatre, the Orpheum, was a huge hit. Kate headlined, producing and directing her own shows, and acted as hostess. Alex acted as host and brought up choice acts, displaying the uncanny knack of the showman, knowing just what people want to see. At the peak, he grossed $8,000 a day.

During the winter of 1900–01, Kate brought home a baby. She claimed to have been taking care of a young girl dying of tuberculosis, pregnant and deserted. On Christmas Eve, 1900—the night she was crowned Queen of the Klondike, the night Johnny Matson first set eyes on her, the night that streaked her hair with candle wax so she had to cut it into an unconventional bob the next day—the baby came. Kate was fetched before the show to hold the dying girl as she uttered her last

*Klondike Kate as a pansy.*

request, for Kate to take care of the baby. A housekeeper took charge as Kate rushed back to the theatre for her legendary performance.

The story is somewhat far-fetched and perhaps a product of her sentimental imagination. No one believed that the baby came that night. Many suspected that the child was hers and Alex's. Some recalled that she had gone South alone for a month at some point that winter, and there were reports that she was ill on arrival in Seattle. It is hard to see how Kate could have been performing in the last trimester, as she must have done, without anyone noticing she was pregnant. It may well be that the baby was abandoned to her, in whatever circumstances.

Still, other women of the time managed to carefully disguise their condition with clever dressmaking, only to go on a trip and return with a foundling.

Whatever the case, Kate was the little bundle's mother for his first three years and she doted on him: "I kept the baby . . . until he became as dear to me as if he'd been my own. At night when I'd go back to the cabin to tuck him in . . . he used to pat my face and say sleepily, 'Do love my dear mummy.'" When he was old enough to start remembering the dance hall life she led, she took him to the States and gave him to foster parents: "I sent money for his college education and he is one of the most successful engineers in the country today. I have never disclosed his identity. He perhaps has never known of me, but I like to think of him as my son."[20]

In the meantime, the Orpheum began to suffer losses. They had to rebuild it three times after disastrous fires. Then the Gold Rush moved to Nome, Alaska and Dawson went into decline. Kate didn't want to leave, but Alex convinced her to join him on a scouting trip for a new business proposition in the States. They flitted about, posing as man and wife, making their way haphazardly to New York. Rumour has it that Kate had once been in Texas and had a gambler as a lover there—perhaps even as a husband—who'd kept her jewelry when she'd moved on. The story goes that Alex was determined to get this loot back, and that the pair managed to do so, hurriedly hopping onto a train to escape a rain of bullets from the gambler.

Not finding what they were looking for, they returned to Dawson until the spring of 1902. Then Alex stayed to wind up their affairs as Kate headed to Seattle with fifty grand in jewels and a hundred grand in gold coin—although some accounts say this sum is exaggerated. He dictated loving letters begging her to stop drinking and saying that he was getting "fat as a pig" with "no one to fight and fuss with . . ." He also reminded her to "always bear in mind that Papa is always in need of ready cash and ever willing to put your savings alongside of his so as to make a good showing."[21]

She ended up in Victoria and bought a nickelodeon with a Biograph machine for $350, adding vaudeville to the bill and performing herself as well as showing early silent films. It was a profitable business but it made Alex livid; he thought films a foolish investment. He must have changed his mind after coming South though, as he then purchased a similar venue in Seattle, naming it the Crystal Theatre, the first of what was to become the Pantages theatre empire. Kate sold her venture and gave Alex the $1500 so he could buy the Strand, a skid row theatre. The businesses grew but they were still short on cash. It was decided that Kate would take her show on the road in Texas, where oil was booming, and send Alex the easy money. She thought of it as an investment in their partnership, expecting to receive equal shares in the theatres.

For almost a year in Texas, Kate read Alex's love letters, which included frequent requests for money alongside the sweet nothings. One vaudeville house where she performed featured a 17-year-old violinist, a refined girl from a respectable family, and the two women contrasted each other—the wild frontier redhead and the innocent, cultured brunette. Her name was Lois Mendenhall and she would change everything for Kate.

Kate came back to Seattle to find Alex distant, but assumed he was preoccupied with business. She performed her new Butterfly Dance at the Crystal. Lois was also performing there. Then Kate went on tour and was in Spokane, her old hometown, when a fateful letter came from a friend in Seattle. Alex had married Lois four days earlier.

Kate fell apart. She hit the bottle hard, sitting slovenly and sad in the saloons, showing up drunk for work. Another letter bucked her back up. Her friend Flossie de Atley wrote that she should make something of herself instead of throwing her life away because of a man.

She pulled herself together, becoming more and more bitter as Alex renamed the Crystal after his wife, stating: "It wasn't until I met Lois that

I knew anything much about good women."²² Two months after the marriage, Kate filed a breach-of-promise suit against Alex in Seattle, on May 26, 1905. The case made the front page of the newspapers. Alex told reporters he didn't even know Kate, then admitted he did but only as an acquaintance. The records of the trial include this same flat denial, but faced with the evidence of hotel registers and love letters, Alex eventually offered an out-of-court settlement. Kate agreed and, in April 1906, she settled for under $5,000, according to her account.

She returned to Dawson but could not bear the memories or the decline of the town and left after four months for a vaudeville tour of the Pacific Northwest. But vaudeville was on the wane while silent films—offered by Pantages theatres—were rising in popularity. When she got a letter from a dance hall friend, the Oregon Mare, inviting her to Fairbanks, where a small hotel was for sale, Kate headed North again. She had just made the final payment on the hotel when it burned to the ground, leaving her with only ashes. She went back on stage, dancing at the famous Flora Dora and at a number of venues in the States.

After a decade of toiling in vaudeville throughout the States, a twisted knee brought on a complete nervous breakdown. She was under doctor's orders to change her life. Her mother had swapped some land in Puget Sound for an Oregon homestead and Kate purchased it from her mother. Neither had seen the property. It turned out to be a small one-room shack in the middle 320 acres of high desert, 40 miles from Bend, Oregon, strewn with rattlesnakes and sagebrush.

Kate flounced about Bend in her dance hall glad rags and big plumed hats, eager to make a strong impression. That she did. With the thrill of some notoriety, she could enjoy the life of a homesteader. With her $3,500 grubstake, she got a hound dog, a saddle horse, some chickens and 42 head of cattle, the latter eventually lost out of neglect. What she loved the most was roaming the desert and collecting rocks; some credit her with pioneering the rock hound craze in Oregon.

She would never be one to completely settle down, though, and often was gadding about the country, picking up dancing and singing gigs to top up the coffers. Then a wagon accident cracked her kneecap and ended her professional dancing career. Unable to hold on to love, now unable to dance, she felt she had lost everything. Restless, she married Floyd Warner on October 26, 1915, a marriage that ended with her falsely accusing her younger husband of beating her after she'd been unfaithful many times.

The government granted Kate her certificate of ownership for the homestead the autumn of 1917, and she wrote a poem to celebrate. It includes the lines:

> I've grubbed a lot of sagebrush;
> I've worn blisters on my hands
> Just to show our Uncle Sammy
> How a woman wins his lands.[23]

At least she had that—she'd proven herself that much. Meanwhile, she was just scraping by, dishwashing in restaurants and scrubbing floors in a whorehouse. Somehow she raised the funds to buy a convalescent hospital, but she sold it within ten months and bought a café, both in Prineville.

There comes an age when the caprices of youth are no longer becoming. There comes a price to pay when all the champagne has been guzzled, all the songs sung, and all the lips kissed. There comes a time when all the good times are gone and the good-time gal becomes a good-for-nothing. All that Kate knew how to do—charm and flirt and kick up her heels—was useless to her now. She had no other skills. Desperate, lost, and broke, she flitted about Seattle, Portland, San Francisco, cooking or serving in logging camps and cheap restaurants. Everywhere she went the marquees of Pantages theatres mocked her. In Los Angeles, the only job she could get was part-time with poor wages.

In worn-out clothes and with a growl in her stomach, she went to her former lover, Alex Pantages, awed by the butlered mansion that was his home now. No one knows what they said to each other, but Kate did say that Pantages handed her six dollars from his wallet. And that the gesture was like a slap in the face.

Back in Bend, Kate devoted herself to her community, especially the fire department, becoming known as Aunt Kate. Somehow she was able to buy a big block of property with a two-storey, six-room house and a magnificent view of the mountains. Throughout the 1920s, in her early fifties, she built up her real estate, constructing rental units next to her house, buying other Bend houses and lots in Seattle, and purchasing a summer home in Washington State. She couldn't have done this on her wages. The evidence suggests that Pantages would send an agent from Portland to bring Kate cash when pressed.

The name Pantages had become a household word. Alex owned 30 theatres and controlled 42 more across the country in the last great year of vaudeville, 1926. In recent years he had been shrewdly adding motion pictures to the variety shows. Just before the crash of 1929, he sold everything to RKO for $27,750,000. Then the trouble started.

In June, Lois Pantages was arrested for manslaughter, her drunk driving having killed a Japanese gardener and injured others in an accident. In August, 17-year-old Eunice Pringle accused Alex of rape. He was arrested for statutory rape and forcible attack. These felony charges were laid on the thirty-third anniversary of the find that started the Klondike Gold Rush: August 16, 1929. Kate was in Seattle for the Sourdough Convention, her presence announced by the *Post-Intelligencer*. Shortly after, a subpoena called her as a character witness for the prosecution. The trial was set for early October. A couple days prior to the trial, Lois Pantages was convicted of manslaughter in the same courtroom that was to try her husband.

After Alex's first day in court, the headlines created suspense about a mystery woman among the prosecution's witnesses. When they discovered it was Kate, the newspapers went wild, telling the old story of the breach-of-promise suit and featuring pictures of her on the front page.

Pantages insisted he was being framed, meanwhile bribing witnesses to falsify their testimony. The verdict was guilty and the maximum penalty—50 years in San Quentin—was requested by the jury in October 1929. Later, on November 27, 1931, he would be acquitted upon appeal.

Although Kate was never called to the stand, she got to have her say on the front page of the Los Angeles *Evening Herald,* illustrated with photos from her glory days. She returned to Bend with a full file of press clippings, saying that justice had been done.

Kate thrived on the media attention and it brought her renewed adulation at the annual Stampede—an event commemorating the Gold Rush—in 1931. A speech paid her tribute, confirming the titles some claim she took for herself:

> To us she was laughter and beauty and song . She was forgetfulness of hardship and homesickness. But she was more than that, she was our friend—a square shooter. Comrades, it is my honor and pleasure to present her again tonight—not Aunt Kate of Oregon but our Kate, the Belle of the Yukon, Klondike Kate, the sweetheart of the Sourdoughs.[24]

They gave her a standing ovation and serenaded her as she posed in the memorable white Worth dress. Fame also gave her back her bombast and charm, and the romance that was to establish her as one of the greatest legends of the Klondike. An old newspaper turned up in a remote cabin on Matson Creek in the Yukon. Johnny Matson read its full feature on Kate during the Pantages trial. He remembered Kate from her Christmas Eve, 1900 performance, and her story elicited nostalgia and sympathy. He wrote her a letter, addressed simply to Klondike Kate—

and it found her. Although Kate would claim that he professed undying love and asked her to be his wife, Matson did not propose in his first letter—he asked if she was the same Kate who used to wear lit candles in her hair in Dawson. Kate responded pretending to remember who he was. From the summer of 1931 to the spring of 1933 they corresponded. Read in their entirety, Kate's letters reveal a manipulative hand: complaining about the trials of poverty she endures while being too proud to ask for help; asserting her strong work ethic and frugal ways; noting proposals from wealthy men she was turning down because she would not stoop to marry for money; warning him of her fame and how everything she did wound up front page news; suggesting she was strong enough to keep him company out in the bush; angling for a new garage, a fur coat, a gold ring.

Matson set up a bank account for her and sent her money. She got her new garage and had her teeth fixed. In the summer of 1933, they met in the lobby of a hotel in Vancouver. He was 70; she claimed to be 53. Spruced up in a new suit for his first trip Outside in decades, Johnny looked like a fresh ticket to Kate. Two weeks later, they married, on July 14, in what was supposed to be a small wedding. Someone tipped off the press and the event headlined papers across the country. The story was too deliciously romantic: famed down-on-her-luck dance hall girl finds true love 33 years after her suitor first fell for her in her crown as Queen of the Klondike.

They went to Dawson for their honeymoon. Kate was appalled to see it had become almost a ghost town. Hardest of all was visiting the deserted Orpheum; she described it as the tomb of her youth. She didn't go out to Matson's claim—she never would. She went back to Bend, ostensibly to settle her affairs in order to move back North, but there she stayed. She would never be happy in the Yukon and he wouldn't be happy anywhere else, so theirs was a strange marriage. Kate would head to Dawson when it was time for Johnny to emerge from his claim near Sixtymile with the year's poke of gold. They'd stay in hotels separately for a week or two, then return to their respective homes, Kate with the money she needed. Matson never visited her in Bend.

Some, like old-timer Steve Cramer, saw that Matson was hopelessly stuck on a hussy who took all his gold and furs. Fran Hakonson, a doyenne of present-day Dawson, knew the couple at the time, as they would stay in the Hakonson's hotel, the Eldorado, Kate teaching Fran's husband, Bill, how to roll his own smokes with one hand. Fran didn't like her one bit: "She was just a gold digger! She never even went out to see his claim!" For Fran, who had run the hotel while Bill was out on their mines, and had on occasion driven 20-ton trucks out to him by herself, this was a betrayal of the frontier spirit.[25] Others believed the couple really cared for each other but were on in years and used to living their own way.

The marriage cemented Kate's celebrity and she was forever after a symbol of the Klondike Stampede. A relentless self-promoter, Kate was always getting invitations to events and features in the papers. At the drop of a hat, she'd break into a buck and wing or pull some stunt, not caring, she said, whether the laugh was with or against her, as long as she got a laugh. She bought old Victoriana at antique stores and would bestow these gifts as "souvenirs" of her days in the Gold Rush. She brought the chief of the police in Portland a crate of baby chicks and a swarm of bees, creating pandemonium. Ever after, the department was her private taxi service whenever she was in town. As Klondike Kate, she did celebrity endorsements, appearing in ads for products like the Oremaster, and had her name emblazoned on her car, suing anyone who used the name without her permission. She was paid for many public appearances throughout the Second World War, marshalling parades and opening shopping centres. Her trademark phrase was "Mush on and smile."

In the early 1940s, Hollywood came calling, a dream come true. They made a movie of her life, starring Ann Savage, and paid her to be an advisor to the film. While she revelled in the press photos of her showing starlets how to roll their own, Kate was infuriated by the B-picture's lack

*Even Klondike Kate's car is a promotional tool. Hillsboro, Oregon, November 1955.*

of authenticity: "Imagine, it showed a train going to Dawson."[26] She told a columnist that she didn't recognize anything in the film as being from her life. Posters for the flick still adorn the restaurant called Klondike Kate's in Dawson.

She was still Aunt Kate as well, generous to a fault. She took on good works: arranging adoptions, visiting prisoners in jail, and even hiding escaped convicts at her place. She raised funds for a Bend accountant, Bill Van Duren, to get surgery on his cataracts.

In the fall of 1946, Matson, who hadn't been seen since April, failed to send Kate his yearly letter. He was supposed to be coming out of the bush for good and she'd prepared a house in Halsey, Oregon for them to share. She contacted the Mounties and flew North dressed in gold nuggets and dramatic black, causing more headlines. Her letters to Matson lay unclaimed at the post office. Trapper Joe Sestak made a search and found Matson's bones scattered in a ten-mile radius around Seven Mile by wolves or bears. Sestak tripped and gouged out an eye leading the Mounties to the body; he sued the government for $3,072. Kate had Matson buried at his claim, still not setting foot there herself. She tried to find his fortune but tracked down a disappointing $1,600. She couldn't find anyone to work the claim and signed it over to Sestak.

Two years later she married Bill Van Duren, keeping two hundred guests waiting as she was late for her own wedding. It was April Fool's Day, 1948 and both bride and groom were 71. Kate joked, "I was the Flower of the North, but the petals are falling awful fast, honey."[27]

The pair left Bend for a happy life together in Willamette Valley. Kate had a back condition necessitating a brace and cane, but still made public appearances, including on the Groucho Marx televison show in 1954. To the end, it was fame more than money that fed her.

She died at home in her sleep on February 21, 1957 at age 81. *Newsweek* and *Time* marked her passing as the end of an era.

There will never be another woman like Klondike Kate in the Yukon, but perhaps we don't need one anymore. Maybe we are less impressed by the sensational, more drawn to substance. Thousands flocked to the Klondike unprepared to meet its hardships and dangers because they were caught up in the hype of the Gold Rush. They stayed gullible, fleeced left and right by card sharks and gold diggers who would roll them for their poke, all because they were dazzled by flash. Perhaps there is a kind of innocence that should be lost.

*Klondike Kate and last husband, Bill Van Duren, in Sweet Home, Oregon, 1956.*

# 9

*Nellie Cashman*
## THE MINER'S ANGEL

*Portrait of Nellie taken sometime during the 1880s.*

*The backs of the huskies undulate, a sinuous grey calligraphy, as the dog team flows around the corner. The driver calls for them to stop and applies the snow brake. Obedient but reluctant, they pause, some curling into a comma and others scribbling around each other, tangling their ropes. The driver ties the sled securely to a post and swings open the door of the saloon, unwinding a scarf, unbuttoning a heavy Mackinaw, shaking grey hair out of a fur hat. Simply, without formality, all the men rise to their feet at the sight of the diminutive woman. They smile, nod, lift a hand, or touch their caps. She greets some by name in her rolling Irish brogue, calling out teasing questions and tossing out laughs as full and rich as bags of gold dust.*

*She strides to the back room, picks a spot where she can watch most of the gaming tables, and waits for the chips in the middle of one of the tables to pile high enough. When the time is right, she strikes—a cheery cobra—leaning across the green baize to sweep the jackpot into her poke. The men's jaws drop. "Okay, boys!" she says. "This is for the hospital. You've all had the good of it, you low down blankety-blank varmints— and if you got the money to throw away at poker, you can give it to them hard-workin' Christian women that's takin' care of the sick."*[1]

*They can't mind. Many have been nursed or grubstaked by her. She is Nellie Cashman, the Miner's Angel, and they know that throughout a score of gold rushes every nugget she's ever taken from the ground she has given away.*

Queenstown, County Cork, Ireland is the birthplace of the most renowned female miner in history. Nellie Cashman was born around 1851 into the brutal realities of the potato famines and British colonialism, an "unequal contest between want and oppression,"[2] as she would later describe it. In their teens, and accompanied by their mother, she and her sister Fanny joined the almost a million emigrants fleeing to find a chance to know what a full belly might feel like. They landed in Boston, possibly in 1868. With much of the male population engaged in the Civil War, positions were open to women that had been the preserve of men. Nellie got one of these jobs and it gave her an anecdote for the history books:

I remember when I met General Ulysses S. Grant. I was a bellhop in Boston at the time. He was easy to talk to, like everyone I ever knew, and when I told him I wanted to do things, because I had to if I wanted to live, he said, "Why don't you go West, young woman? The West needs people like you."

Well, we had gone west when we left Ireland, and I certainly didn't expect to spend the rest of my life being a bellhop or an Irish servant girl in Boston.[3]

She went West. Taking advantage of Union Pacific's special forty-dollar immigrant rate, Nellie and Fanny slept on the crowded floor of a train in 1869. They arrived in San Francisco and found it less than civilized. There were few women, so most got more marriage proposals than mosquito bites. The sisters had only been in town a few months when Fanny was snapped up by Thomas Cunningham and in 1870 settled down to start a family.

Some friends were surprised that Fanny married first, as they thought it was Nellie who possessed superior beauty and charm, with her fair complexion, ebony hair, and deep eyes. Such were the attitudes of the day: the prettiest girl wins the diamond ring, a prize that all women wanted to win. It might not have occurred to anyone that marriage was the last thing in the world a woman like Nellie would want. Although Nellie preferred the company of men, she was never tempted by one. For starters, she was fiercely independent and, as she would later say in a January 7, 1925 *Arizona Star* interview, she "preferred being pals with men to being cook for one man." For Nellie, such friendly familiarity would breed some contempt over the years, as is clear in the same interview: "Why, child, I haven't had time for marriage. Men are a nuisance anyhow, now aren't they? They're just boys grown up. I've nursed them, embalmed them, fed and scolded them, acted as mother confessor and fought my own with them and you have to treat them just like boys."

What Nellie did want she couldn't name, but she knew it wasn't in San Francisco. She headed to Nevada at the age of 23 and worked as a cook in several mining camps. Here she got a taste of what she would hunger for the rest of her life: the big strike, that shiny, hard treasure paid for with risk and toil but only granted by rare luck, a bounty she could bestow on the sick, the poor, the unlucky. Around Pioche, Nevada, she started doing her own prospecting, to no avail.

While the common practice for male prospectors was to get a business owner to grubstake them, this was not an easy option for a woman starting out. It occurred to her that she could become that business owner and grubstake herself. From then on, she would always establish herself with a restaurant or store in a boom town to finance her mining. In Pioche, it was a boarding house, first advertised on September 4, 1872. As a business woman, she expected the men to treat her as an equal because she acted like one, as she explained to the *Arizona Star*:

> Some women in business think they should be given special favors because of their sex. Well, all I can say after years of experience is that those special favors spell doom to a woman and her business. It gives me a feeling of pride to be able to go back every place I've ever been and look folks straight in the eye and know that I've paid my bills and played the game like a man.

Nellie made many friends among the miners. When the ore in Nevada started to dwindle, she and six men debated whether to move on to the gold in Canada, or the diamonds in South Africa. Legend has it that Nellie flipped a twenty-dollar gold coin to decide the matter: the posse headed for the Cassiars in northern British Columbia and the southern Yukon. In all, two hundred miners from Nevada would migrate to the Canadian strike. Dates are unclear for this period; some sources say they headed out in 1877, while others make it a few years earlier.

Despite the almost impassable Stikine Trail, Nellie became the first white woman to make it into these mountains. In the March 6, 1875 edition of the *Daily British Colonist,* a reporter who'd met her on the trail described her with awe: "The woman was on snowshoes and as jolly as a sand-buoy. At the Boundary Pass she lost the trail and was twenty-eight hours exposed to the pitiless pelting of a storm, without shelter or blankets."

This was a woman lighter than a hundred pounds and hardly five feet tall. Unlike many of the women who would trek the Klondike, Nellie pragmatically wore men's clothes and didn't give a hoot for those who might be shocked at her unfemininity. As she would tell the *Daily Colonist* on February 15, 1898, years later: "You would like to know how I dress when on such expeditions, eh? Well, in many respects as a man does, with long heavy trousers and rubber boots. Of course, when associating with strangers, I wear a long, rubber coat. Skirts are out of the question up north as many women will find out before they reach the gold fields."

Of course, there was considerable social pressure on women in the frontier to conform to the elaborate—and unhealthy, with its tight corsets—feminine dress of the day. The respect the men had for Nellie's exceptionality as a crackerjack miner allowed them to ignore her apparel; she was always described as being both "very feminine" and tougher than a pickaxe. Nellie expressed her appreciation of their regard in her January 11, 1925 *Daily Colonist* interview: "The farther you go away from civilization, the bigger-hearted and more courteous you find the men. Every man I met up north was my protector and any man I ever met, if he needed my help, got it, whether it was a hot meal, nursing, mothering, or whatever else he needed."

After prospecting for a while, Nellie was visiting Victoria in the winter of 1874–75 when she heard the tales of a scurvy epidemic raging in the remote mining camps she'd left. She immediately spent all her money ordering fruits and vegetables, especially potatoes, and organizing a rescue party of six men. The winter was so fierce that it took 77 days to get to the camps. Customs officers in Wrangell tried to talk her out of the trip, calling it crazy, but she kept on. A First Nations local then reported finding a dead white woman. As Nellie was the only known white woman around, soldiers were sent on a search. They found her enjoying a tea break by a cosy fire in the bush. She refused to return with them.

Through mile after mile of deep snow, sharp wind, and rough terrain, Nellie strained at the neck harness to pull a laden sled behind her, her feet shuffling in the long arctic snowshoes. Altogether, they were packing fifteen hundred pounds of supplies. Five miles was all they could do some days, as they had to break a trail on the Stikine River. At night they had to sleep in the snow with only a pair of blankets. Nellie had a tent, but that wasn't always the most secure shelter.

> One night the men put my tent on the side of a steep hill where snow was ten feet deep. The next morning one of the men came to where my tent was to bring me coffee.
>
> It had snowed heavily in the night and, to his surprise, he couldn't find the tent. Finally, they discovered me a quarter of a mile down the hill, where my tent, my bed and myself and all the rest of my belongings had been carried by a snowslide. No, they didn't dig me out; by the time they got there I had dug myself out."[4]

When their journey ended, Nellie went straight to work feeding and nursing the miners. Not one did she lose, a fact she would be proud of all her days. Several had died before her arrival. The men titled her "Angel of the Cassiar," a name that would follow her from camp to camp as they told this legendary tale of her heroism, and their near escape, for decades.

Her next act of compassion was to give all the gold she'd dug—and donations she's pried out of the miners—to the Sisters of St. Ann in Victoria to build St. Joseph's Hospital. Then she went in search of more.

A bumpy stagecoach took her to Los Angeles, which was teeming with stray dogs and lost men. As she would tell the *Arizona Star* in January 1925, Nellie was not impressed—"What dump is this?"—and she left California for Arizona.

Her first stop was Yuma:

Such a place—mosquitoes by the billions everywhere. When we sat down to supper, I asked the driver if he hadn't seasoned the beans rather heavily with pepper.

He looked up and laughed. "Mosquitoes it is, my friend," he said. But we ate the beans just the same. Had to. There was nothing else cooked.

She hit Tucson and was the first white woman to open a business there. The opening of Delmonico's Restaurant was announced in the paper on July 29, 1879. It turned a pretty penny, even though Nellie's lifelong policy was that down-on-their-luck prospectors ate for free.

Within months, she had sold the place to a married woman. A big silver strike had been made a mere 80 miles away in Tombstone, a city only one year old but immediately cosmopolitan due to its fresh riches. She started with a store this time, opening the Nevada Boot & Shoe Store on April 15, 1880, but there were too many purveyors of footwear already. She bought a steakhouse called the Arcade then sold it almost immediately. Then she partnered up with a cattle rancher to offer gourmet meals at Russ House, a restaurant and boarding house. On opening day, over four hundred people squished in for dishes like lobster salad, croquettes with Kirschwasser sauce, and something called "calf head in tortue."

A good Irish Catholic, Nellie was distressed that Tombstone had no Catholic church. She went door to door, even in the seedy side of town, and raised $700. Then she put on a grand ball and a musical comedy as benefits. She got her church. Honouring their deal, the bishop coughed up a priest. She also turned her attention to miners' aid organizations and became treasurer of two of them, one specifically for Irish miners. She would raise funds to help the families of injured miners. No one ever refused her pleas for donations.

Nellie was so popular that folk tales, many of which may well be true, were told about her for years. One of the best ones concerns a customer in Nellie's restaurant making a critical comment about his food:

A lanky, mustachioed man seated at a nearby table took umbrage at the salesman's remarks, drew his revolver, and pointed it in such a way as to cause the complainant an immediate loss of appetite.

"What did you say about Miss Nellie's food, mister?" the gun-wielder asked.

"Food's delicious," the man replied. "Good as I've ever tasted."

A satisfied smirk spread across Doc Holliday's face as he eased his weapon back into its holster and drawled, "Yep, that's what I thought you said.[5]

During this period, Nellie was too busy to do her own prospecting so she grubstaked others for a cut of the take. Then tragedy struck, and Nellie was to have her hands full for a long time.

Her brother-in-law, Thomas Cunningham, was taken by tuberculosis in 1880 and widowed Fanny, also afflicted with the wasting disease, was left alone with her five children. Nellie sold her business and rushed to San Francisco. The city was in a bad depression with high unemployment so she moved the family back to Tombstone with her, buying back Russ House. The brood moved into a modest adobe dwelling. Then the sisters opened a boarding house—the American Hotel—which caught fire three times, the women becoming experts at the bucket brigade. Nellie always carried lots of fire insurance so could cover even $2000 worth of damage.

Other dangers abounded. There was the famous shootout at the O.K. Corral between Wyatt Earp and the Clanton Gang on October 26, 1881; nephew Mike, at seven years old, brought water to the injured and saw the bodies being carried away. Then Nellie had a close "squeak." She was in a buggy going to get a female friend in a nearby town but had to pull over when Apache chief Geronimo and his war party galloped by on their way to raid a farmhouse, their battle cries spooking the horses but not Nellie.

The next time she was not afraid was in Baja California. A miner from Mexico passed her a garbled tip about a find in the Santa Rosalia area. She raised an expedition, including a saloon owner and a lawyer, and they coached to Guaymas, Mexico, ferried across the Gulf, and hit Santa Rosalia. There they purchased burros for a gruelling 20-mile trek through the desert to the Golo Valley. There was no map, they refused to hire a guide, and although they had promised the authorities that they would drop markers on the trail, they had lied because they didn't want any claim jumpers to find the same treasure. Walking beside the water-bearing burros in the midsummer swelter, sand gritting their eyes, they hit dead ends, went in circles, took wrong forks in the road. On the fourth day, the dehydrated, heat-stroked men decided to go back. But where was that?

Nellie alone still had her strength, so she went in search of help. As the Legend of the Lost Cashman Mine goes, she stumbled onto a trickle of water in a parched stream and, bending to drink, spotted gold nuggets spicing the bed of pebbles. A shadow crossed her grasping hands as she greedily picked up the gold. She looked up to see a priest, Father Pedro, who invited her back to his mission for a meal. After she'd been fed, he told her that her find was the only thing supporting the people who had lived on this land for hundreds of years, and that if word got out hordes would arrive to steal their livelihood. She promised to keep their secret. When she headed out the next morning, he gave her a guide, mules, and provisions that helped the wayfarers back to the Bay of California. She didn't say a word. The men were so relieved to have escaped becoming bleached bones scattered in the sand that they didn't ask questions.

On their return crossing, the captain was wild with drink. The miners unceremoniously tied him up in the hold and got two sailors to help them home. The second they landed, they were thrown into a foul Mexican jail for mutiny and the American consul had to free them. The entire escapade became a good joke in the papers back in Arizona.

Such horrors make entertaining stories, unlike real tragedy, which carries a pain that can't be told. Fanny finally succumbed to the tuberculosis that killed her husband. Nellie was left with five orphans to raise on her own. She was a loving and firm parent who rescued the children from their misadventures, broke up neighbourhood fights, and doled out delicious desserts with her lectures on sportsmanship and self-control.

When five men were sentenced to death for a robbery shootout that killed three bystanders, Nellie went down to the jail to be their spiritual advisor, baptizing two of them. They confided their woes to her: rumours that the townspeople were building a grandstand and selling tickets to their hanging as if it were a rodeo and that their bodies would be stolen for medical practice.

Nellie convinced the sheriff and the mayor to impose a curfew to prevent a riot. Then she spread word to her cronies to meet her at the grandstand at two in the morning. At that surreptitious hour, she distributed pickaxes, sledgehammers, and crowbars, being the first to wield her weapon and smash it into the scaffold. By dawn, the grandstand was a pile of splinters in a nearby ditch.

After the execution, two miners slipped out of Russ House under cover of darkness to camp on the graves for ten nights in a row, until they were sure the bodies were safe from grave robbers.

Nellie was to perform one more act of heroism before leaving Tombstone. The price of silver was falling but the huge costs of keeping the shafts from flooding stayed the same. The big mining companies economized by cutting wages and the miners went on strike in 1884. Nellie's sympathies lay with the miners until she heard they were going to lynch E. B. Gage, one of the managers. She drove out to his place and got him to take a buggy ride with her, driving him slowly through town so as to avert suspicion. Then she put the whip to it and drove hell bent for leather to Benson, getting him on the train to Tucson to give tempers time to cool. People started calling her the Angel of Tombstone.

But bad times soon forced her to quit the town. An employee sued her. Fires destroyed expensive equipment at two of the big mines. The value of silver dropped further. The boom town was busting. Schools closed down, crime went up, people left in droves. In 1885, around age 35, Nellie took the children with her as she went from mining camp to mining camp in Montana and Wyoming. Her prospecting brought in enough to keep them going but no claim produced a rich enough yield to make it worth staying. And few of these settlements had schools for the children.

Wanting to give her nieces and nephews the education she didn't get, Nellie sent them to California to attend Catholic boarding schools. She travelled around New Mexico and Arizona, going from goldfield to goldfield, and even went to South Africa in search of diamonds. But she never hit real pay dirt.

Then came the news of the Klondike bonanza and Nellie knew that was where she'd find her motherlode. Newspapers announced her intention to go, the free publicity allowing her to advertise for a backer and companions for her trip up. She was not able to raise a party to join her but got financing for her expedition. She left Tucson in February 1898 and went to San Francisco then Victoria to start the long journey to the Yukon, at around age 50.

America was on the verge of war with Spain. In her March 9, 1898 *Daily Colonist* interview, Nellie said she'd abandon her trip if war was declared: "I do not value all the gold in Klondike as much as I would a chance to fight those treacherous Spaniards." When asked by the incredulous reporter if she wanted to ship out to the battle herself, she answered that she "couldn't be kept out of it"; in fact, "I would not only go myself but I would organize a company of women in the state of Nevada who would all go, and who would be of some effect in a battle."

But the Spanish-American War had yet to begin, so Nellie headed for Dawson, intending to take the Stikine River route, through the Cassiars. She left Victoria on March 9, 1898 on the S.S. *Centennial.* Arriving in Wrangell on March 13, Nellie felt as if she were coming home. These were the old stomping grounds of her younger days, the country that had honed her, hardened her, made her see just how far she could go.

But the route was all slush due to the early spring thaw, making it almost impassable. Nellie had to change her plans. She returned to the *Centennial* and headed for Skagway, Dyea, and the Chilkoot Pass.

In spite of her age, Nellie pulled her own weight, perhaps with some help by packers. It usually took 35 trips of six-hour climbs spread over two months to get the required thousand pounds of supplies over the Pass. She had nine hundred pounds and made her last haul to the Summit within three weeks.

At the Summit, Nellie was inspected by the NWMP to ensure that she did indeed have the legislated provisions to make it through a year. She sweet-talked her way through.

The appearance of Nellie Cashman was cause for some comment on the trail. She was travelling all by herself, an impressive sight in her men's pants and Mackinaw, with a single dog to pull her much-laden sled, when other stampeders chanced upon her close to Lake Laberge. The men let her tie her sled to theirs for a while and eat with them but they didn't think it fitting for a woman to camp with them, and she continued on alone.

Winter conditions forced Nellie to cool her heels at Lake Laberge until spring breakup. At this time of year, all river travel is suspended for as long as the ice is unreliable. A dog sled might fall through weak patches over a strong current. Boats can't be used until all the ice is gone because huge chunks can ram into and sink a craft. Once the boats were built, the river trip through Miles Canyon and the infamous rapids amazed Nellie—the speed of the current was an experience she never wanted to repeat.

She hit Dawson in mid-April 1898. By June 18, the *Midnight Sun* was already reporting on her charitable activities: "Misses Nellie Cashman and Georgie L. Osborne returned Friday morning from a trip up the creek, where they solicited for the benefit of the hospital . . . Miss Cashman is the pioneer woman in this country and is widely known for her good deeds." The subscriptions collected, and no doubt some of Nellie's own funds, helped build a three-storey addition to the hospital. Nellie was especially pleased to help, because the Sisters of St. Ann, whom she'd canvassed for in Victoria during her Cassiar days, were to take it over.

She was also overjoyed that her nephew Tom finally caught up with her that summer and would stay on, helping out with all her enterprises. She already had "a tomato can loaded with dust"[6] from the four claims she owned.

True to form, Nellie also worked hard to open another restaurant called Delmonico's. Restaurants she owed during her seven years in Dawson included the Cassiar Restaurant, one adjacent to the Donovan Hotel, and one out on Bonanza Creek. Although she could charge high prices for quick meals, she let many eat on the house.

She made her killing with mine No. 19 near the strike at Bonanza Creek. It yielded over a hundred grand, every penny of which she used to stake more claims, prospecting al over the remote creeks by snowshoes or dog sled.

*Nellie in front of her Dawson store, June 23, 1898.*

Travel in the region was always time-consuming; on occasion it was life-threatening. In October of 1899, returning from a supply trip, Nellie experienced the wreck of the steamship *Stratton*. She and the other passengers lost everything but the clothes on their backs and had to walk the two hundred miles back to Dawson. All her provisions were gone but she carried on with her mines regardless.

Over one thousand women were involved in mining in the Klondike—as owners of mines, investors in claims, cooks in their spouse's mining camp or, very rarely, working their own claim. As a female miner, Nellie faced discriminatory obstacles. Unmarried women weren't allowed to file claims; they were only permitted to buy claims that had already been filed. This rule meant that Nellie had to partner with or hire men.

Also, corruption was rife. The mining records had lines cut out of them or pasted over. Boundaries between claims were unclear. Claim jumping was common, especially as those who went Outside for months to raise capital were often unaware that prolonged absences could cost them their rights to the claim. All was confusion and controversy, and more than one miner lost the pay dirt that was rightfully his or hers.

The records in Dawson show that Nellie staked her first Klondike claim on May 3, 1899, out at Rosebud Creek, but the grant is missing. As is the grant for the Monte Cristo claim she staked on March 1, 1900. Nellie bought and sold claims like trading cards, and it is impossible to keep track of all her dealings. But she was to get into trouble with two mines in particular.

The first was the Jeandreau (also recorded as Johndrew) claim out on Little Skookum Creek. Mrs. Jeandreau sold her claim to Nellie. There are no records of Mrs. Jeandreau having staked this claim, although she is recorded as having staked claims on Swedish Creek and on Bonanza. Instead, it was M. E. Russel who had recorded it as his in March 1898.

As a married woman, Mrs. Jeandreau should have been able to record the claim herself. As an unmarried woman, Nellie should also have been able to list the claim upon purchase because it had been previously listed. Nellie believed the claim rightfully hers and hired a surveyor to establish her boundaries. The surveyor did his work but Nellie wanted Mining Inspector H. H. Norwood to confirm her entitlement.

Hearing that Norwood was involved with Belinda Mulrooney, the owner of the Fairview Hotel, Nellie hinted to him that a certain person in town would get some compensation if he cooperated. She then went to see Belinda and made similar suggestive comments. Nellie was hoping to bribe Norwood through Belinda. Dominion Lands Commissioner William Ogilvie—who would be responsible for cleaning up the mining office's act—began an investigation. He went to Nellie's cabin to question her. Nellie admitted everything but accused Belinda of playing a trick on her.

It was a messy business all around and it was only Nellie's previously spotless record and sterling reputation that saved her from ignominy. Still, she was galled to have been had by another woman, especially one who had a higher status in the community than herself.

The next case involved the same M. E. Russel. He and another miner named William Thompson complained that Nellie was encroaching on their claims. She had filed for a placer grant on January 24, 1899 for a claim she'd bought for $1,500 around Monte Cristo Gulch. It was just above the claim she'd tried bribing Norwood about. Ignoring the charge, Nellie put $4,000 into getting the mine going. The ruling, made by Commissioner Senkler, was in favour of Russel and Thompson.

Nellie engaged lawyers and appealed. It took two years for Senkler to succumb to pressure and agree that Nelllie had acted in good faith. He still didn't believe she deserved compensation, but the rest of his department did. The case dragged on. On November 30, 1901, Senkler granted Nellie ten claims on Soap Creek, but these didn't amount to much.

She spent most of 1902 and 1903 prospecting, despite undergoing intestinal surgery necessitating a hospital stay from November 1902 to February 1903, and continued to involve herself in the good works of the Sisters of St. Ann. Her treks sometimes got in the papers. On January 26, 1904, the *Dawson Daily News* reported that she had just hiked alone for 21 miles in temperatures of minus 60.

Are there roadhouses on the Bullion Trail? Well I should say. One night I occupied the top bunk in the fifth story of a series. The bunks were put up more for catching quick transients trade than for stability, and they collapsed under the heavy superimposed weight of humanity. Ah, Lucky day. I came down on top. The bottom victim is there yet.

She bought claims on Madeline, Sheep, and Bullion Creeks in Alsek country west of Whitehorse, then went on a jaunt South to visit family and investors around Arizona and in St. Paul, Minnesota (where a niece was in a convent). She was still travelling around her claims at the age of 60. This gallivanting made for lively news copy. On February 28, 1904, the *New York Times* called her a "Klondiker with as much energy and enterprise as any of the men who ever went over the trail."

No matter what how her claims fared, Nellie always had her businesses to back her up. She ran a grocery store out of the basement of the Hotel Donovan, and it became a kind of clubhouse for the miners. As an alternative to the saloons, she set aside an area for the prospectors to rest and write letters. She called it the Prospector's Haven and Retreat and would spend hours there giving out smokes and getting the news—no doubt a few lucrative tips as well.

She was so well respected that every man would stand when she entered a room.

Often she'd run into pals from the old days in other gold rushes. Wyatt Earp and his wife, Josephine, were up for a while. And John Clum, of the *Daily Citizen* in Tucson, was on a business trip establishing postal services when he heard a familiar voice pressing for a charitable donation in the photography shop. Immediately, he called out to Nellie in recognition of her voice and mission, amused she hadn't changed her ways.

When the Dawson Rush slowed in 1904, Nellie moved on to

*Last night at the Fair in the Palace Grand Theatre to benefit Nellie's favourite charity, the St. Mary's Hospital. Faith Fenton reported on the events in the* Paystreak.

Fairbanks, Alaska for a few years. Having already been a benefactress of St. Mary's Church and Hospital in Dawson, she became known in Fairbanks for scooping up the poker jackpots for the Episcopalian St. Matthew's Hospital. A medical missionary described her as having a freckled, wrinkled, and weathered face and said of her that "a more colorful and entertaining highwayman never mushed the trails of the Yukon."[7] It was still her habit to tour the mining camps in the bush, shaking the miners down for donations for the hospital.

She opened an outfitting and grocery store, with a profit of six grand in its first year, but Fairbanks was too tame for her. There was a place that seemed wild enough. A mining camp called Coldfoot had been established about 60 miles north of the Arctic Circle on the Upper Middle Koyukuk River. Not only was this the most remote country she could find, with the kinds of challenges she relished, she was sure this was where she'd find her motherlode.

She left on July 14, 1905. Shooting some rapids, their raft broke up on a rock. They made it to shore with only four of the logs, fixed it up, and carried on. Nellie knew there would always be something interesting happening here, something real. In the January 11, 1924 *Arizona Star* interview, she described her experience of the Far North:

> It takes real folks to live by themselves in the lands of the north. Of course there are some rascals everywhere, but up north there is a kindly feeling towards humans and a sense of fair play that one doesn't find here, where men cut each other's business to hack and call it "competition." It takes the solitude of frozen nights with the howl of dogs for company, the glistening fairness of days when nature reaches out and loves you . . . to bring out the soul of folks. Banging trolley cars, honking cars, clubs for catty women and false standards of living won't do it.

At the same time, there was the potential for violence. At least one of the outlaws Nellie knew of in Alaska was a murderer—the "Blueberry Kid"— who was caught in 1912 and faced the full force of the law. He had killed "Dutch Marie" and "Fiddler John" for their gold pokes as they returned from Nolan Creek, where Nellie's claims were. But she still didn't believe violent force was required to keep northern folks in line. When the post of deputy U.S. marshal came open in 1921, she was recommended to fill it. She told the *Arizona Star* that she wouldn't be a "two-gun man":

> I wouldn't think of using force on anybody, particularly those boys up there. You see, they look upon me as a sort of mother and they

wouldn't think of doing anything wrong while I'm around. I've been all through Alaska dozens of times but I've never been troubled by bad men. There isn't a man in Alaska who doesn't take off his hat whenever he meets me—and they always stop swearing when I come around, too. I wouldn't have any trouble in keeping order, because everybody's orderly when I'm around anyway!"

One of the ways in which Nellie had earned such respect was by being one of the very few women—some say 1 per cent of all miners in the Klondike—who sometimes worked her own mines—back-breaking, grubby work, often in extreme conditions. In the Klondike, she'd done placer mining. All winter, miners would thaw the ground with wood fires or with boilers, when these were brought North. They'd shovel out as much dirt as had been softened, digging a hole deep into the mountain, through to permafrost and then to below bedrock. The excavated dirt would make a huge pile that was sluiced in spring cleanup. For sluicing, a flume is built so that river water can pour down it, then gravel from the dug-up pile of dirt is shovelled in to be washed away, leaving the gold flakes and nuggets in riffles along the bottom. Dirt that had gone through the sluice would then be panned for any gold that had gotten away from the riffles. Nellie would have likely been standing in freezing water as she heaved the gravel into the sluice or bent with icy fingers to pan for gold.

Nellie staked her first Alaskan claim on July 27, 1905 on Nolan Creek. She was to have many more: Bunker Hill Bench, Sweet Marie Bench, Eureka Claim, Fay Gulch, Sullivan Gulch, and even Cashman Gulch. The Koyukuk ground required shaft mining, which relied on expensive equipment. In 1908, she went to Fairbanks and brought back unwieldy and pricey boilers not only for herself but for her neighbours as well. Her mines produced hefty profits until 1919, when it became clear that only improved technology would continue to wrest the gold from the ground.

*Nellie in her mid-seventies, 1923.*

In the winter of 1918, she was more interested in fighting battles abroad than working her mines. She managed to convince a group of Alaskan men to follow her to the Great War from their remote camps in Koyukuk. They mushed the hundreds of miles to Fort Gibbon only to learn that the Armistice had been signed.

After the war, an engineer building roads in Alaska asked why she didn't go and she retorted, "I started to go, but your ———— roads were so infernally bad that the war was over before I got there."[8]

Nellie would make frequent trips Outside to raise capital for her claims, forming Midnight Sun Mining Company in 1922 and selling stocks. Large mine owners like Big Alex MacDonald and E. B. Gage often grubstaked her. They considered it an indirect way of giving to charity, because that's where Nellie's gains always ended up, as donations for hospitals or churches. Her nephew also contributed but just as often she refused to take his money, giving his uncashed cheques for up to $10,000 to a banker in Fairbanks for safe keeping.

Her trips South gave her a chance to visit her nieces and nephews. Always, her arrival would be remarked upon, as in this January 10, 1924 Associated Press article:

> Miss Nellie Cashman, a slight figure and worn by years of prospecting and mining in the north, fully maintained her reputation of being the champion woman musher of the north in the opinion of pioneers here, when she came to Seward recently to take a steamship to the States. To reach Seward, Miss Cashman mushed, that is to say, part of the time she ran behind a dog sled and part of the time rode by standing on the runners, seven hundred fifty miles in seventeen days. In the seventeen days, with a good dog team and the lightning fast ice that precedes the heavy snows, she traveled along the Yukon and Tanana Rivers from Koyukuk, Alaska to Nenana whence she rode the cushions of the government's Alaska railroad.[9]

Biographer Suzann Ledbetter compares this trip with the feat of Iditarod musher Susan Butcher, who holds the 1990 record for 1,100 miles mushed in 11 days: Susan had 150 dogs (and handlers at rest stops) and was 36; Nellie had one team and was in her seventies. A marathon mush was the perfect send-off for Nellie. That would be her last trip.

She caught a cold traipsing around New York City, Washington, D.C., and Bisbee, returning to Nolan Creek on a mail plane. When she didn't get better, Nellie went to the Sisters of St. Ann in Fairbanks, beneficiaries of much of her charitable work. Their hospital diagnosed double pneumonia, and Nellie was sent down to Victoria, again to the Sisters of St. Ann. For nine weeks she worsened, then rallied for two days before going "Up There with all them fellers I used to know."[10] She died on January 4, 1925.

She was buried next to the Sisters of St. Ann plot in the Ross Bay cemetery in Victoria. Eulogies appeared in newspapers all over the continent. The *Arizona Star* wrote: "She had beauty without ostentation, wisdom without education, and a flaming, unquenchable spirit

*Nellie visits Arizona in 1924*

that was nonetheless familiar with the paths of humility."[11] In 1984, she was inducted into the Arizona Women's Hall of Fame. Her old friend newspaperman John Clum wrote a short biography of Nellie, in which he said:

> She was one of the first of a band of daring women to invade the frozen, uncharted fields of the North, and a little later, with her favorite team of huskies, she followed the winter trails until she became known as the champion woman musher of her time.[12]

Shortly after her death, new hydraulic methods proved that she'd been right on the money about her Nolan Creek claims. From Tombstone to the Cassiars to the Klondike to Alaska, there was hardly a gold rush that Nellie Cashman missed. To this day she is known as the foremother of all female miners.

# *10*

*Faith Fenton*

# THE FAITHFUL CORRESPONDENT

*Portrait of Faith Fenton.*

*The execution is scheduled for eight in the morning, but she has her copy written hours before. Her plan should allow her to scoop all the other journalists in Dawson City. The official mail won't be going out for two more weeks, but a man named Sandison will be leaving for*

*Outside at seven and he has agreed to take her envelopes, although he steadfastly refuses to wait just one more hour so she can complete the telegram that reports on the hangings.*

*She hurries past the barracks, where already the doctors and reporters are heading toward the sentry guarding the entrance. Her small figure turns down a side street, her ankle-length skirts swirling over the powdery snow dusting the boardwalk. It is the first day of November and the sun won't rise over the mountains until well past ten. The sky until then is a suffocating dark grey. She catches her breath outside the saloon, reassured by the dog team waiting in its harnesses outside, the sled packed lightly, all in readiness.*

*Inside, the private mail carrier is wolfing down pancakes, anxious to be off. She hands him two sealed enveloped then pauses over the unsealed telegram. The time is checked—it is after seven now. The man still will not wait three-quarters of an hour so she can finish her story. He remains unmoved by the intentness of her dark eyes; the resoluteness of her narrow, elegantly plain face; or her musical voice, which pleads forcefully. She invents the most probable ending, describing the four men swinging in the wind, seals the telegram and hands it over with the three-dollar fee. She follows Sandison, watching him mush his dogs out onto the frozen river. Relieved she heads back to bed for an hour's nap.*

*When she wakes, it is to unsettling news: the executions have been stayed for 24 hours. She tells herself it will be all right, amounting to only a slight error in her column, a date that is a mere day off. The whole town is holding its breath. Then it comes, the second reprieve. The condemned men now have four months, maybe more, to live. While they must be startled with renewed hope, the female correspondent for Toronto's* Globe *is seized with panic. She runs to Colonel Sam Steele of the Mounted Police and begs for help. Within an hour, the fastest runner in the Yukon is sent to retrieve the telegram that would kill her career. He catches Sandison almost 50 miles away and returns to collect her fifty dollars, an exorbitant sum but the speed of recovery was worth any price.*

*Word of mouth travels much faster than mail in the Klondike, as she humorously notes in the column she writes to expose her folly. "The story of that hotly-pursued telegram was carried up and down the river, and related with zest in many a miner's cabin, usually with the facetious comment that the* Globe *correspondent was the only official in Dawson who showed no hesitancy in carrying out the sentence of the law.*[1]

*Correspondent Faith Fenton was never known to be hesitant, especially not with sentences. In a time when women with ambition were castigated as traitors to femininity, she knew what she wanted and she got it: to become one of Canada's first women journalists.*

Faith Fenton was born Alice Matilda Freeman on January 14, 1857 in Bowmanville, Ontario, with wilfulness in her blood. Both sets of grandparents had eloped. Her maternal grandmother was a well-born Irish girl who ran away with an English soldier. Her paternal grandmother was an opera singer and actress who eloped with a songwriter. Her parents married for love in 1851, both 21 at the time.

They had their first child, named Mary for her mother, the same year in London, England. Three years later, they moved to Brooklyn, New York and had their second child, a boy named Henry, after his father. As Tories, they were disenchanted with the United States and moved to Canada in 1856, settling in Bowmanville the year Alice was born.

Alice's father, William Henry, was a carpenter by trade and a musician by inclination. In the Bowmanville years, he often neglected both his furniture-making business and his burgeoning family for the sake of his passion. He played cornet and violin and was the Orono Band's bandmaster. Alice's mother, Mary Ann, bore 12 children, all surviving infancy. Such a large brood wore her out and taxed the family finances. The eldest daughter was often kept from school to help in the home, as was Alice. For Alice, this was truly a hardship. Clever, an avid reader and aspiring poet, she hungered for education. Perhaps this is why she was given away when she was ten, like a character in the novels of Jane Austen or Charles Dickens.

The family had moved to Barrie, where there were no bands to distract William Henry, who gave up music and concentrated on his furniture store. But Alice was sent back to Bowmanville to live with Reverend Thomas Reikie, a Nonconformist preacher, and his wife, Margaret. While Alice was hurt by her unexplained exile, her new situation would offer her better opportunities. On the practical level, she had her own room in the Fowler's octagonal house and could attend school religiously. On a more personal level, she became deeply attached to her foster mother.

Margaret was a lonely woman whose husband was often away spreading the Word. She was also of delicate health and refined sensibilities, and a secret poet herself. She and Alice soon became fast friends. Margaret taught Alice etiquette and encouraged her in school, where Alice won awards for every subject with the ironic exception of English composition. If the example of her mother set Alice against the imprisonment of marriage and motherhood, the example of Margaret increased her ambition to be a "real writer," instead of a woman who scribbled verses furtively.

Margaret succumbed to a fever in 1871, at age 46. Fourteen-year-old Alice was devastated. Back with her family in Barrie for the summer, she had one of Margaret's poems published in the local newspaper as a tribute to the woman who had loved and understood her. Somehow Alice also managed to return to school in Bowmanville, even though the Reverend had scandalously married a woman 30 years younger and moved back to Scotland. Alice's own poems commemorating Margaret appeared in the paper shortly before his swift remarriage. Alice was now on her own and learning the power of the published word.

At 15, in 1872, she moved to a boarding house in Toronto and began six months of studies at the Toronto Normal and Model Schools, earning a Third Class teaching certificate. She played the part of Japonica in *The Crowning of the Rose* for graduation, and won both a Second Prize in Science and a First Prize in English. At 16, in 1873, she stayed in a Mennonite community near Fort Erie for six months to complete the practice teaching that qualified her to earn her Second Class Certificate back at the Toronto Normal and Model Schools in 1874. At 18, in 1875, she was employed by the Toronto Board of Education to teach Fifth Division at the Palace Street School. At Front and Cherry streets, this posting was a tough school at the very edge of the city and she earned less than half the salary of a male teacher. In 1877, she taught at the more central but just as tough Niagara Street School. In 1881, she switched to younger grades at the John Street School. And, in 1883, she settled into the Ryerson School, where she would teach for 11 years, while living with her brother's family and beginning her journalism career.

By all accounts, Alice was a gifted and gentle teacher with an inspirational love of learning. She was well respected by her colleagues and adored by her students. But teaching was her livelihood, not her life. Her dream, deferred but undeterred, was still to become a writer.

Her first big break came in the summer of 1886. She convinced the *Northern Advance* newspaper in Barrie to let her write a two-part series on her adventures, accompanied by two women friends, on a lighthouse supply boat from Detroit to Sault Ste. Marie. Here she initiated her signature style: focusing on the human face of places and issues by giving anecdotal descriptions of the emblematic or unusual people she met.

The series was so well received that Alice began publishing almost weekly articles for the paper under the pseudonym Stella. She was 29 years old and finally apprenticing in her craft, writing in the sentimental, inflated style of the day. Her turf was Toronto, and her letters for the ladies of Barrie commented on fashion, theatre, social occasions, political events, and civic figures. In 1887, she covered the Toronto mayoral campaign, which was controversially won by a temperance advocate. Many thought it was the large turnout of women voters that had swayed the outcome; single and widowed women with independent living quarters had been given the vote in Ontario in March 1884. That an election could be affected by women voters, and that the political coverage of this could be written by a female journalist, must have given hope to the literate ladies of Barrie still largely restrained by strict Victorian gender roles.

It also gave Alice her foot in the door at a larger newspaper. At the end of 1887, she began writing for the "Our Young Folks" children's section of the *Globe* weekend edition. It was then that she chose the *nom de plume* with which she would become famous: Faith Fenton. For almost a decade, she would lead a double life, restricted by the proprieties of her role as teacher Alice Freeman by day and freed by the intrepid new position of female journalist Faith Fenton by night. She was living with her brother Fred and his wife and so could not hide her nocturnal work from her family, who helped keep her secret identity under wraps.

Her career took off when she got her own column, "Woman's Empire," in the new Toronto paper, the *Empire,* created by John A. Macdonald and the Conservative Party as a mouthpiece for their views. As Faith Fenton, she was one of the first female columnists to write under a woman's name.

Still, she was paid less than male columnists, who made little enough to begin with. It would be years before she could quit her day job. She would go undercover at night as an indigent woman seeking refuge at a homeless shelter, then teach school all day and write up her exposé without having slept. She visited and reported on orphanages, kindergartens, old age homes, hospitals, and women's prisons, calling for donations and social justice. Like any good journalist, she caught not only the meticulously researched details of her subject but also the individual human story that was its beating heart. She took a woman's point of view that female readers could relate to even as she argued for controversial reforms.

She advocated the emancipation of women, but did so most often in a gentle and optimistic voice, a savvy strategy against the charges of stridency that were often made against the suffragettes. She also mixed her more political pieces in with descriptions of fashion, profiles of actresses, reviews of plays, and travel pieces on her vacations to places like Niagara Falls, thereby reassuring readers by couching subjects still considered beyond the domain of women with those that were firmly within their limited sphere. Despite such tactics, there was no mistaking Faith Fenton's belief in women's rights, which she made daringly plain on occasion in her *Globe* column: "We say not now: 'tis the will of Allah,' and cover our heads in harem seclusion; but we enter into the world's arena, and in critical debate argue the pro and con, or in open revolt fight it out."[2]

Faith could get away with such calls for rebellion by taking a heart-to-heart tone that spoke directly and confidentially to her readers: "I speak as a woman to women. I know, for you have told me, in often unconcious plainings, of your searchings, your restless questionings and blind outreachings towards the far-off thing that seems always a greater good."[3] The readers responded: women from every kind of background wrote her from all over the world, as did men. She gradually became a popular voice uniting Prairie homesteaders with Maritimers, reaching out to women across the country. She also was one of the first women to join the Imperial Federation League of Canada.

In her travel pieces, Faith served as both an example of an independent woman claiming her right to roam and as a conduit, passing along the stories of the women, and men, she met on her journeys. In 1889, at age 32, she took another trip on a lighthouse boat in the summer, this time for a six-week tour along the St. Lawrence River. In the

Thousand Islands, she extolled the beauty of the scenery. In Montreal she revelled in the cosmopolitan ambience. In Lake St. Louis, she discovered a widow with two daughters who'd kept her post as a lighthouse keeper for 13 years after the death of her husband. In Kingston, she visited both women and men in the penitentiary and openly took a stand against the imprisonment of petty criminals. She also toured an insane asylum, which she approved of because it was nicely decorated. And, in Sault Ste. Marie, after travelling back across Lake Ontario, through Lake Huron, up past Georgian Bay and farther into Lake Superior, Faith proved her daring. She hired two First Nations men to take her on an adventurous trip through the rapids, a feat that left her euphoric. She also described First Nations villages and reported on how Europeans stole the traditional offerings left at sacred burial grounds. In Port Arthur, she demonstrated her intrepid spirit again by ascending the ladder of one of the highest grain elevators of the world to gaze out at the even higher mountains and the shining water below.

It was an exhilarating summer but the return to teaching in the fall left Faith dispirited. She was depressed at finding herself still single in her mid-thirties, working to exhaustion at two demanding careers, and living two opposing identities. In a column entitled "The Art of Growing Old" she wrote, "A woman's bitterest moment, I think—especially if she be a woman unloved and therefore lonely—is when she turns from the mirror realizing for the first time that the fair flush of youth has vanished." In December, Faith covered the speaking engagement of 71-year-old women's rights advocate Susan B. Anthony, which gave her a renewed sense of purpose and faith.

She began to speak out more strongly about issues such as sexual harassment on Toronto streets, the lack of public bathrooms for women downtown, the health detriments of corsets, and women's need for exercise. In October 1891, Faith interviewed many of the speakers at the Association for the Advancement of Women Conference in Toronto, again taking a softer approach to make this controversial event, and its goals, making them less threatening to the average woman. She was confident enough in her position to openly criticize her editor in her column for not allowing her to cover a club meeting because she was a woman: "My particular editor is not advanced in his views concerning our sex. He doesn't believe that women should be in medicine or law, or on the platform, or in politics—or anywhere except home—and I shouldn't be surprised if sometimes he didn't want them even there."[4]

By 1892, her fame had grown to the extent that her column was lengthened and, beyond the distinction of a regular byline, her *nom de plume* was often featured in the headline of her article, as in "Faith Fenton goes to . . ." Fan letters, flowers and gifts poured in. As her renown grew, she increasingly favoured her commitment to writing above her teaching responsibilities and would take many leaves of absence to travel to the United States, Quebec, Ottawa, and Muskoka.

The big event of 1893 was undoubtedly the Chicago World's Fair, which drew enormous crowds, as well as female entrepreneurs like Belinda Mulrooney. Alice Freeman took unpaid leave from her teaching position so that *Empire* correspondent Faith Fenton could cover the International Council of Women held at the exposition in May, organized in part by Chicago socialite Martha Munger (Black). Faith served on the advisory council, representing the press, under her real name as well as her *nom de plume,* thus finally revealing her true identity in public. By describing the women who participated in the Council as unthreateningly feminine and by refraining from revolutionary exhortations, Faith beat the drum for the cause of women's rights in her reportage.

She also made an important alliance at the Fair. Lady Ishbel Aberdeen was a speaker at the Council when she received word that her husband had been appointed Governor-General of Canada. Meanwhile, the Canadian delegates were forming the National Council of Women of

Canada (NCWC) and finding an ardent supporter in Faith Fenton. The founders asked Lady Aberdeen to become the first president of this new umbrella organization and she accepted. Through a correspondence that lasted almost 15 years, Tory Faith Fenton and Liberal Lady Aberdeen plotted to advance women's causes, with Faith as the duo's public voice and Ishbel as the behind-the-scenes political force.

By February 1894, Faith's status had risen enough that she could finally quit her teaching job for good at age 37. She began publishing more widely, with articles in the *Canadian Magazine* and the *New York Sun*. No longer was Faith relegated to the ladies' section at political events; she could now join the press gallery.

Faith was also now of such stature that she was invited to attend the functions of the higher echelons of Canadian society. She became increasingly enamoured of the upper classes. Though her original strength as a journalist had been to speak directly to her readers as a woman of the people, she began to hide her early origins as a tradesperson's daughter and her working life as a schoolteacher. At the same time, she was soon to face some major setbacks in her career.

The *Empire* was dismantled and Faith lost her job when a merger created the new *Mail and Empire.* In 1895, she freelanced for Toronto's *Evening News* and the *Ottawa Citizen,* among others, before receiving a plum job offer. Faith was chosen to become the first female magazine editor in Canada at the new *Canadian Home Journal.* In Faith's hands, the *Canadian Home Journal* became an arm of the NCWC, always waving a promotional flag for Lady Aberdeen. Faith ignored increasing complaints against the pre-eminence of Lady Aberdeen, who was not admired in Toronto, and continued to use her position to support Her Ladyship.

Suddenly, in early 1897, Faith was fired as editor of *Canadian Home Journal.* She had just turned 40 and was reduced to living on dwindling savings. A regular column in the *Evening News* and freelance pieces for other papers could not restore her former prestige and income. It was this professional setback that prompted her decision to join the stampede of the Klondike Gold Rush.

Faith had recently interviewed Dominion Minister of the Interior William Ogilvie. He had assured her that respectable women were going to the Yukon to make an honest living, that these women were perfectly safe because law and order prevailed in the territory, and that marriage prospects were excellent there for single women. It was this last information that most piqued her interest. As a woman, she was determined to go in search of a husband. As a woman journalist, she was eager to report on this great historical event.

It took months to prepare for her adventure. As a correspondent for Toronto's *Globe,* Faith would be travelling in the company of four members of the Victorian Order of Nurses and the Yukon Field Force, an army unit sent to protect the border with Alaska. Hamilton, Ontario industrialist Senator William E. Sanford and his manufacturing company sponsored them all. Once again, Lady Aberdeen was instrumental. It was she who gave a recommendation to the Victorian Order of Nurses, one of her causes, for Faith to accompany their representatives to the Yukon. She also promoted the Klondike series to British newspapers and arranged for the government to supply Faith with rations, as it was doing for the nurses and soldiers.

Faith's proposed journey was announced by a society columnist in the *Ottawa Free Press,* by a featured paragraph in Toronto's *Globe,* and by Prime Minister Wilfrid Laurier himself, who wrote to the *Mail's* Alfred Harmsworth praising Faith as a writer. Faith went to Ottawa and was interviewed by the press. Showing a flair for public relations, she did not mention her teaching career, or that her father had owned a store, and said that she had been born in Toronto. The interviewers were impressed and described her as courageous trailblazer who had opened up the field of journalism to women.

Late in April, Faith joined the four VON nurses, Amy Scott, Margaret Payson, Georgia Powell, and Rachel Hanna, at the Ottawa railway station. A North West Mounted Police officer's wife, Mina Stames, was also coming along to join her husband in Dawson City. The party was seen off in style by Lord and Lady Aberdeen, Sir Sandford Fleming, and notable local families. In early May, with much military fanfare, Wilfrid Laurier and the Aberdeens, sent off the army unit.

Because she would be accompanying Canadian soldiers, who could not appropriately march through U.S. territory, Faith would take the Stikine River route through Canada to the goldfields. On May 15, the

*Faith Fenton,* Globe *correspondent, in the Stikine River Canyon, British Columbia, on her way to the Klondike in 1898.*

public turned out in droves to see Faith, the nurses, and the army board *The Islander.* By May 16, they were in Wrangell, an American shanty-town which, like Skagway, was ruled by thugs. Because an army official had objected to her travelling skirt, which she had shortened to little more than knee-length, Faith had to make a trip into town to see a seamstress. Black satinette, the only material available, was used to lengthen the skirt, to scarcely less risqué effect.

As the boat then began its journey up the Stikine River, Faith was struck by the sudden climactic changes of the North, how a day's travel took her from wintry chill to summery warmth, how the river rose and fell suddenly, stranding steamships on sandbars. She was awed by the vivid landscape, especially the two-mile-wide Grand Glacier's azure gleam. But her delight waned briefly when their boat was forced to tie up in the rain belt, as revealed in her article "A Scow Tie-up on the Stikine," which ran in the *Globe* on June 21, 1898.

> The low bank is like a slimy sponge; the Devil's Club and other thorny astringent plants spring thick from the soaking ground, permeating the air with a faint, offensive flavour. Coarse mosses of varied texture and shade climb the tree trunks and throttle the slender branches. The snow-streaked, mist-curled mountains lock us chillingly about, and the rain falls with a steadiness born of long-asserted custom.

On May 24, they landed in Glenora, and the army ritualistically shot off its rifles to honour Queen Victoria's birthday. For a week the party camped here in their tents and prepared for the gruelling hike ahead: the 150 miles of the Telegraph Trail.

At this time of year, the sun shines warmly enough to cause perspiration, while ice still tinges the ponds left by the melted snow. In their long, full skirts, the women bushwhacked through dense forest and hopped on

*Faith and other stampeders going to Glenora, British Columbia.*

little hillocks of humus in dank swamps, often slipping into deep mud and always battling swarms of vicious mosquitoes. Despite it all, according to party member Georgia Powell, Faith and the nurses "went trampling, leaping, springing, and climbing, a strain that only the strongest and most sinewy women could bear."[5] Faith even carried a small golden cat with her the whole trip. They rose at two in the morning, were marching by five, and didn't stop until about ten o'clock in the evening, making the same dozen miles a day as the accompanying troops.

Faith, at 41, demonstrated not only courage but also a striking optimism. Her columns, passed on to travellers heading back to civilization for posting, made light of the hardships she and the others endured and celebrated the stampeders she met along the way. In her August 20, 1898 *Globe* article "Packing on the Trail," she made special mention of a Scottish-American woman who wore a short skirt and had already traversed

Telegraph Trail twice with her husband. And she gently mocked a packer named Murphy for "the crudeness of his thought regarding women":

> "White women are not much good," says Murphy, "savin' your presence. They won't work. A klootchman (Indian woman) is best. She don't ask no questions, and she does what she's ordered. A klootchman's worth five dollars a day to any man out in these parts."
>
> He looked across the camp fire meditatively.
>
> "Can you cook?" he queried. "Can you wash blankets? An' I suppose you couldn't round up cayuses? No? Well, you see, you really wouldn't be no use to a packer. A klootchman 'ud be far better."
>
> And Murphy is a bachelor.

It wasn't until the middle of August that the group reached Teslin Lake, and this was almost too late to make the rest of the trip before the rivers froze. The army was headed to Fort Selkirk, another four hundred miles up the Hootalinqua River, then to the Yukon River to the mouth of Pelly River. Dawson City, the heart of the goldfields, was still farther. The troops built about 50 boats, almost all with sails, and the party headed out en masse. Faith gloried in the comparative ease of river travel, the excitement of the Five Finger Rapids, and the camaraderie of the evening campfire. The beauty of the northern sunset inspired her awe and her pen.

> From deepest velvety purple, through shades of violet and heliotrope, to delicate pearly grey, the higher mountains stood like richly mantled kings, while the lower hills, pine green to the timber line, caught the sun upon their bald, moss-covered brows in a harmony of browns. The lake stretched its half-mile of blue from bank to bank, while far off between the lower heights three snow-capped peaks caught the one touch of scarlet.[6]

*Faith and* Globe *photographer H.J. Woodside with the Yukon Field Force on the Teslin Trail, British Columbia, June 1898.*

Faith reached Dawson on September 15, 1898. On September 28, the *Klondike Nugget* noted the arrival of "a brilliant Canadian writer of magazine and newspaper fame." By autumn, Faith was squatting in a tent at the NWMP barracks in Dawson City while the VON battled the epidemic of typhoid. She was gaunt, sickly, broke, and already chilled even before the river had turned to ice. The police dogs had ripped her cat apart. Her ink was frozen solid. Things could not have looked more bleak. But on October 1, Dr. John Nelson Elliot Brown, head secretary to William Ogilvie and a long-time fan of Faith's work, came and offered her a position as Ogilvie's assistant private secretary. The doctor was already in love with Faith and would always recall in detail the first day he'd seen her, September 12, walking by the river.

After typing and taking shorthand all day, Faith prowled the streets at night looking for news stories to write up for the *Globe*. Soon she was firmly established in all levels of Dawson's community, a familiar figure among swells and *hoi polloi* alike. The booming Gold Rush town was a bonanza of material and Faith's sharply observant articles mined it thoroughly. Many of her observations of the North ring just as true today as they did then, as when she describes a hike up the Dome, along a trail familiar to Klondike Kate and Alexander Pantages, Martha Munger Purdy and George Black, and all the courting couples of Dawson:

> Yesterday we had a glorious climb up the heights that rise directly behind the half-mile width of swamp land that constitutes Dawson's town site. Up and up and up, pausing every little while to regain our breath and take a view. Up, and up again, over a well-marked trail; catching at twigs, moss tufts, saplings, any stanch

*Faith in the Yukon, 1898.*

thing, to swing ourselves on over the almost perpendicular height. The cluster of log cabins and white tents grew more diminutive as we ascended, until they appeared like a speckled bit of low-lying river bank. The mountain tops came into view—those snowclad peaks that are always present in these sub-arctic regions. We stooped here and there to pluck a flower—tiny bluebells and a bit of golden rod or a spray of wild sage."[7]

The only difficulty was in getting her copy to the newspaper in Toronto. When a public execution of four men was scheduled for early in the morning on November 1, Faith came up with a scheme to scoop the other journalists. Instead of waiting two weeks for the regular mail to go out, she'd send her report on the hangings out with a private mail carrier who was leaving that morning. The problem was that he was insistent on leaving an hour before the actual event. Faith fabricated a plausible report and sent it off, fully expecting her article to be borne out within the hour. Instead, there was a four-month postponement of the hanging and she had to pay a runner fifty dollars to retrieve the false news. Her folly became a legendary Klondike story, and she later wrote it up in her February 18, 1899 *Globe* article "Mail Carrying on the Yukon."

> It was an expensive recall but the correspondent learned the lesson that even with the death chant ringing and the trench grave dug, with the noose almost about the victim's neck, there is still no surety of death. While, from a journalistic point of view, even with several weeks delay involved, it does not do to take advance chances to the extent of three-quarters of an hour.

The unreliability of the postal system created a number of crises. Edith Tyrrell, who had known Faith in Ottawa and had been on *The Islander* for the trip north, did not receive her husband's letter telling her not to come to Dawson because he would be out in the bush prospecting. She arrived in the overflowing town in December to find herself and her toddler daughter stranded and homeless. An acquaintance gave her his room at the Fairview Hotel, owned by Belinda Mulrooney, but it had no lock, and next door cursing, brawling drunks were kicking up a ruckus. Crying with fear, Tyrrell and her daughter piled their suitcases in front of the door and curled up in bed until Faith appeared, brought by the desk clerk to comfort her. Soon, Faith had Tyrrell not only calm but laughing. The next day, Faith came with the wife of a government official and arranged for mother and child to stay in their home.

Faith wasn't the only, or even the first, female journalist to come to the Klondike. Among others, she was preceded by the illustrious Flora Shaw of *The Times* (London), one of the world's first female international correspondents, who had been instrumental in foreign affairs from Gibraltar to Australia. Shaw's coverage of the Trail of '98, and her accusations of corruption in the mining office, so offended Faith that she publicly criticized her in her own article, "Winter Days in Dawson," in the January 28, 1899 *Globe:* "There are difficulties of administration that even Miss Shaw, with all her ability, could not possibly comprehend within the limits of two or three weeks stay in the territory."

William Ogilvie's investigation into such corruption became one of the big stories of this year, so perhaps part of Faith's pique was that she had been scooped. As his private secretary, Faith was in a prime, if not entirely impartial, position to report on the story. And, as a stampeder who had her own gold claims that would produce a couple of thousands of dollars, she was also able to give precise coverage of mining regulations, methods, and profits in the Klondike. In her March 6 *Globe* piece "Vivid Picture of Dawson," she even went to so far as to make predictions based on her comprehensive knowledge: "Some day all this vast body of gravel will be worked by haudraulics. Then you will hear of such an output of gold as will startle the world. The benches and hills will far exceed the creeks in the output of gold."

Another top story of 1899 was the April fire that razed the town and, as a full-time resident of Dawson, Faith was on the spot. For her female audience, she also detailed her intimate knowledge of the unique northern lifestyle: the difficulty of skiing in skirts, the lack of flowers for funerals in the long winter months, the plague of ravens that infested garbage sites, the awesome cataclysm of the river breaking up, the sudden green wonder of spring. If Flora Shaw was dismayed by the growing pains of this new city, Faith was exhilarated by them: "One feels as if witnessing the birth of a nation."⁸ Dawson was becoming a cosmopolitan city and Faith was undeniably a part of it. When the Telegraph Company started up at the end of September, Faith was given the honour of the inaugural telegram. With a brief announcement of this new development, she sent a "Hurrah!" to the *Globe*.

Another distinction granted to Faith was editorship of the six-issue paper published to promote the St. Mary's Bazaar, a cause that Émilie Tremblay and Nellie Cashman contributed to diligently. Suitor Dr. John Elliot Brown and another man helped Faith put together the *Paystreak* for the six days of revelry at the Palace Grand in the middle of a 50-below cold snap. In the December 23, 1899 issue of this magazine, Faith captures the wonder of winter in Dawson City in "In the Yukon":

Still, white and windless—what a splendid place is this Yukon valley for winter festivities! The months may be, nay, are indeed, one long winter carnival; one picturesque drama.

Look at the material that lies about us—icy river, snow-covered hills; grey valley shadows; sun-lit summits; dog teams; trail travellers; uniformed police and military; moss chinked cabins; curious costumes; everywhere that which is picturesque, amusing, dramatic.

Her Christmas Day coverage of the opening night of the bazaar in "The Opening" is equally celebratory:

> From eight o'clock onward guests arrived in a continuous stream. They crowded galleries and boxes, then overflowed down to the main floor. They laughed and chatted, drank café noir and fished in the water lily pond; they tried the wheel of fortune, visited the gipsy proprietress, purchased bon-bons, listened to the music, and when it grew irresistible, threw severity and formality to the winds, and danced—making the pretty picture more charming yet.

In the December 28 edition, Faith made special mention of her suitor. A blackboard had tumbled from the stage onto the head of a Mrs. Ward Smith, and "Dr. J. N. Elliot Brown who was present attended to her injuries and before the evening was over she was sufficiently recovered to reappear for a few moments." No doubt the journalist and the doctor were constant companions at the bazaar, as they worked closely together to put out the *Paystreak* under less than ideal conditions: "Type was scarce; so was the paper supply; and it was 'take what you get when you get it and be thankful' with the busy printing staff."[9]

After a lengthy courtship, which included many long hikes into the surrounding mountains and valleys to enjoy the splendour of nature, Faith accepted the good doctor's proposal. One could hardly imagine a more suitable husband for Faith. Also Ontario-born to small-town Empire Loyalists, John had dreamt of being a writer and had begun his career as a teacher. In 1888, he had taken a degree in medicine at the University of Toronto, winning the Silver Medal when he graduated in 1892. His first position was at Toronto General Hospital as a house surgeon. His second was at St. Michael's Hospital as chief obstetrician. A passion for nature and a longing for adventure made him impulsively abandon this enviable post to accompany William Ogilvie to the Gold

Rush in August 1898. He was 36 to Faith's 42 years (although she put 39 on the marriage certificate).

Hardly was their engagement announced when they were wed. On New Year's Day, 1900, St. Paul's Church was filled with rare mid-winter flowers for the evening wedding. Faith's younger sister, Edith, had joined her in the summer to work as a typist in Ogilvie's office and she stood as bridesmaid, while John's brother was present as best man. The marriage was reported, with glowing praise for both the personages and the professional standing of bride and groom, in all the Dawson newspapers, as well as in papers in Bowmanville, Barrie, and Toronto.

The distinguished and popular newlyweds moved into a one-room cabin at Seventh and Mission, with a little kitchen and big storeroom attached to the back. They had a shared study curtained off from the bed and the dining table but no parlour. In a city like Dawson, this did not prevent Faith from holding her at-homes for the society matrons on Wednesdays. Her guests included all of the *crème de la crème,* including Martha Black, who was also friendly with Émilie Tremblay. These connections were made prior to her marriage: "Before marrying Dr. Elliot Brown and joining the ranks of the home-makers, Faith Fenton had been a shining example of the kind of respectable, unmarried woman who could occupy a prominent place in Dawson society."[10]

By March, Faith had quit her job in Ogilvie's office but she continued to write for the *Globe,* under her new byline, Faith Fenton-Brown. Concerned about how the rush to Nome was emptying the streets of Dawson, Faith used her column for unabashed boosterism, claiming over and over that Dawson was still being swarmed by gold seekers and respectable women: "In the summer of '97 Dawson could count only forty women. The summer of 1900 sees at least one thousand, and the large majority of these are wives and mothers who have come to make homes for husbands and sons."[11]

The rough and tumble world of the Klondike had not diminished Faith's regard for the elite: "Dawson society is especially fortunate in having at its head women of more than ordinary culture and standing . . . of travel and taste who form a social world quite equal in brilliance and intelligence to any of the *monde* in bigger cities."[12] Known as one of these women herself, Faith was often called upon to be the entrée into this rarified society. Such social standing enabled her to participate in the August visit of Lord and Lady Minto, the Governor-General and his wife (the Aberdeens having returned to England). Faith was invited to the reception and the tour of the mines as a prominent society matron, not as a journalist. This did not prevent her from devoting two columns to the Mintos' trip.

By 1901, though, Faith preferred the privileges of being a socialite wife to the pressures of being a diligent correspondent, and she gave up her regular column for the *Globe*. In the future, she would only publish sporadically, when specifically inspired by an intriguing subject. Leisure was a well-deserved luxury for the hard-working woman who had spent so many years performing two demanding jobs at once. She had chosen her husband well, and she did not have to sacrifice her independence to play the role of wife. In July, she left John in Dawson to make her first visit back down South since she'd arrived. Transportation in the territory had so improved that it took only two weeks to reach Ottawa, where she was interviewed by the *Ottawa Journal* about her plans to see Toronto and Montreal again before heading home to the Yukon in September.

Back in the Yukon, Faith and Edith were joined by younger sister Florence, who was soon very active in the community, attending the Tennis Club dance, singing for the amateur opera society's production of *The Bohemian Girl,* and playing piano at a fundraiser for the library. Within two years, she too had found a Klondike husband. Her wedding to lawyer John K. Sparling on October 15, 1903, in the same church as Faith's, was considered the fanciest in Dawson history. The 31-year-old groom was a powerful man, representing two of the major British mining companies operating in the Klondike and being the only collection agent in town. The guests reflected his esteemed status. The bride was 32 but imitated her sister and claimed only 26 on the certificate. Dr. John Brown escorted her down the aisle and Faith stood as matron of honour. Edith had gone back Outside to resume a career in journalism, inspired by her elder sister.

Faith herself left for a visit South in the summer of 1904, joining her husband as he was to train at Toronto's General Hospital and Baltimore's Johns Hopkins University in bacteriology. His intention was to improve medical expertise in the Yukon, as well as to bring back an X-ray machine. But no X-ray machine would be coming to Dawson, for Faith and John did not return. While they were on their trip, a political skirmish deposed Commissioner Congdon, whom John had served since Ogilvie retired in 1901, and eliminated the post of territorial secretary. John no longer had a job in the Klondike. Their cabin was, like so many still standing in Dawson, abandoned with all their possessions left in perfect order, waiting for the owners who would never come back to claim them.

For the remainder of her life, Faith's career would take a back seat to her husband, although she definitely retained a mind of her own, especially in regard to politics. Unlike Martha Black, Faith was comfortable remaining a Conservative while her husband was a Liberal. But she no longer had a full-time career. In July 1905, John returned to Toronto General Hospital as medical superintendent and house surgeon, and Faith relegated herself to the role of supportive wife.

Surprisingly, more writing by John was being published at this time than by Faith, who only occasionally did a freelance piece. John's articles were usually in connection with his work, but he also wrote an article on Oliver Wendell Holmes, whom Faith had once interviewed, suggesting some merit to suppositions that Faith was largely responsible for writing that appeared under her husband's name. It seems amazing that he would have had the time for this output, considering his demanding schedule as both practising doctor and hospital administrator.

Toronto General renovated a house on their grounds for the couple to live in, and in return John contributed some of his own money to the many improvements he spearheaded in the hospital. A dedicated innovator, he travelled all over the United States and Europe to study examples of different hospital administrations. Faith often accompanied him.

Faith did not completely disappear from the publishing world. In 1907, the publishers of *Songs of a Sourdough,* the first volume of poetry by Robert Service, had her read the manuscript and offer advice. And she also met frequently with the Canadian Women's Press Club, an organization founded after the 1904 St. Louis World's Fair, when 13 female journalists from Canada converged by happy accident in the same railway car.

Faith kept her oar in and, in 1912, wrote an article about her move to the States. John had accepted a position as medical superintendent of the Henry Ford Hospital in Detroit. Faith encountered a few snags at the border, with immigration problems possibly due to the Scottish citizenship of her personal maid and customs difficulties definitely due to her sealskin coat. Since she could not tell the inspectors where the seals had come from, they suggested that she put the fur in storage in Windsor and pay it hour-long visits on those occasions when she felt a powerful urge to wear it.

Faith was still in America when World War I broke out, and she played a leadership role in the Red Cross before returning to Toronto in 1918 for good. The Browns settled into a house on Bloor Street, eventually moving to Blythwood Avenue, and finally, to Mount Pleasant Road. John started a private practice, became a contributing editor for a variety of medical publications, was elected as president of the Yukon Sourdoughs' Association, acted as a secretary for the British Hospital Association, and founded the Canadian Hospital Association. Faith joined a reading club for women and wrote many letters to old friends. Childless themselves, both John and Faith doted on the children in their extended families, helping with their educations and spending hours with the youngsters, especially Faith's niece Olive, who travelled with them.

In 1935, Faith wrote her will and started collecting all her published writing, as if preparing a book. At the beginning of 1936, the *Globe* published an article on her days as their Klondike correspondent, as well as a fresh poem she had written about the land of the midnight sun. Almost immediately after this tribute, on January 10, she died of pneumonia.

*Two women are front and centre in the crowd waiting for the mail at the Dawson City Post Office.*

January 14, 1936 should have been Faith's eightieth birthday. Instead, it was the day of her funeral, attended by hundreds of mourners. Headlines in all the largest newspapers announced the demise of this icon of the Klondike, celebrating her as one of Canada's first, and most popular, women journalists, who had given an entire generation the vicarious thrill of her Gold Rush adventures.

Faith's husband tried unsuccessfully to honour her by writing her biography. In 1937, he wed Faith's niece Olive, who at 45 was almost 30 years his junior. The marriage shocked their family and friends, creating unresolvable rifts and causing Olive to be shunned by those disapproving of the scandalous match. When John died in 1943, he was buried in Toronto's Mount Pleasant Cemetery next to Faith. Olive rests with her parents.

Like Klondike Kate, Faith Fenton seized her independence early and eschewed the retiring modesty expected of femininity to shamelessly seek fame. Like Anna DeGraf, she worked tirelessly and without complaint to make a life for herself. Like Émilie Tremblay, she discovered the joys of matrimony in the Klondike and contributed to the community as a socially prominent wife. Like Martha Black, Belinda Mulrooney, and Nellie Cashman, she was a pioneer who went against the strictures of Victorian society to succeed at a profession traditionally barred to women.

And, like all of these intrepid women of the Gold Rush, Faith Fenton proved beyond a doubt that a woman could march into the wilds of the North, take the town by storm, and "mush on and smile" no matter what hardships were to be endured, what obstacles were to be surmounted, what summits were to be scaled.

# *11*

## GRANDES DAMES OF DAWSON

⌒⌒⌒⌒

The women of Dawson City today have much in common with their sisters of a hundred years ago. They venture North with the same sense of adventure and they stay because they fall under the same Spell of the Yukon. They mine at remote family claims; kick up their heels at Diamond Tooth Gertie's Casino; own and run stores, restaurants, and hotels; raise children on the trapline; and work to implement the Land Claims Agreement that recognizes the First Nations' right to self-government.

I met many of these *grandes dames* of Dawson City during my seasons there and each is my personal heroine for her strength, humour, and courage.

The grandest dame of all is Fran Hakonson, matriarch of one of the town's most established mining families. Fran is 78, and her hands are now curled like autumn leaves, afflicted with the arthritis that often comes from too many years of extreme cold. Walking is painful and she doesn't get out much, so she graciously invited me to her comfortable home for our talk. Outspoken and lively, Fran painted a proud picture of her many years as a mother, miner, and businesswoman. She first came to the Yukon in 1944 but settled in Dawson on June 9, 1946 because she and her husband Bill had claims in the area. She hated it at first. "I couldn't stop feeling cold. I was just always cold," she says. The early years were a struggle. While Bill worked their mines, Fran raised the children and ran a grocery store in town, which burnt down. Dawson then was "a pit," says Fran, with few entertainments and little culture. But the mines produced and their fortunes grew. Soon Fran and Bill embarked on a new enterprise that would become one of the landmarks of Dawson: building the Eldorado Hotel. This was where Klondike Kate lodged when she came to visit her husband Johnny Matson—"That woman! She just married him for his money! I didn't like her at all. But Bill did, didn't you, Bill? She taught Bill to roll a cigarette with one hand!"—and it is still considered *the* miner's hotel, where all the prospectors stay when they come in from the creeks to do business.

Bill was often needed to run their mining operations, so Fran ran the hotel much of the time. Occasionally, she'd have to drive a 20-ton truck by herself out to a claim. Fran enjoyed the revival of Dawson's Klondike culture, which started in the 1970s and continues today. Now that they are retired, Fran and Bill are just as active in the community and proud of their grown children's contributions. Many of the younger Hakonsons work family claims of their own, and son Greg is helping to establish a foundation year visual arts program through the Dawson City Arts Society and the Klondike Institute of Arts and Culture. Fran wouldn't want to live anywhere else. She gestured to the panoramic view of the mountains of West Dawson and said, "Where else would you find all this? A place with so much beauty and such great people? The people in Dawson are the best you'd meet anywhere. Some may be eccentric but they're all individuals, salt of the earth!"

One of those salts of the earth is Leslie Chapman, who has a family mine out on the creeks and a store—Forty Mile Gold—in town. Leslie is 46, but looks 20 years younger, with long ash-blonde hair and a face of beauty and calm assurance. She grew up in Calgary and was registered in university when, at 19, she came to Dawson for the summer to visit her boyfriend, who was working for Parks and Recreation. She never left, and that was 27 years ago. The boyfriend became her husband. They were part of the back-to-the-land movement and wanted to be self-sufficient, living in the wilderness. Out at Fortymile River they built a six-sided log cabin with a peaked roof, which now features three additions spoking out in different directions and a solar panel to run a computer and a radio phone. They didn't intend to become miners but the old-timers told them that their creek had lots of gold in it. They realized that "even in the Yukon, you can't be completely independent of society. You need money. Well, you could live without it but you'd be living *really* basic. Mining was a good solution for us because we could do it at home and not have to come to town to get jobs."

Leslie says that placer mines are the family farms of the Yukon. "It's a really good family lifestyle as you're together all the time and everybody contributes. The kids learn the realities of life: if you want to be warm, you have to chop wood. And it's fun because you're together and can enjoy the beauty of the land all around you."

Leslie taught her children to read when they were two, then did home-schooling from kindergarten to grade 12. Her son is finishing grade 11 and her daughter just graduated from the University of British Columbia.

While her husband is doing innovative research on the effects of mining on the environment and developing new mining technologies, Leslie is the full-time expediter, ordering parts and supplies, keeping the books, writing reports. Everyone pitches in to run the equipment. She says women today do much the same work as the female miners of the Gold Rush, like Ethel Berry, Émilie Tremblay, and Nellie Cashman: "Women often have the job of panning to separate the gold from the black sand left in the riffles after sluicing because it's a meticulous job."

What she loves the most about mining is that it is a seasonal lifestyle. Mining shuts down in the winter and then she is free to ski everyday, learn to weave on a loom, practise goldsmithing. When the Top of the World Highway is plowed out in April, she and her husband start bringing in supplies and equipment, and then they sluice from May to September. Since she opened Forty Mile Gold, Leslie has spent summers in town. She sells gold nuggets, jewelry that she and other artisans have made, paintings and prints by local artists, and First Nations art like beaded baskets and moosehide mitts, almost everything created in the Yukon. After this busy season, fall is spent getting all the provisions in for the winter before the ferry goes out and the road is closed and she can breathe a sigh of relief.

This is a lifestyle that Jennifer Flynn knows well. At 18, Jennifer came to the Yukon from Ottawa in 1973. Her first job was serving 900 meals a day to tourists at Lake Bennett. Her second job was cooking out at a mining camp, where she volunteered to do the panning after a full day begun at 4:30 in the morning. Her decision to come up North was inspired by the thrilling tales told by her grandmother, a First World War nurse who'd returned from the war to battle the tuberculosis epidemic in Northern Ontario, living in wall tents and canoeing to remote First Nations communities around Red Lake near Kenora. "She was one of three nurses that went up to work with the gold miners and the Native people of the area," Jennifer says proudly.

Jennifer married a man from an old Dawson family—his grandmother was Tagish—and spent four years with her babies at the family claim. She held her own but admits it was hard work having to haul water to wash diapers. She says that "especially as mothers, women need connecting with others more than men do so the bush lifestyle is not as attractive."

Now that her children are in high school, Jennifer works as the receptionist at the nursing station in Dawson, where she's on a first-name basis with the entire town. I didn't expect her to know me when I stopped by for a prescription, but she greeted me with "So how's Jake and Megan's new baby? I can't wait to see him!"

Bonnie Nordling is another woman who came to the Yukon as a young woman in 1973. Bonnie has a dramatic delivery. One can easily imagine her commanding a stage. She was one of the first local dancers at Diamond Tooth Gertie's Casino: "Previously dancers came from southern cities and no one knew them. It was really fun having someone on stage that everyone knew. It was easy to joke with the miners in the crowd. But it was good, clean fun! One year I got in with a particulary clean-living string of girls. Some ran marathons, some studied natural medicines and some went to church the next morning. No smokin,' no cussin,' no spittin.' Just lots of cancan energy!"

Bonnie was able to get a commercial fishing license; after she married and had children in Dawson, the family would spend summers out on the river scooping up the salmon. "It was a great life for our kids," recalls Bonnie. "As parents, my husband and I gave them a lot of freedom and the responsibilities that come with it. The kids helped with everything from driving the boat to cleaning fish. It produced an independence and confidence that remains with them today. As a teenager, my daughter is secure in her town and a victim to no one."

A few years ago, Bonnie gave up her fishing license as she felt there was too much competition for salmon. Now Bonnie spends most of her time in an office at Social Services: "I sure miss getting out on the river!" she confesses.

Tracey Horbachuk, striking and self-assured, is another "Gertie's girl" who has gone on to other endeavours in Dawson. Like Klondike Kate, she came to Dawson as a professional dancer. Dancing was all this Vancouver woman had ever wanted to do, and since the age of 15 she'd performed professionally all across Canada, in Japan, and on cruise ships, on stage, and in film and television. She was auditioning in New York City when she got the call to take a five-month contract in Dawson. She came up in April of 1998 at age 24, met the man who is now her husband, and decided to settle. "The more I was away from the city, the more I didn't want to go back to it. I'm not like some people in town who go back to the city and freak out and can't handle it. I still have the city in me. But I like being able to walk down the street and say hello to everybody. The natural beauty of Dawson is a real draw. And, you have really unique people here—some might say crazy! They are unique whether they were born and raised here or came up, decided to change their way of life, and became real, authentic Dawsonites."

For four summers she danced three shows a night six nights a week at Gertie's, and on more than one occasion male tourists, having taken too seriously the legends of the Klondike, asked the woman playing Gertie how much her girls were—"Too much for you!"—and whether "business" was conducted in the back room.

Tracey and her husband bought the homey Fifth Avenue Bed and Breakfast, and now Tracey understudies the role of Diamond Tooth Gertie instead of dancing herself. She misses the camaraderie and nights like the one when she got into a shaving cream fight on stage.

Wendy Cairns also came to Dawson as a cancan dancer for Diamond Tooth Gertie's, where she helped start a union for employees. She came in 1986 after having spent a year in the Middle East, studying Arabic at university and teaching aerobics to women in the summer. When Kim Bouzane arrived from Vancouver in 1992, the two women got to talking about how they were both looking to own their own businesses so they could be their own bosses. By the ferry docks, there was a beautiful, but boarded-up and run-down, building that had been Bombay Peggy's bordello decades ago. I took pictures of it on my first visit because, despite its decrepit condition, it had real architectural charm. Wendy and Kim wanted to restore it to its former glory, as a bar and inn this time, but it was in a poor location. With an inheritance from Wendy's mother and financing from the bank, they had the building lifted up and hauled across town to the corner across from the Oddfellows Hall, which was being renovated to house the Arts Society offices, ballroom and art gallery.

Wendy and Kim had to act as their own contractors during the construction, and were almost crushed by the financial strain and the physical effort. Wendy says, "We almost gave up a dozen times. It took a real toll." Kim agrees, "We'd just put so much into it that there came a point where we couldn't give up, we would lose too much."

Their daring and hard work paid off. Bombay Peggy's is now a daily meeting place for many locals and visitors, especially those involved in classes or events at the Arts Society across the street. Wendy and Kim are cheeky enough to have a red light glowing outside, a photo of the real madam Bombay Peggy hanging in the bar, and a framed pair of tattered pink silk bloomers, found behind one of the walls during renovation, displayed in the inn. The inn has theme rooms like the Lipstick Room or, my favourite, the Attic Room, which has a white colour scheme, minimalist furnishings, and an old clawfoot bathtub right in the room.

Diana Holt came to the Yukon to get away from such luxuries and live in the wilderness. Born in the late 1960s, Diana grew up in Toronto but had such a yearning for nature that she would gaze out her classroom window and imagine the buildings turning into mountains, the streetlights into trees, the streets into rivers. Her older sister moved to the Yukon, married a trapper, and began living the bush lifestyle. Diana went up 17 years ago and partnered with another trapper who taught her how to live in the wilderness. "He was very patient. I didn't know *anything*. I couldn't even get a good fire going," she recalls. They lived in a cabin that was 11 feet by 11 feet and she'd bang her head on the four martens and part of a moose that hung from the rafters. It was close quarters for two people who didn't really know each other.

But proximity and the Yukon worked their spell. They fell in love and married, and Diana made the Yukon bush her home, where she and her husband have been raising two children. It takes five days to go around the trapline—which uses humane traps—and there are cabins every nine miles for resting and skinning. They painstakingly broke one hundred miles of trail that need to be cut again every year because of regrowth. First, she would snowshoe out, cutting branches, then double back and use the dog sled to pack down the snow. It took a long time and had its own hazards: "Dog mushing is a bit tense because anything can happen, like you might twist your leg, and there's no way to get any help. Once I was chopping a branch off a tree over me and I stuck the axe into my knee. It was nine miles to the nearest cabin. I thought, This could turn into a life or death situation. There's no way to communicate really. My husband will say he'll try to be back in ten days, but you never really know."

Later, forest fires swept their area and planes had to douse their main cabin. Burnt trees are too hard to break trail through. They had to build caches and cabins farther out. But this takes money, so they took jobs in town. This was a big change for her husband, who hadn't really been out of the bush for a decade.

Now they try to get out to their trapline, with their children, for at least four months every winter. It can take a month to get there because so many supplies must be hauled, requiring many trips with 400-pound sleds over the 25-mile trail from the first cabin to the far cabin. To build the far cabin, Diana and her husband worked 18-hour days finding the right trees, cutting them down, then hauling about 50 huge logs for miles.

Chores include grinding grain and cooking up food to feed the dogs, getting water, chopping wood, heating water for cleaning, cooking on a wood stove, and home-schooling. Cabins are one-room affairs and family are the only people they'll see for months. "I work really hard to be mentally and physically healthy so that I'm okay to be around in that tiny cabin. You develop a really intense relationship with your kids and husband. You're everything to your children: parent, teacher, playmate."

Diana finds the isolation especially hard: "Women want to be around other people," she believes. "The First Nations didn't do it alone. They travelled with family and friends. At least two families would camp together. The women would talk to each other and the kids play together and everyone would have a grand old time. It's no life to be on your own out there. There's a lot of boring chores to do everyday. I wouldn't even notice those chores if I had another woman doing them with me. It's the fact of being isolated that makes it unpleasant because it's just you and your thoughts running around in your head. It's lonely. I can be on my own but I need my art, my music, my books, projects to do. And seven months a year is enough, then I want to go to town and see my friends."

But that's not always so easy. Diana had a gruelling trip in July 2002. They had to walk out, a journey of five days, with 12 dogs that had to be kept separated to prevent fights. Breakup had left the river too high and it flooded the cabin they were staying in and the outhouse; it was sweltering hot, and the swarms of mosquitoes were the worst she'd ever seen. They all carried packs, the two boys and the parents, and she and her husband were going from six in the morning to two the next morning every day. They had to hike through muskeg with hillocks drowning in swampy water from the flooding. Once they had to build a bridge to get over a creek. Every day her husband said, "The worst is yet to come." At the next difficulty she would ask, "Is this the worst part?" But it wasn't the worst part until they hit a long stretch of spagnum moss. She'd take a step and sink to her waist. But what really broke her spirit was the dog.

The whole way, she had to keep a particularly rambunctious dog on a leash. A dog that dogged her heels. That butted his head into her. That smashed her into trees. Finally, she confesses, she lost it and burst into tears. She says this as if it is a really bad thing to do; that's how strong her morale usually is.

Nevertheless, Diana wants to go back out with her family. While she recognizes some downsides to the bush, it is the life she loves best. "You get really persnickety," she admits. "Have to have a certain mug, your chair in a certain place. Everything has to go your way. And you can't imagine living in town because the world goes your way in the bush, except for a few natural disasters. It's an empowering feeling to have that much control over what happens in a day. You're always accomplishing something. And you're outside most of the time, getting exercise. There's a feeling of balance."

As a First Nations woman, Georgette McLeod was raised mostly in the bush by her grandparents. Until the age of 14, when her grandmother died, Georgette understood the Han language always spoken by her grandparents. They sometimes lived in Dawson, but when Georgette was five their house in town on Second Avenue was destroyed by the flood of 1979. "While they were rebuilding, we went downriver. We lived off and on in the bush. My grandfather would take us berry-picking—I love blueberries! We spent a lot of time out at my family's camp. A great moose-hunting area in the fall. We had this old trap that my grandfather had built. We lived in canvas tents by the creek and had a moose rack ready. Sometimes we'd go to Moosehide. We did a lot of fishing. My uncles would be around a lot. People would visit and sometimes get a salmon to take way."

But eventually Georgette's grandparents could no longer take care of her. "I lived with a non-First Nations family for a number of years and as I got a bit older I noticed a difference between my identity and theirs, in subtle ways. Some say First Nations people are quiet and it takes a long time for them to trust people. It took me a long time. My [birth] family didn't show closeness in a demonstrative way. The bond was there but it was expressed in a different way. The family I lived with were affectionate. They liked to hug a lot. It took a long time to get used to it. And another thing was, I ate a lot of moose, caribou, and rabbit—I loved rabbit—as those were our staples. There was a lot of their food that I'd never had before. Lasagna. Clam chowder. Hamburgers. Once I got used to it, it became the norm. I became very close to this family."

One of the things the gentle and shy Georgette appreciated was that she felt safe with this family: "I still saw my family. They weren't a perfect family. There was drinking, drugs, violence. A number of my uncles and aunts had been through the residential schools. And they're still dealing with it today, their sense of identity, the abuse they received. And sometimes they deal with it by drinking. Some of my family have overcome that, made a positive change. And I feel really good about that. I can feel that people are working towards not only healing themselves but working together as a community to heal."

Georgette attended high school in Dawson until grade 9, then she moved to Whitehorse with her second family and completed grade 12. She went to Juneau, Alaska for university, earning a Bachelor in Education, because it was close to home. She returned to Dawson to become the first guide for the Interpretive Centre. Then she worked for the Tr'ondëk Hwëch'in government collecting archeological, archival, and oral history research for heritage projects. When I spoke with her, she was teaching art at the Robert Service School. "I've been gone for ten years," she explained. "I came back three years ago and worked in the First Nations. I wanted to come back and find out about my family and background. I'm still meeting more family and learning a lot. I feel lucky and honoured to be part of this community. I want to be here and be able to make a difference. It's something I feel strongly about. I think if we can resolve the past, it's going to make a big difference for our future. People need to get involved and make things happen. And that's a big change for people to make when they've been put into a dependent position for generations. There are some very strong First Nations women in this community who take on roles like chief and counsellor. And I have great admiration for how hard they work to make things better for our people."

Because of what has happened to her people, Georgette has a different perspective on the Gold Rush. "I've lived in those two worlds—First Nations and non-First Nations, and my blood is 50 per cent of each. I've seen the hardships that the First Nations have gone through because of changes that were forced upon them, whether they were displaced from their homes to go live on reserves or just not given the same rights as everybody else. There's a carry-over from the Gold Rush period. I want to take the best of both worlds. And I think that's true of most First Nations people. We want to make our own decisions for our community and environment. We want non-First Nations to take responsibility."

Lisa Hutton is another woman of the First Nations raised in the Yukon. A Dawsonite born to an Australian father of English and Scottish heritage and a Tr'ondëk Hwëch'in mother who also has some Irish in her background, Lisa feels that "it is a blessing to come from an ethnically diverse background. It gives more respect for other cultures."

Lisa's maternal grandfather had an Irish father and a First Nations mother, so the family was considered white under the Indian Act, which was both blessing and curse. Blessing because they were then spared the residential schools. Curse because their Indian status was denied, along with their benefits under the Act. "The Indian Act made people decide who was who and I don't think anyone has the right to decide that," Lisa says.

In 1985, Bill C-31 demanded that they prove to the government that they were 50 per cent First Nations. This Bill split families between Status and Non-status Indians. Lisa was able to prove her status: "Basically I have a number now that says I'm Indian."

While the First Nations government was negotiating land claims for the future of the Tr'ondëk Hwëch'in, Lisa worked in the Finance and Housing departments as part of the staff that kept the day-to-day operations going. The land claims were settled in 1998. The new agreement both addresses the inequities of the past and recognizes the First Nations' right to full self-government. All of Yukon society will benefit from this agreement, as it establishes processes of consensus decision making and community-based resource management that set precedents for a ground-breaking system of government that is truly inclusive. Lisa says,

"The Indian Act no longer exists in the Yukon and that's a step up! Brings us back to our own decisions."

Lisa worked with Wendy Cairns to start the union at Diamond Tooth Gertie's and recently ran for Member of the Legislative Assembly of the Yukon Territory. Until the last few years, Lisa has been involved in Moosehide Gatherings, open cultural celebrations and meetings of the First Nations that take place every two years. At one, she was shocked to see her grandmother speaking Han to relatives from Eagle, Alaska. She didn't know her grandmother had the tongue; the language has not been passed down in her family. Now there are Han language classes in the school and the Tr'ondëk Hwëch'in have a say in the curriculum. And they have stories to tell.

Lisa tells how the Tr'ondëk Hwëch'in saved their heritage: "The First Nations people are really resilient to have held on to their culture. Chief Isaac, chief during the Gold Rush, had the foresight to protect the language and dances and songs. He asked our neighbours and relatives in Eagle, Alaska to take them and keep them until the Tr'ondëk Hwëch'in were ready to receive them back. The influx of non-Native peoples, the diseases, being removed from their fishing grounds—it didn't kill them. The First Nations people have been an integral part of this city since they moved into town from Moosehide in the 1950s. They played active roles in the community. We make up part of the city. And what Chief Isaac did really saved the First Nations culture here. Almost a hundred years later, the First Nations decided it was time. Following traditional ways, they contacted the people in Alaska and asked what the protocol was to get the songs and dances back. There were certain ceremonies the people in Dawson had to learn, certain rules they had to follow, and once they were ready, they began earning the return of that traditional knowledge. And that's been going on for about ten years now."

Having seen Lisa on video performing one of these dances at Moosehide, I knew women were playing a big part in this reawakening.

She agrees that all women in the Yukon are brave. "Women are a hell of a lot tougher in the North. It was much harder all those years ago, but they made it. My great-grandmother packed over the Chilkoot. And look at the women that came up—they were very enterprising and made a stake for themselves. I look at pictures from back then and how big the community was and I just can't imagine—houses all up the hillsides—it's mind-boggling. Certainly we have a rich history in the Gold Rush but we also have an extremely rich history of the First Nations that we're willing to share. We want to share our culture, our heritage, our language. The more people that you share it with, the more it is going to be remembered."

People around Dawson City live with layers of history. You can walk into a defunct hundred-year-old store at Fortymile and find shovels with their turn-of-the-century price tags still on them. At Lousetown, you can find the empty bottle from a prostitute's perfume, the bone needle of a Tr'ondëk Hwëch'in woman from hundreds of years ago, a chip of ivory from a mastodon tusk from thousands of years ago. There is a keen awareness everywhere you go of the women and men who broke the trail. Of the brave women who were here from time immemorial and those who struggled long and hard to get here. Of female miners, moguls, members of Parliament. Whether they succeeded or failed, each serves as a compelling example of the frontier spirit. And that is the real gold there is to find in Dawson, as the women of Dawson make history again.

# NOTES

CHAPTER 1

1 Quoted in Jill Downie, *A Passionate Pen: The Life and Times of Faith Fenton* (Toronto: HarperCollins Publishers, 1996), pp. 271–72.

2 *Martha Black,* Third edition, Flo Whyard, ed. (Anchorage: Alaska Northwest Books, 1998), p. 22.

3 Faith Fenton, "Winter Days in Dawson," *Globe,* Jan. 28, 1899.

4 *Paystreak,* Vol. 1, no. 1, December 23, 1899, p. 1

CHAPTER 2

1 Quoted in Ian Macdonald and Betty O'Keefe, *The Klondike's "Dear Little Nugget"* (Victoria: Horsdal & Schubart Publishers, 1996), p. 43.

CHAPTER 3

1 Quoted in Rab Wilkie and the Skookum Jim Friendship Centre, *Skookum Jim: Native and Non-Native Stories and Views about his Life and Times and the Klondike Gold Rush* (Whitehorse: Heritage Branch, Department of Tourism, Government of the Yukon, 1992), p. 76.

2   Pierre Berton, *Klondike: The Last Great Gold Rush, 1896–1899,* Revised edition (Toronto: McClelland & Stewart, 1993), p. 39.

3   George Carmack's letter quoted in James Albert Johnson, *Carmack of the Klondike* (Seattle, WA and Victoria: Epicenter Press and Horsdal & Schubart, 1990), p. 94.

4   Virgil Moore, "George W. Carmack," *Klondike News,* Apr.1, 1898.

5   *Seattle Post-Intelligencer*, Sept. 1, 1898.

6   Ibid., July 26, 1899.

7   *Seattle Times,* July 27, 1899.

8   Quoted in Johnson, *Carmack of the Klondike,* p.117.

9   *Weekly Star,* Apr. 2, 1920.

CHAPTER 4

1   Father Marcel Bobillier, *Madame Émilie Tremblay: A Pioneer Woman of the Yukon,* unpublished manuscript (Yukon Archives, Whitehouse), p.10.

2   Ibid., p. 4.

3   Sam Holloway, "Madame Tremblay: Une Pionnière du Yukon," *Northern Journal,* vol. 4, no. 10 (Aug. 1986), p. 15.

4   Bobillier, *Madame Émilie Tremblay,* p. 23.

5   Applications #30691 and #29957.

6   *Dawson Daily News,* Feb. 24, 1921.

7   *Alaska Weekly,* Jan. 8, 1937.

8   *Dawson Daily News,* Sept. 29, 1938.

9   *Alaska Weekly,* Aug. 23, 1946.

10  *Dawson Daily News,* Oct. 16, 1924.

11  *Whitehorse Star,* Apr. 29, 1949.

CHAPTER 5

1   Anna DeGraf, *Pioneering on the Yukon 1892–1917,* Roger S. Brown, ed. (Hamden, CT: Archon Books, 1992), p. 12.

2   Ibid., p. 28.

3    Ibid., p. 78.

4    Ibid., p. 108.

5    Ibid., p. 109.

6    *Dawson Daily News,* Jan. 8, 1924.


CHAPTER 6

1    Belinda Mulrooney Carbonneau and Helen Lyon Hawkins, "New and Wonderful," 1928. University of California, Berkeley; Bancroft Library, BANC Mss 77/811928.

2    Ibid.

3    Ibid.

4    Ibid.

5    *Seattle Times,* Aug. 12, 1962.

6    *Alaska Journal,* vol. 10, no. 2 (Spring 1980), p. 67.

7    Carbonneau and Hawkins, "New and Wonderful."

8    *Klondike News,* Apr. 1, 1898.

9    *Dawson Daily News–Special Mining Edition,* September 1899.

10   Carbonneau and Hawkins, "New and Wonderful."

11   Ibid.

12   Ibid.

13   *Klondike Semi-Weekly Nugget,* June 7, 1900.

14   Carbonneau and Hawkins, "New and Wonderful."

15   *Yukon World,* Feb. 7, 1907.


CHAPTER 7

1    Martha Louise Black, *My Ninety Years* (Anchorage, AK: Alaska Northwest Books, 1977), p. 17.

2    Ibid., p. 20.

3    Ibid., p. 28.

4    Ibid., p. 29.

5    Ibid., p. 59.

6  Frances Backhouse, *Women of the Klondike* (Vancouver: Whitecap Books, 1995), p. 99.

7  Quoted in Emily Kendall Wheeldon, "U.S.-Born Woman Is Canadian Lawmaker," *Buffalo Evening News,* March 27, 1937.

8  Ibid.

9  Quoted in Jean Johnston, *Wilderness Women* (Toronto: Peter Martin Associates Limited, 1973), p. 231.

10 Ibid.

11 Wheeldon, "U.S. Born Woman Is Canadian Lawmaker."

12  Ibid.

13 Quoted in Joyce Hayden, *Yukon's Women of Power* (Whitehorse: Windwalker Press, 1999), p. 49.

14 Quoted in Flo Whyard's Epilogue to Martha Black, *My Ninety Years,* p. 162.

15 Ibid., p. 141.

16 Ibid.


CHAPTER 8

1  Quoted in Lael Morgan, *Good Time Girls of the Alaska-Yukon Gold Rush* (Vancouver: Whitecap Books, 1998), p. 141.

2  Sam Holloway, "The Life and Times of Klondike Kate," *Yukon News,* July 29, 1987.

3  Sam Holloway, "The Sorry Tale of a Queen and her Princes," *Yukon News,* May 20, 1994.

4  Ellis Lucia, *Klondike Kate: The Life & Legend of Kitty Rockwell* (New York: Hastings House Publishers, 1962), p. 31.

5  Quoted in Rolv Schillios, "Dance Hall Girl," *Alaska Sportsman,* March, 1956.

6  Ibid.

7  Ibid.

8   Ibid.

9   Lucia, *Klondike Kate,* p. 78.

10  Quoted in Schillios, "Dance Hall Girl."

11  Quoted in Morgan, *Good Time Girls,* p. 145.

12  Holloway, "The Life and Times of Klondike Kate."

13  Quoted in Lucia, *Klondike Kate,* p. 95.

14  Quoted in Bay Ryley, *Gold Diggers of the Klondike* (Winnipeg: Watson & Dwyer Publishing, 1997), p. 28.

15  Doris Anderson, *Ways Harsh and Wild* (Vancouver: J.J. Douglas, 1973), p. 38.

16  Quoted in John Kirkwood, "Her First Letter Was Cautious, Friendly," *Winnipeg Free Press,* January 9, 1960.

17  Anderson, *Ways Harsh and Wild,* p. 38.

18  Quoted in Lucia, *Klondike Kate,* pp. 112–13.

19  Quoted in Morgan, *Good Time Girls,* p. 149.

20  Quoted in Lucia, *Klondike Kate,* p. 134.

21  Quoted in Morgan, *Good Time Girls,* p. 151.

22  Quoted in Lucia, *Klondike Kate,* p. 142.

23  Ibid., p. 77.

24  Ibid., p. 43.

25  Interview with Fran Hakonson in Dawson City, January 29, 2002.

26  John Stevenson,"Queen of the Klondike," *Frontier Days in the Yukon,* Garnet Basque, ed. (Langley, B.C.: Sunfire Publications Limited, 1991), p. 35.

27  Quoted in Lucia, *Klondike* Kate, p. 283.

CHAPTER 9

1   Don Chaput, *"I'm Mighty Apt to Make a Million or Two": Nellie Cashman and the North American Mining Frontier* (Tucson, AZ: Westernlore Press, 1995), p. 118.

2   Harriet Rochlin, "The Amazing Adventures of a Good Woman,"

*Journal of the West,* Apr. 1973, p. 283.

3 Frank Cullen Brophy, "God and Nellie," *Alive,* Oct., 1973, p. 2.

4 Mary W. Anderson, "They Called Her 'The Angel'," *National Tombstone Epitaph,* Nov. 1990, p. 11.

5 Suzann Ledbetter, *Nellie Cashman: Prospector and Trailblazer* (El Paso: Texas Western Press, 1993), p. 19. She is repeating an anecdote taken from C.L. Sonnichsen's *Billy King's Tombstone* (Tucson: University of Arizona Press, 1972), p. 24.

6 Chaput, *"I'm Mighty Apt,"* p. 103.

7 Quoted in Chaput, *"I'm Mighty Apt,"* p. 118.

8 C.L. Andrews, "Nellie Cashman," *Alaska Life,* Apr. 1945, p. 53.

9 Melanie J. Mayer, *Klondike Women: True Tales of the 1897–1898 Gold Rush* (Athens, OH: Swallow Press/University of Ohio Press, 1989), p. 226. Mayer found the article, from Seward, Alaska, in W.C. Fonda's scrapbook housed in the University of Washington's Northwest Collection.

10 Ivan C. Lake, "Irish Nellie: Angel of the Cassiar," *Alaska Sportsman,* Oct. 1963, p. 44.

11 Quoted in Ledbetter, *Nellie Cashman,* p. xi.

12 John Clum, *Nellie Cashman,* booklet reprinting article from *Arizona Review,* Jan. 1931.

CHAPTER 10

1 Faith Fenton, "Mail Carrying on the Yukon," *Globe,* Feb. 18, 1899.

2 Quoted in Jill Downie, *A Passionate Pen: The Life and Times of Faith Fenton* (Toronto: HarperCollins Publishers, 1996), p. 101.

3 Ibid.

4 Ibid., p. 229.

5 Georgia Powell, "The Klondike Nurses," *Globe,* Oct. 1, 1898.

6 Fenton "A Scow Trip Down the Yukon River," *Globe,* Oct. 22, 1898.

7 Fenton, "Mr. Ogilvie's Work," *Globe,* Nov. 24, 1898.

8    Quoted in Downie, *A Passionate Pen,* p. 268.

9    Fenton, "A Reminiscence," In *The Northern Light,* M. Wilma Sullivan, ed. (Dawson City: n. p., July 1904).

10   Frances Backhouse, *Women of the Klondike* (Vancouver: Whitecap Books, 1995), pp. 180–81.

11   Faith Fenton-Brown, "The Dawson of Today," *Yukon Sun Special Edition: The Dawson of Today,* Sept. 1900.

12   Ibid.

# SOURCES

Three books already published on women of the Klondike Gold Rush proved essential for both background on and the details of all the female stampeders: Frances Backhouse's *Women of the Klondike* (Vancouver: Whitecap Books, 1995); Melanie J. Mayer's *Klondike Women: True Tales of the 1897–1898 Gold Rush* (Athens, OH: Swallow Press/University of Ohio Press, 1989); and Claire Rudolph Murphy and Jane G. Haigh's *Gold Rush Women.* (Anchorage: Alaska Northwest Books, 1997). Barbara Kelcey's unpublished master's thesis, "Lost in the Rush: The Forgotten Women of the Klondike Stampede," was also of great assistance (University of Victoria, 1989). I also relied upon countless news items from the Gold Rush period and after in the *Seattle Times, Seattle Post-Intelligencer, Klondike Weekly, Klondike Nugget,* and *Dawson Daily News.* The *Alaska Sportsman* of later decades featured articles remembering women of the Gold Rush and interviewing those who remained.

The following books provided the most comprehensive and useful histories of the Klondike Gold Rush: Charlene Pirsild's *Gamblers and Dreamers: Women, Men and Community in the Klondike* (Vancouver: University of British Columbia Press, 1998); Pierre Berton's *Klondike: The Last Great Gold Rush:*

*1896–1899* (Toronto: McClelland and Stewart, 1987); and Richard J. Friesen's *The Chilkoot Pass and the Great Gold Rush of 1898* (Ottawa: National Parks and Sites Branch, 1981).

Finally, the studies done by Julie Cruikshank and Catharine McClellan on the First Nations of the Yukon remain an inspiration for their respectful inclusion of First Nations' values in recording traditional knowledge from elders. Catharine McClellan's book (written with Lucie Birckel, Robert Bringhurst, James A. Fakll, Carol McCarthy and Janice Sheppard), *Part of the Land, Part of the Water: A History of the Yukon Indians* (Vancouver: Douglas & McIntyre, 1987), gave me an understanding of the background of this subject. I also consulted her Ph.D. dissertation "Culture Change and Native Trade in the Southern Yukon Territory" (Department of Anthropology, University of California, Berkeley, 1950); her article "Wealth Woman and Frogs among the Tagish Indians" in *Anthropos,* vol. 58, pp. 121–28; her book *My Old People Say: An Ethnographic Survey of Southern Yukon Territory* (Ottawa: National Museums of Canada Publications in Ethnology, no. 6, 1975); and her entries "Tagish" and "Inland Tlingit" in the *Handbook of North American Indians: Volume 6, Subarctic,* edited by June Helm (Washington DC: Smithsonian Institution, 1981).

Works by Julie Cruikshank explore Shaaw Tláa's life and the story of the Bonanza Creek find from the perspective of the First Nations. Her titles include *Life Lived Like a Story: Life Stories of Three Yukon Native Elders* (Vancouver: University of British Columbia Press, 1990); *Reading Voices: Dän Dhá Ts'edenintth'é; Oral and Written Interpretations of the Yukon's Past* (Toronto: Douglas & McIntyre, 1991); and *The Social Life of Stories: Narrative and Knowledge in the Yukon Territory* (Vancouver: University of British Columbia Press, 1998). Also consulted were her unpublished manuscript, "Becoming a Woman in Athapaskan Society: Changing Traditions on the Upper Yukon River," found in the Dawson City Museum Archives (a later version was published in the *Canadian Journal of Anthropology,* vol. 5, no. 2, 1975). Further background was provided by her book, written in collaboration with Angela Sidney, Kitty Smith, and Annie Ned, *Early Yukon Cultures* (Whitehorse: Department of Education, Government of Yukon

Territory, 1982) and the book by Angela Sidney, Kitty Smith, and Rachel Dawson, as told to Julie Cruikshank, *My Stories Are My Wealth* (Whitehorse: Council for Yukon Indians, 1977).

PREFACE

Additional information on Lucille Hunter was found in the *Whitehorse Star* and the *Yukon News*. There are many sources for Ethel Berry, including, among others, her sister Alice Edna Berry's memoirs, *The Bushes and the Berrys*. (San Francisco: C.J. Bennett, 1941.); Ethel's own story, "How I Mined for Gold on the Klondyke," in the *San Francisco Examiner Sunday Magazine*, August 1, 1897; reports in the *Dawson Daily News* and the *Klondike Nugget;* and stories in Harry L. Bennett's "Official Guide to the Klondyke Country and Gold Flats of Alaska: Written in 1897" in *Gold!*, Spring 1972, pp. 34–59; Norman Bolotin's *A Klondike Scrapbook: Ordinary People, Extraordinary Times* (San Francisco: Chronicle Books, 1987); and William Bronson's *The Last Grand Adventure* (Toronto: McGraw-Hill Ryerson, 1977). For Marie Joussaye Fotheringham, I examined the following court documents in the Yukon Archives: *Kilpatrick vs. Fotheringham* and *Rex vs. Fotheringham*. Carole Gerson's "Only a Working Girl: The Story of Marie Joussaye Fotheringham" in *Northern Review*, no. 19, Winter 1988, provided essential background on this subject. Mary E. Hitchcock's memoir, *Two Women in the Klondike* (New York: Putnam's Sons, 1899), was invaluable and entertaining. For Mae Fields, and for background information on Klondike prostitution, these books were comprehensive resources: Bay Riley's *Gold Diggers of the Klondike* (Winnipeg: Watson & Dwyer Publishing, 1997); Lael Morgan's *Good Time Girls of the Alaska-Yukon Gold Rush* (Vancouver: Whitecap Books, 1998); and Jay Moynahan's *Red Light Revelations: A Peek at Dawson's Risqué Ladies, 1898 to 1900* (Spokane WA: Chickadee Publishing, 2001).

CHAPTER 2

For descriptions of the days of the Gold Trickle, I consulted a reprint of George Dawson's *Report on an Exploration in the Yukon District, 1887* (Whitehorse: Yukon Historical Museums Association, 1987); Michael Gates's *Gold at Fortymile Creek: Early Days in the Yukon* (Vancouver: University of British Columbia Press, 1994); and William R. Morrison's *True North: The Yukon and Northwest Territories* (Toronto: Oxford University Press, 1998). Amongst other early studies and journals, William Ogilvie's works were of assistance: *Early Days on the Yukon* (Ottawa: Thornburn & Abbott, 1913) and "Historical and Descriptive Sketch of the Yukon Territory" (from the *Yukon Sun Special Edition*, September 1900).

I read over a hundred books and articles on the Klondike Gold Rush and all enriched my understanding, but the following sources proved most memorable. Some first-hand and period accounts were: *The Official Guide to the Klondike Country* (Chicago: W.B. Conkey, 1897); Tappan Adney's *The Klondike Stampede* (New York: Harper and Brothers, 1900); T. Mullett Ellis's *Tales of the Klondyke* (Toronto: Copp Clark, 1898); John William Leonard's *The Gold Fields of the Klondike: Fortune Seekers' Guide to the Yukon Region of Alaska and British Columbia* (Chicago: A.N. Marquis and Co., 1897); and Arthur Newton Christian Treadgold's *Report on the Goldfields of the Klondike* (Toronto: G.N. Morang, 1899). These books gave a woman's point of view: Laura Berton's *I Married the Klondike* (Toronto: McClelland & Stewart, 1982); Eudora Bundy Ferry's *Yukon Gold: Pioneering Days in the Canadian North* (New York: Exposition Press, 1971); and Emma B. Smythe's (as told to Hugh D. Maclean) *Yukon Lady: A Tale of Loyalty and Courage* (Surrey, B.C.: Hancock House Publishers Ltd., 1985). Other works that added important background information were: Allan Duncan's *Medicine Madams and Mounties* (Vancouver: Raincoast Books, 1989); Hal Guest's *A Socioeconomic History of the Klondike Goldfields, 1986–1966* (Ottawa: Parks Canada, 1985); Edward Burchall Lung's *Black Sand and Gold* (Portland, OR: Binford and Mort, 1967); and the revised and expanded edition of Archie Satterfield's *Chilkoot Pass: The*

*Most Famous Trail in the North* (Anchorage: Alaska Northwest Books, 1988).

For other understandings of the Yukon First Nations, I delved into George Dawson's "Notes on the Indian Tribes of the Yukon District and Adjacent Northern Portion of British Columbia, 1887" from the *Annual Report of the Geological Survey of Canada*, vol. 3 no. 2. The works of Kenneth S. Coates were also helpful in this regard: *Best Left As Indians: Native-White Relations in the Yukon Territory, 1840–1973* (Montreal: McGill-Queen's University Press, 1993) and "On the Outside in Their Homeland: Native People and the Evolution of the Yukon Economy" from the *Northern Review*, vol. 1, no. 1, 1988.

For further research into the First Nations of the Dawson City area, I consulted the following: Helene Dobrowolsky's "Hammerstones: A History of Tr'ondek Village/Dawson City" from the *Northern Review*, no. 19, Winter 1998; John R. Crow and Philip R. Obley's "Han" from the *Handbook of North American Indians: Volume 6, Subarctic*, edited by June Helm (Washington, DC: Smithsonian Institution, 1981); and Sally Robinson's unpublished manuscript, "Part II, The Han: A History of Change, 1847–1910," from the Dawson City Museum Archives. Also helpful were the works of Cornelius Osgood, *Contributions to the Ethnography of the Kutchin* (New Haven, CT: Human Relations Area Files, 1970) and *The Han Indians* from *Yale University Publications in Anthropology*, no. 74, 1971; and articles by Richard Slobodin, "The Dawson Boys" from *Polar Notes*, vol. 5, no. 3, 1963, and "Kutchin" from the *Handbook of North American Indians: Volume 6, Subarctic*.

## CHAPTER 3

While the works of Catharine McClellan and Julie Cruikshank, as well as newspaper accounts from the time of Shaaw Tláa's life, proved to be the most reliable sources, I also consulted George Carmack's *My Experiences in the Yukon* (privately published by Marguerite P. Carmack, 1933); James Albert Johnson's biography *Carmack of the Klondike* (Seattle: Epicenter Press and Horsdal & Schubart, 1990); and Seattle's Sourdough Stampede Association's *The Alaska Yukon Gold Book: A Roster*, published in 1930. Also helpful was Rab Wilkie and the Skookum Jim Friendship Centre's pamphlet "Skookum Jim: Native and Non-Native Stories and Views about his Life and Times and the Klondike Gold Rush" (Whitehorse: Heritage Branch, Department of Tourism, Government of the Yukon, 1992).

For background on the Tlingit and Tagish First Nations, I consulted Sheila Greer's *Skookum Stories on the Chilkoot/Dyea Trail* (Carcross, YT: Carcross-Tagish First Nation, 1995) and Erna Gunther's translation of Aurel Krause's *The Tlingit Indians* (Seattle: American Ethnological Society, 1976), among other sources.

For first-hand accounts from First Nations participants in the Bonanza find, I read the transcripts of interviews from the Skookum Jim Project, including Patsy Henderson's taped interview "Early Days at Caribou Crossing: The Discovery of Gold on the Klondike," as recorded by Jennie Mae Moyer (available in the Yukon Archives pamphlet collection).

## CHAPTER 4

Émilie Tremblay's memoirs were printed as a pamphlet entitled *Une Pionnière du Yukon: La première femme blanche qui franchit la Chilcoot Pass* in Chicoutimi in 1948. Father Marcel Bobillier translated and added to this account in his unpublished manuscript *Madame Émilie Tremblay: A Pioneer Woman of the Yukon* (found in the Yukon Archives), and this proved to be the most comprehensive source on this subject. Sam Holloway's "Madame Tremblay: Une Pionnière du Yukon" in *Northern Journal,* August 1986, vol. 4, no. 10, pp. 11–19 was useful. Victoria Faulkner's unpublished manuscript *Canadian Department of Indian Affairs and Northern Development Historical Sites, 1960–1962* from the Yukon Archives details the history of Émilie's store, as does Joanne Whitfield's unpublished manuscript "Madame Tremblay's Store" from the Dawson City Museum Archives. Many newspaper items on Émilie were found in *Alaska Weekly, Dawson Daily News* and *Whitehorse Star.* Émilie's scrapbook entitled "Madame Nolasque Tremblay" can be found in the Victoria Faulkner Collection at the Yukon Archives, in rather fragile condition.

CHAPTER 5

Anna DeGraf's memoirs, as edited by her descendant Roger S. Brown and published as *Pioneering on the Yukon 1892–1917* (Hamden, CT: Archon Books, 1992), captured Anna's stalwart and eager voice and were the best resource on her life. Besides newspaper items, other sources on Anna DeGraf included Victoria Faulkner's unpublished papers from the Yukon Archives and Michael Parfit's article "The Untamed Yukon River" from *National Geographic*, July 1998.

CHAPTER 6

The best biography of Belinda Mulrooney is Melanie J. Mayer and Robert DeArmond's *Staking Her Claim: The Life of Belinda Mulrooney, Klondike and Alaska Entrepreneur* (Athens, OH: Swallow Press/Ohio University Press, 2000). Melanie J. Mayer was also very generous in assisting with requests for photo permissions. From this biography, I learned of and consulted the 1928 transcripts of tapes of Belinda speaking as recorded by Helen Lyon Hawkins, entitled "New and Wonderful" from the University of California at Berkeley's Bancroft Library (BANC Mss. 77/811928). The following sources were also helpful: *Pierre Berton's Canada.* (Toronto: Stoddart, 1999); Norm Bolotin's "Klondike Lost" from the *Alaska Journal*, Spring 1980; Stephen Franklin's "She Was the Richest Woman in the Klondike" from the *Vancouver Sunday Sun Weekend Magazine*, July 7, 1962; Wallace Vincent Mackay's "The Saga of Belinda Who Gained Fame Among Rough Men" from the *Seattle Times*, Aug. 12, 1962; and Pam Whitener's "Her Tongue, Wit Made Her Rich" from *The Calendar*, August 29–September 4, 1978. I also consulted several news stories, including those from the *Alaska Journal, Skagway News, Yakima Daily Republic, Yukon News,* and *Yukon World*.

CHAPTER 7

The primary sources for Martha Louise Black were her own autobiographies, published as *Klondike Days* (Victoria: Acme Press, no date); *My Ninety Years*

(Anchorage: Alaska Northwest Books, 1976); and as *Martha Black,* edited by Flo Whyard (Anchorage: Alaska Northwest Books, 1980). Martha's papers from the National Archives of Canada and her scrapbook and correspondence from the Martha Louise Black Collection in the Yukon Archives were also enlightening. I also read many articles written by Martha, under various bylines. For example, she wrote as Martha Munger Black in her passionate description "Flowers of the Yukon" in the *Dawson Daily News* of July 21, 1909, and as Mrs. George Black in her brief memoir "Between Campaigns in the Yukon" in *Saturday Night,* March 8, 1924.

Carol Martin's *Martha Black: Gold Rush Pioneer* (Toronto: Douglas & McIntyre, 1996) is a concise biography. Martha is included in many books about famous women, such as: Jean Johnston's *Wilderness Women* (Toronto: Peter Martin Associates, 1973); Susan E. Merritt's *Her Story: Women from Canada's Past* (St. Catharine's, ON: Vanwell Publishing, 1993); and Joyce Hayden's *Yukon's Women of Power* (Whitehorse: Windwalker Press, 1999). Some articles about Martha Black include Emily Kendall Wheeldon's "U.S.-Born Woman is Canadian Lawmaker" in the *Buffalo Evening News,* Saturday, March 27, 1937; Loraine Carter's "Martha Black" in *Western People,* January 3, 1985; and Liza Sardi's two *Yukon News* pieces, "Lawn Ceremony Cements Black's Stature," July 21, 1993, and "Martha Black 'Wasn't Just a Pretty Face,'" July 16, 1993.

CHAPTER 8

My primary sources on Kate Rockwell Matson were Joe Sestak's papers (Kate's letters to Johnny Matson and details on Matson's burial) and her own correspondence, scrapbook, and papers, found in the Yukon Archives. Victoria Faulkner's unpublished manuscripts "'Klondike' Kate Rockwell" (Whitehorse, 1962) and *Canadian Department of Indian Affairs and Northern Development Historical Sites, 1960–1962* were also found in the Yukon Archives. Ellis Lucia's colourfully written biography *Klondike Kate: The Life & Legend of Kitty Rockwell* (New York: Hastings House Publishers, 1962) provided many facts. Kate

Rockwell Matson's voice was most apparent in her recollections, as told to May Mann, in "I Was Queen of the Klondike" in the *Alaska Sportsman,* August 1944. A number of books include details about Kate's life, including: Bay Ryley's *Gold Diggers of the Klondike* (Winnipeg: Watson & Dwyer Publishing, 1997); Doris Anderson's *Ways Harsh and Wild* (Vancouver: J. J. Douglas, 1973); Richard O'Connor's *High Jinks on the Klondike* (Indianapolis, IN: Bobbs-Merrill, 1954); and Kathryn Winslow's *Big Pan-Out* (New York: Norton, 1951).

Kate generated a massive amount of press, and a number of journalists wrote several stories about her. Ron Moxness wrote articles for the *American Weekly* : "Klondike Kate's Strange Love Idyll." (April 13, 1947) and *"Klondike Kate's Persistent Suitors"* (May 16, 1948). Rolv Schillios wrote pieces for the *Alaska Sportsman:* "Dance Hall Girl" (March 1956) and "Dreams and Reality" (April 1956). John Kirkwood wrote for both the *Winnipeg Free Press*—"The Boys Went Wild"(January 9, 1960)—and the *Toronto Daily Star*—"How a $1-a-Dance Won for Klondike Kate" (December 16, 1959) and "Kate Put Out Fiery Drapes with Bare Hands" (December 19, 1959). Sam Holloway wrote a series for the *Yukon News:* "The Sporting Women of the Klondike" (May 13, 1987); "The Life and Times of Klondike Kate" (July 29, 1987); and "The Sorry Tale of a Queen and her Princes" (May 20, 1994). Other useful articles were Warren Hall's "Queen of the Yukon." in *Esquire* (May 1951); Paul Hosmer's "Rags and Riches of Klondike Kate" in the *Oregonian's Northwest Magazine* (January–February 1934); D.H. Howard's "The Truth about Klondike Kate" in the *Westerner* (May–June 1972); Maurice Kildare's "Klondike Strumpet: She Warmed the Miners' Hearts—and Stole Their Gold" in the *Westerner* (December 1970); Cy Martin's "Klondike Gold Rush Girlies" in *Real West Annual* (Summer 1970); Jack Richards's "Sourdoughs' Sweetheart Has Host of Memories" in the *Vancouver News-Herald* (November 7, 1946); Delores Smith's "The Romance That Became a Klondike Legend" in the *Whitehorse Star* (February 14, 1996); and John Stevenson's "Queen of the Klondike" in *Frontier Days in the Yukon,* edited by Garnet Basque (Langley, BC: Sunfire Publications Limited, 1991).

CHAPTER 9

Primary sources included Nellie Cashman's files of mining claims in the Yukon Archives; her file in the Elmer E. Rasmuson Library of the University of Alaska, Fairbanks; and her papers in the Archives of the Sisters of St. Ann, Victoria, B.C. Also useful were letters from Sister Mary Loyola regarding Nellie, found in Robert C. Coutts's papers in the Yukon Archives. Two comprehensive biographies provided many essential details: Don Chaput's *"I'm Mighty Apt to Make a Million or Two": Nellie Cashman and the North American Mining Frontier* (Tucson, AZ: Westernlore Press, 1995) and Suzann Ledbetter's *Nellie Cashman: Prospector and Trailblazer* (El Paso: Texas Western Press, 1993). Shorter biographies are John P. Clum's booklet *Nellie Cashman,* reprinted from the *Arizona Historical Review,* January 1931, and Rosemary Neering's chapter on Nellie in her book *Wild West Women: Travellers, Adventurers and Rebels* (Vancouver: Whitecap Books, 2000). Nellie is also mentioned in Sister Margaret Cantwell and Sister Mary George Edmond's *North to Share: The Sisters of Saint Ann in Alaska and the Yukon Territory* (Victoria: Sisters of St. Ann, 1992). The following articles also proved very useful: Mary W. Anderson's "The Miner's Angel" in *Canadian West* (October–December 1991); Helen Berg's "The Doll of Dawson" in the *Alaska Sportsman* (February 1944); Louise Cheney's "Angel of the Gold Camps" in *Wild West* (September 1970); Harriet Rochlin's "Nellie Cashman: Gold Digger of '77" in *Ms. Magazine* (September 1974); and Ivan C. Lake's two pieces, "Irish Nellie, Angel of the Cassiar" in the *Alaska Sportsman* (October 1963) and "Nellie Cashman Blazed the Frontier Trails" in *Real West* (November 1965). Newspapers that featured items about Nellie include the *Alaska Weekly, Anchorage Daily News, Arizona Daily Star, Daily Alaskan, Daily British Colonist, Midnight Sun, Victoria Daily Colonist, Victoria Daily Times,* and *Yukon Catholic.*

CHAPTER 10

Jill Downie's biography *A Passionate Pen: The Life and Times of Faith Fenton* (Toronto: HarperCollins Publishers, 1996) proved an extremely detailed resource. Faith's own writings were also highly descriptive sources. The most pertinent of her articles for the *Globe* were: "A Scow Tie-Up on the Stikine" (June 21, 1898); "Packing on the Trail" (August 20, 1898); "A Scow Trip Down the Yukon River" (October 22, 1898); "Mr. Ogilvie's Work" (November 24, 1898); "Winter Days in Dawson" (January 28, 1899); "Mail Carrying on the Yukon" (February 18, 1899); and "Vivid Picture of Dawson" (March 6, 1899). Other articles that had special relevance include: her writings for the *Paystreak;* "The Dawson of Today" in the *Yukon Sun Special Edition* (September 1900); and "A Reminiscence" in the *Northern Light,* edited by M. Wilma Sullivan (Dawson City: n.p., July 1904). As well, the following books and articles contained helpful references to Faith: Anna-Shane Devin's "Homes and Homemakers of Alaska" in *Pacific Monthly* (June 1906); Edith M. Tyrrell's *I Was There: A Book of Reminiscences* (Toronto: Ryerson Press, 1938); Tanya Lester's *Women Rights/Writes* (Winnipeg: Lilith Publications, 1985); editor Lorraine McMullen's *Re(dis)covering Our Foremothers: Nineteenth-Century Women Writers* (Ottawa: University of Ottawa Press, 1989); and editor Greenhous Brereton's *Guarding the Goldfields: The Story of the Yukon Field Force* (Toronto: Dundurn Press, 1987).

## CHAPTER 11

The following women graciously granted me interviews in Dawson City: Fran Hakonson, (Jan. 29, 2002); Leslie Chapman (May 24, 2002); Jennifer Flynn (May 7, 2002); Bonnie Nordling (Jan. 23, 2002); Tracey Horbachuk (May 7, 2002); Wendy Cairns (Jan. 24, 2002); Kim Bouzane (Jan. 24, 2002); Georgette McLeod (May 24, 2002); Lisa Hutton (May 23, 2002); and Diana Holt, (Nov. 28, 2001), who chose to use a pseudonym because she is involved in trapping, which is controversial to animal rights activists.

# PHOTO CREDITS

AHS: Arizona Historical Society
DC: Duncan Collection
DCM: Dawson City Museum
NAC: National Archives of Canada
VCA: Vancouver City Archives
YA: Yukon Archives

PREFACE
p.3: DCM. Photograph by Dow.

CHAPTER 1
p.5: DC. Photograph by Janice Cliff.
p.11: DC. Photograph by Jennifer Duncan.
p.24: DC. Photograph by Jennifer Duncan.
p.29: DC. Photograph by Jennifer Duncan.
p.31: Yukon Territorial Government Collection. Photograph by Ryan Leef.

CHAPTER 2

p.41: YA, H.C. Barley Collection, Vol. 1, #4771.

p.42: YA #2426.

p.50: DCM #984R-216–59. Photograph by Goetzman.

p.52: University of Washington Libraries, University Archives, Manuscript, Special Collections, LaRoche #2049. Photography by LaRoche.

p.58: YA, MacBride Museum Collection, Vol. 1, #3795. Photograph by Larss & Duclos.

p.60: YA, MacBride Museum Collection, Vol. 2, #3872.

p.61: YA, Bill Roozeboom Collection, #6290. Photograph by Goetzman.

CHAPTER 3

p.63: YA, James Albert Johnson Collection, 82/341 #21.

p.74: YA, James Albert Johnson Collection, 82/341 #15.

p. 76: YA, James Albert Johnson Collection, 82/341 #22.

p.80: VCA, Major Matthews Collection, PORT N317.1.

p.81: VCA, Major Matthews Collection, PORT N317.3.

CHAPTER 4

p.83: *Glimpses of Alaska* by Veazie Wilson.

p.87: YA #1186.

p.89: YA #2141.

p.94: YA, MacBride Museum Collection, Vol. 1, #3739. Photograph by Larss & Duclos.

CHAPTER 5

p.102:  Collection of Roger S. Brown.

p.105:  Collection of Roger S. Brown.

p.114:  Collection of Roger S. Brown.

p.117:  Collection of Roger S. Brown.

## CHAPTER 6

p.119:   Yakima Valley Museum.

p.126:   Alaska State Library Historical Collection, PCA 87–682. Photograph by Winter & Pond.

p.130: DCM #984R-44–1–1.

p.139: *Seattle Times.*

p.144: Collection of Candy Waugaman.

## CHAPTER 7

p.145: YA, Martha Louise Black Collection, #3253.

p.156: YA, Martha Louise Black Collection, #82/218 H-14.

p.160: YA, Martha Louise Black Collection, #3258.

p.162: YA, Clayton Betts Collection, #9423.

## CHAPTER 8

p.167: DCM #984–98–4.

p.177: YA, MacBride Museum Collection, Vol. 2 #3880. Photograph by Larss.

p.182: YA, National Museum of Canada Collection, #818.

p.191: YA, Dawson City Museum Collection, #6372.

p.193: DCM #984R-98–2.

## CHAPTER 9

p.195: Collection of the Sisters of St. Ann, Victoria, British Columbia.

p.208: AHS #1134. Photograph by Clum.

p.212: YA, MacBride Museum Collection, Vol. 1 #3816. Photograph by Larss & Duclos.

p.215: AHS #2090. Photograph by N. H. Rose.

p.217: AHS.

CHAPTER 10

p.219: Glenbow Archives NA-2883–28.

p.230: NAC PA-016892. Photograph by H.J. Woodside.

p.232: NAC PA-016148. Photograph by H.J. Woodside.

p.234: NAC PA-017213. Photograph by H.J. Woodside.

p.235: NAC, Yukon Territory Collection, C-008066.

p.244: YA, McLennan Collection, #6487. Photograph by Hegg.

# ACKNOWLEDGEMENTS

First of all, I kiss the hems of goddesses: my editor, Martha Kanya-Forstner, and my agent, Anne McDermid. Without Martha—who had the idea in the first place and remained true throughout her daughter's birth and my jinxedness—and Anne—who gave me my wings—this book would not exist.

Secondly, I thank my brother, Jake Duncan, for being the stellar guy he is and for helping me settle into the Yukon again and again. To my father, Rod Duncan, I owe both gratitude and apology for the car that didn't make it back. The same debt is owed to my aunt, Susan Duncan Patterson, for her generosity and understanding. Thanks to Gord and Sandi Bricker for continual moral support. Kudos to all my cousins—Geordie, Duncan, Josh, and Daniel—for growing up so fine. Thanks also to my new nephew, Rory Phelan Waterman Duncan, for being born, even if it was bum-first.

I thank my friends down South for always keeping in touch: Elizabeth Gold, Anna Roosen-Runge, Robin Gorn, Kent Wakely, Trish Salah, Sina Queyras, Danielle Bobker, Lesley Grant, Tracey Burke, Cate Barnes, and Miguel Bolullo.

Up North, debts of gratitude have accumulated over the years to Megan Waterman, Jeremy Roht, Janice Cliff, Karen McWilliam, K.C. Woodfine, John Overell, Martin Kienzler, David Curtis, Jocelyn Martel, and Mary Ellen Jarvis.

These fine folks saved my butt: Greg Skuse was unbelievably kind to loan me his trailer two years in a row; Wayne "Potsy" Potoroka supervised my internship; Jonathan "Howl" Howe took me dog mushing; Willy McIntyre traded me his air miles for my charred car; Kim and Shelby gave me rides when I was stranded; and Heidi let me use her bath when I was stinky.

And these pals I thank for inviting me to their parties: Mikin, Laurence, Gerry Couture, Chera, Kendra, Tammy, Mindy, Melissa, Joanne Dyck, James McNaughton, Dominic, Dominique, Jen, Dylan, Kyla, Tara, and, at KIAC, Karen, Gary, Mike, and Paul. Anybody whose name I neglected to mention or misspelled, I owe you a beer.

A huge whack of gratitude goes to the fine women who let me interview them for hours: Fran Hakonson, Leslie Chapman, Jennifer Flynn, Bonnie Nordling, Tracey Horbachuk, Wendy Cairns, Kim Bouzane, Diana Holt (not her real name), Georgette McLeod, and Lisa Hutton.

Likewise, I appreciated the invaluable assistance of Cheryl Thompson, Sue Parsons, and Paul Thistle at the Dawson City Museum Archives and Heather Jones at the Yukon Archives. Many thanks are also due Ryan Leef, Candy Waugaman, Melanie J. Mayer, and Roger S. Brown, for going out of their way to contribute photos for the book.

# INDEX

## A

Aagé, 66, 68, 76–77

Aberdeen, Lady Ishbel, 227–230

Adams, Alex, 176, 179

*Alaska Weekly,* 98–99

Alexander, Jennie Bosco Harper, 43, 81

Alexander, Robert, 44

Allmon, Danny, 174, 176, 180

Ancient Voices, 23

Anglo-French Klondike Syndicate, 136

Anthony, Susan B., 148, 226

*Arizona Star,* 197–198, 201, 213, 217

Arizona Women's Hall of Fame, 218

Association for the Advancement of
    Women Conference, 226–227

Athapaskans, 65

Atlin, 59

Aubert, M., 95

avalanche, 54, 84, 92–93

## B

Banff, 98

Bear Creek, 9, 22, 27–28, 36–37

Bend (Oregon), 185

Bering Strait, 91

Berry, Ethel, 2, 97, 249

Berton House, 30

Bettis, Francis Allison, 169–170

Black, George, 98, 159, 235

Black, Martha, 4, 19, 40, 96–99, 227,
    235, 240, 245
    birth, 146
    birth of Lyman, 156
    Chicago fire, 145–146

in Dawson City, 154–159

death, 166

death of brother George, 164

death of Lyman, 163

death of Warren, 164

early life, 146–149

marriage to Black, 159

marriage to Purdy, 149

move to Whitehorse, 165

in Skagway, 151

Speaker of the House of Commons,
162-163

in Vancouver, 160–161

"Blueberry Kid," 213

*Bohemian Girl, The,* 241

Bombay Peggy's, 21, 30, 37–38,
252–253

Bompas, Charlotte Selina, 45, 79

Bonanza Creek, 2, 23, 45–46, 74, 93,
99, 207, 209

Boundary Pass, 199

Bouzane, Kim, 252

Bowmanville, 221

Braeburn's Lodge, 7, 18

"Bride of the Klondike,"
see Berry, Ethel

Brown, Dr. John Nelson Elliot, 234,
238-239

Bullion Creek, 211

Bush, Tot, 2

Butcher, Susan, 216

C

Cairns, Wendy, 252–253, 259

Canadian Bank of Commerce, 141

*Canadian Home Journal,* 228

*Canadian Magazine,* 228

Canyon City, 174

Carbonneau, Count Charles Eugène,
131–132, 134–135, 136–137,
140–143

Carbonneau Castle, 142–143

Carcross, 78, 154

Caribou Crossing,
see Carcross

Carmack, George, 45, 61, 69–75, 137

Carmack, Kate, 4, 45, 61, 99, 137

in California, 75, 78

daughter, 69

death, 80

family, 66

finding gold, 73–74

first marriage, 68–69

Graphie Grace, 71, 74, 77–79

later life, 79–82

lifestyle, 70–71

origins, 65

physical description, 63–64

second husband, 69

separation from George, 77–79

Carmack, Marguerite, 80

Carmacks, 17

Cashman, Fanny, 196–197, 202

death, 204

Cashman, Nellie, 4, 94, 97,
    136-137, 238, 245, 249
  Alaskan claims, 214
  "Angel of the Cassiar," 199–200
  Angel of Tombstone, 205
  in Arizona, 201–206
  birth, 196
  death, 217
  early life, 196–198
  in Fairbanks, 212
  Legend of the Lost Cashman Mine,
    203-204
  problems with claims, 209–210
  Prospector's Haven and Retreat, 211
  restaurants, 207
  as spiritual advisor, 204
  U.S. Marshal, 213–214
  in the Yukon, 205–218
Cassiar Restaurant, 207
Chandindu River Salmon Weir, 22
Chapman, Leslie, 248–250
"cheechako," 6, 13, 40, 58, 74
Cheiro, 149
Chicoutimi, 85–86
Chief Isaac, 59, 259
Chilkat, 53, 65
Chilkoot Pass, 2, 7, 45, 49–53, 56, 65,
    68–70, 84, 86–87, 97, 99–100,
    150–151, 161, 174, 206
Circle City, 44

*City of Topeka,* 124, 137
Clanton Gang, 203
Clum, John, 211, 218
Cohoes, 91–92
Corbeil, Father, 93
Cramer, Steve, 190
Crane, Alice, 55
Cripple Creek, 51
Crow (clan), 65
Crystal Theatre, 184
Cummings, Belle, 137
Cunningham, Thomas, 197, 202

D
*Daily British Colonist,* 199, 206
*Daily Citizen,* 211
Dak̲l'aweidí, 66
Dawson, George, 56
Dawson Charley, 45, 70–74, 76–79, 81
Dawson City Arts Society, 21, 29, 34,
    248
Dawson City Music Festival, 16
*Dawson Daily News,* 97, 99, 131, 210
Dawson fire, 157
*Dawson News Clean-up Edition,* 95
de Atley, Flossie, 184
DeGraf, Anna, 4, 44–45, 99–100, 245
  birth, 104
  in Dawson City, 111–117
  death, 118
  early life, 104–105

in Juneau, 105–107

the "Samaritan," 113

Deisheetaan, 66

Delmonico's Restaurant, 201, 207

Denver, 51

Desmarais, Father, 93

Diamond Tooth Gertie Lovejoy, 161, 181

Diamond Tooth Gertie's Casino, 10, 14, 30, 247, 252, 258

Diego Marulanda & Pacande, 16

Dome City Bank, 141

Donovan Hotel, 207, 211

*Dory,* 91

Duncan, Jake, 6, 7–11, 13–14, 17, 20, 23, 25, 26, 28, 29, 34, 36, 37–38, 251

Duncan, Jinx, 36

Dutch Kate, 45, 99–100

"Dutch Marie," 213

Dyea, 51–52, 70, 86, 151, 206

Dyea Trail, 51, 84, 100


E

Earp, Wyatt, 203, 211

École Émilie-Tremblay, 101

Eldorado Creek, 46, 99

Eldorado Hotel, 248

*Empire,* 224, 227–228

Endelman, Max, 136

*Evening Herald,* 188

*Evening News,* 228

*Excelsior,* 46

Excelsior Creek, 154, 158


F

Fairview Hotel, 130–131, 140, 144, 210, 237

Fashion Nugget, The, 20

Fenton, Faith, 4, 10, 32, 47, 49

at Chicago World's Fair, 227

birth, 221

in Dawson City, 234–242

death, 244

early life, 221–223

early writings, 225–227

editor, 228

goes to Yukon, 229–232

"In the Yukon," 238

later writings, 228

"Mail Carrying on the Yukon," 236

marriage to Brown, 239–240

*nom de plume,* 224

as teacher, 223–224

in Toronto, 242–245

in the U.S., 243–245

"Women's Empire," 224

Fenton-Brown, Faith, *see* Fenton, Faith

"Fiddler John," 213

Fields, J. B., 137

Fields, Mae, 2–3

*Five Apples,* 36

Five Finger Rapids, 7, 51, 56, 154, 233

Fleming, Sir Sandford, 230

Flynn, Jennifer, 250–251

Fort Gibbon, 215

Fortin, Joe, 92–93

Fortin, Marie-Émilie,
   *see* Tremblay, Émilie

Fortin, Mary, 93

Fort Nelson, 44

Fort Reliance, 43, 44

Fort Selkirk, 49, 56, 71, 233

Forty Mile Gold, 248, 250

Fortymile River, 43–44, 71, 73–74, 84,
   88-89, 91, 99, 260

Fotheringham, Marie Joussaye, 2

Freeman, Alice Matilda
   *see* Fenton, Faith

Freeman, Mary Ann, 222

Freeman, William Henry, 221


G

Gage, E. B., 205, 215–216

Gage, Eli, 150

Garcia, Madeline, 172–173

George M. Dawson Chapter of the
   Imperial Order Daughters of the
   Empire
      *see* IODE

George V, King, 161

George VI, King, 97

Geronimo, 203

Glenora, 49

*Globe,* 220–221, 224–225, 229,
   231–232, 235–238, 241, 244

Gold Bottom Creek, 46, 72

Golden Stairs, 53

Gold Hill Hotel, 136

Gold Run Mining Company, 140–141

Gold Trickle, 2, 43

Grand Forks, 97

Grand Forks Hotel, 136, 144

Grant, General Ulysses S., 197

Gravel, Onésome, 92–93

Gus'dutéen, 66

Gwich'in, 43


H

Hakonson, Fran, 190, 247–248

Han, 43, 59–60, 72, 89, 256, 259

Hanna, Rachel, 230

Harmsworth, Alfred, 229

Harper, Arthur, 43

Hayden, Joyce, 156

Hegg, Eric, 50

Henderson, Bob, 72

Henderson, Patsy, 72, 74

Henry, Percy, 25

Historical Society of Chicoutimi, 99

Hitchcock, Mary, 2

Holliday Doc, 202

Holloway, Sam, 100

Holmes, Oliver Wendell, 242

Holt, Diana, 253–256

Hootalinqua River, 233

Horbachuk, Tracey, 251–252

Hunker Creek, 23

Hunter, Charles, 1–2

Hunter, Lucille, 1–2

Hurricane, 15

Hutton, Lisa, 258–260


I

Imperial Federation League of Canada, 225

International Council of Women, 227

IODE, 97, 159, 161


J

Jackson, Gertie, 174

Jarvis, Mary Ellen, 23

Jeandreau, Mrs., 209–210


K

Ḵaachgaawáa, 66

Ḵáa Goox̲

  *see* Dawson Charley

Kaska, 43, 65

Keish

  *see* Skookum Jim

Kelly, Emma, 55

KIAC, 21–22, 29, 248

King, Florence, 48

King Solomon's Dome, 154

Kirsten, 15

Klondike City, 59

Klondike Institute of Arts and Culture

  *see* KIAC

Klondike Kate, 10, 40, 55, 98, 235, 245, 248, 251

  birth, 169

  death, 192

  early life, 168–173

  her baby, 181–183

  later life, 189–193

  law suit against Pantages, 185

  living with Pantages, 180–181, 183

  marriage to Bill Van Duren, 192

  marriage to Floyd Warner, 186

  marriage to Johnny Matson, 189

  Orpheum, 89, 181, 183

  Soubrette Extraordinaire, 176

  vaudeville tour, 185

  in Victoria, 184–185

*Klondike News,* 75

*Klondike Nugget,* 234

Klondike River, 14, 26, 35, 45, 56, 72, 155, 158

Koolseen

  *see* Henderson, Patsy

Kooyáy, 69

Koyukuk, 43, 44

Koyukuk River, 213

L

Lac-St-Jean, 85

Ladies of the Golden North, 98

Ladue, Joe, 56, 72, 106, 107

Lagrois, Louis, 99

Laimee, Marguerite, 78

Lake Bennett, 51, 54–55, 70, 88, 100, 151, 153–154, 157, 175, 179, 250

Lake Laberge, 56, 206–207

Lake Lindeman, 51, 54, 93, 153

Lake Louise, 98

Lake Marsh, 70, 154

Lake Tagish, 70, 154

Lamore, Gussie, 180

Land Claims Agreement, 23

LaRoche, Frank, 50

Laurier, Prime Minister Wilfrid, 229–230

Ledbetter, Suzann, 216

Lehman, Harry, 97

Liard Hot Springs, 28

Little Skookum Creek, 209

London, Jack, 42

Lousetown, 59, 155, 157, 260

Lungs, Ed, 176

Lynn Canal, 86


M

MacDonald, "Big Alex," 215

MacDonald, John A., 224

McLeod, Georgette, 256–257

McQuesten, Jack, 89, 108

McQuesten, Katherine, 43–44, 81–82, 89, 108

McQuesten, Leroy, 43, 44

Madeline Creek, 211

*Mail,* 229

*Mail and Empire,* 228

Malaspina Glacier, 49

*Manchester Guardian,* 46

Matson, Johnny, 181, 188–189, 191–192, 248

Matson Creek, 188

Maximilian's General Store, 37

Mayo, Al, 43

Mayo, Margaret, 43

Mendenhall, Lois, 184

*Midnight Sun,* 207

Midnight Sun Mining Company, 215

Miles Canyon, 18, 51, 55, 88, 154, 174, 207

Miller Creek, 85, 91

Miners' and Woodmens' Lien Ordinances, 159

Minto, Governor-General Lord, 241

*Moccasin Square Gardens,* 36

Monte Cristo Gulch, 210

Moore, Virgil, 75

Moose Creek, 90

Moosehide, 22, 43, 59–60, 256, 259

Moosehide Han, 74

Mulrooney, Belinda, 4, 57, 99, 210,
  227, 237, 245
  birth, 120
  in Dawson City, 137–140
  death, 143
  divorce from Carbonneau, 141
  in Fairbanks, 140–142
  in France, 139–140
  law suits, 139–143
  marriage to Carbonneau, 138
  in Yakima, 142–143
Munger, George, 146
Munger, George Merrick, 146
Munger, Martha Louise
  *see* Black, Martha
Munroe, Father, 91
Murphy, Martha Alice, 169
*My Ninety Years,* 147–148, 165

N
Nadagaat' Tláa, 69
National Council of Women of
  Canada
  *see* NCWC
NCWC, 227–228
*Newsweek,* 192
*New York Sun,* 228
*New York Times,* 211
Noble, Jesse, 141–142
Nolan Creek, 213–214, 216, 218
Nome, 59

Nordling, Bonnie, 251
*Northern Advance,* 223
North West Mounted Police, 54–57,
  88, 174, 206, 230, 234
Norwood, Captain N. H., 129,
  136–137, 209–210

O
Odd Gallery, The, 21
Ogilvie, William, 70, 73, 210, 229,
  234, 239–240
O.K. Corral, 203
Osborne, Georgie L., 207
*Ottawa Citizen,* 228
*Ottawa Free Press,* 229
*Ottawa Journal,* 241
Ottawa Senators, 37
Overland Trail, 50, 56
Owens, Susan, 146

P
Palace Grand Theatre, 10, 29
Pantages, Alexander, 180–181,
  187–188, 235
Payson, Margaret, 230
*Paystreak,* 238–239
Peabody's Photo Parlour, 20, 37
Pelly River, 233
Pioneer Women of Alaska, 143
Pius X, Pope, 95
Planet Smashers, 16

Pointer Brothers, 12, 16

Poirier, Madame, 95

Porsild, Charlene, 39

*Portland,* 46

*Post-Intelligencer,* 47, 75, 77, 187

Powell, Georgia, 230, 232

Prince Rupert, 18

Pringle, Eunice, 187

*Province,* 136

Purdy, Will, 149


R

Raymond, Violet, 136

RCMP, 24–25, 38, 57–58, 79, 158

Red Lake, 250

Reikie, Reverend Thomas, 222

Renewal Resource Council and Salmon
    Fishing Association, 25

*Roanoke,* 75

Rockwell, John W., 169

Rockwell, Kate
    *see* Klondike Kate

Rockwell, Kathleen Eloisa
    *see* Klondike Kate

Rockwell, Klondike Kate
    *see* Klondike Kate

Rosebud Creek, 209

Royal Canadian Mounted Police
    *see* RCMP

Ruser, August, 142–143

Russel, M. E., 210

Russell, Lillian, 149

Russ House, 201–202

*Rustler,* 86


S

St. Andrews Church, 71

St. Joseph's Hospital, 201

St. Mary's Catholic Church Bazaar and
    Banquet, 96

St. Mary's of Notre Dame, 148

St. Michael, 49, 91

Sanford, Senator William E., 229

*San Francisco Bulletin,* 99

"Santa Baby," 34

Santa Rosa, 98

Satejdenalno
    *see* McQuesten, Katherine

Sauter, Captain, 171

Savage, Ann, 190

Savoy Theatre, 174

Savoy Theatrical Company, 175

Scales of the Pass, 54

Scott, Amy, 230

Seentahna
    *see* Harper, Jennie Bosco

Senkler, Commissioner, 210

Service, Robert, 42, 50, 243

Sestak, Joe, 192

Shaw, Flora, 47, 153, 237

Sheep Camp, 53–54, 152

Sheep Creek, 211

Silance, Baron de, 95

Sisters of St. Ann, 86, 91, 201, 207, 210, 216–217

Sitka, 91

Sixtymile River, 43, 85, 96, 189

Skagway, 19, 50–51, 97, 157, 174–175, 206, 231

*Skagway News,* 47

Skagway Trail, 51

*skookum,* 13

Skookum, Jim, 45, 66, 69, 70–74, 76–79, 81

Smith, Mrs. Ward, 239

Smith, Soapy, 19, 51, 151

Soap Creek, 210

Society of the Ladies of the Golden North, 96

*Songs of the Sourdough,* 243

sourdough, 6, 40, 98, 157

Sparling, John K., 241–242

Spencer, Captain, 150, 154

Spokane Falls, 169

S.S. *Bertha,* 91

S.S. *Centennial,* 206

S.S. *Nora,* 97

S.S. *Provence,* 95

S.S. *Topeka,* 86

S.S. *Walla Walla,* 91

S.S. *Yukon,* 91

Stames, Mina, 230

Standor, Anton F., 136

Steele, Colonel Sam, 54, 220

Stewart River, 43

Stikine River, 49, 200, 206, 230–231

Stikine Trail, 1, 199

St-Joseph-d'Alma, 85

Stone House, 54

*Stratton,* 208

Stringer, Reverend, 79

*Stroller's Weekly,* 100

Strong, Annie Hall, 47

Suzuki, Troy, 36

Swedish Creek, 209


T

Taber, C.W.C., 161

Tacoma Hotel, 153

Taft, President, 142

Tagish, 1, 42, 53, 65–66, 70–71

Taiya River, 52

Taiya River Valley, 87

Taku, 65

Tanana, 43

Terry, Ellen, 149

Teslin, 1, 49

Teslin Lake, 233

Teslin River, 49

*The Crowning of the Rose,* 223

*The Islander,* 231, 236–237

The Pit, 11–14, 17, 20, 24

"The Row," 59

*The Times of London,* 153, 237

Thompson, William, 210

*Time,* 192

Tláa, Shaaw

    *see* Carmack, Kate

Tlákwshaan, 66

Tl'anaxéedakw, 81

Tlingit, 43, 51–54, 65–66

Tombstone, 202

Treadgold, A. N. C., 46

Treat, Captain, 150

Tremblay, Edmond, 92–93

Tremblay, Émilie, 4, 23, 45, 73, 238,
    240, 245, 249

    adoption of niece, 95

    birth, 85

    church involvement, 94–95

    in Cohoes, 92

    in Dawson City, 96–97

    death, 100

    early life, 85

    known priests, 93–94

    marriage, 85–86

    second marriage, 99

    trip to Europe, 95

    in the Yukon, 86–102

Tremblay, Émilie Fortin

    *see* Tremblay, Émilie

Tremblay, Jack

    *see* Tremblay, Pierre-Nolasque

Tremblay, Pierre-Nolasque, 85, 96–97

Tr'ondëk Hwëch'in, 22–23, 59, 72,
    258–260

Tucson, 201

Tutchone, 43, 56, 65

Typhoid Charlie, 16

Tyrrell, Edith, 236–237


U

Unalaska, 91


V

Valentine, E., 100

Van Buren, Edith, 2

Van Duren, Bill, 191–192

Victorian Order of Nurses, 229–230,
    234


W

Walker, Bill, 179

*Walking After Midnight,* 18

Warner, Floyd, 186

*Weekly Star,* 80

Westminster Hotel, 12

Whitehorse, 7, 27, 29, 36, 39, 56, 79,
    88, 97, 154, 211, 257

Whitehorse Rapids, 55, 154, 174

*Whitehorse Star,* 100, 166

White Pass, 20, 51–53, 78, 97, 174

Whyard, Flo, 156

Willamette Valley, 192

Willard, Frances E., 148

*Willie Rosenfeld,* 172

Wilson, Harry Leon, 143

Wilson Post, 86

Windy Arm, 88

Wolf (clan), 65

Women's Alaska Gold Club, 48

Women's Klondike Expedition
Syndicate, 48

Woodfine, K. C., 36

Woodward, Vernie, 54

World Trade Center, 27

Wrangell, 49, 200, 206, 231

Y

Yakima and Alaska Investment
Company, 142

Yakutat Bay, 49

Yellowhead, 28

Yukon Field Force, 229

Yukon Hygeia Water Supply Company,
135

Yukon Infantry Company, 161

Yukon Order of Pioneers Auxiliary, 96,
134

Yukon River, 14, 26, 45, 49–51,
56–57, 72, 81, 86, 154, 233

*Yukon Wildflowers,* 165

*Yukon World,* 141